A Living History Of

The Kenya Police

Written By Those Who Served

Compiled And Edited
By
Jennifer Reeve – Police Granddaughter
And
John Newton – Policeman

Published By
THE KENYA POLICE ASSOCIATION
Leighton Buzzard

Published in the United Kingdom by The Kenya Police Association Under The Imprint of Next Century Books, Leighton Buzzard

April 2015

Line Drawings by John (Steve) Stephenson
(Except where stated)

Cover Design and Layout by Steve Hanlon

Photographs donated by various former Members of The Kenya Police

Hardback Edition
Printed and bound in the UK by Berforts Information Press
www.bookprinting.co.uk

Dedication

This Living History is dedicated to all those brave Kenya Police Officers, African, Asian and European, who gave their lives in the service of Kenya and its People during seventy years of Colonial Policing.

Drawn By Jill Fielding

Acknowledgements

The editors thank all those who delved into their memories of life sixty and more years ago to dig up and contribute witty, interesting and absorbing stories of their time Policing and serving the people of Kenya during the closing days of Colonial rule.

Our Contributing Artist

In particular we thank John (Steve) Stephenson for the wonderful line drawings throughout this book, so full of life they leap from the page and enhance already excellent stories.

Chronology

The stories in this Living History are placed in no specific order, chronology or timeline.

The Northern Frontier District Of Kenya

The NFD exerts a special fascination for all who served in that wild, lava-strewn, mountainous and desert area, more than twice the size of the rest of Kenya. The NFD is peopled by mostly pastoral tribes who eke a living from cattle, so valuable to their survival, a great deal of stock raiding and theft between tribes goes on. The main targets are sheep, goats and camels along with cattle.

The NFD borders four countries, Somalia, Ethiopia, The Sudan and Uganda. In addition to the Kenya tribes stealing from each other, much stock raiding originates from Somalia and Ethiopia with well-armed parties invading across the borders to attack villages for cattle and women and general stealing and murder.

A line of Forts and Police posts along the four borders protect the NFD as far as possible, given the extreme nature of this massive area. During the Colonial era, young Policemen, often only a few weeks arrived from Britain, would undertake camel and foot patrols of up to ten days from Police Stations and Posts with many thousands of square miles of desert and mountain to regulate and control.

All appear to have sought out and enjoyed the experience.

Alec Abell – Police Officer

A Ride From Marsabit To Moyale – The Preparation

In 1958 as a young Police Inspector I was stationed in Moyale district on the Kenya/Ethiopian border, in the remote semi-desert Northern Frontier District (NFD) of Kenya. Our headquarters was some four hundred miles to the south at Isiolo.

I was in charge of the Moyale police station in addition to a small horse section based nearby at Hiellu. I had learned to ride as a child in England – my mother was a keen rider.

One of my responsibilities at Moyale was running the Hiellu horse section, a duty I enjoyed. Three or four mornings a week I would go for an early morning ride accompanied by a couple of Askaris. This would be before breakfast and before being in the office promptly at eight.

My duties also included being an ex-officio Customs and Immigration Officer. We were only six Europeans in the Boma and the same number of Goan Asians who were clerical staff. We also had an Indian Brahmin medical officer who was very popular and who was an absolute whiz at Liar Dice.

We had a squash court and I always thought how typically British to leave squash courts dotted around in the most unlikely places in their empire. I know of one that eventually became a store for famine relief food and another that was used as an overflow from the local prison.

If we happened to be playing squash at 1800 hours when the flag was lowered and the last post played on a bugle we would immediately stop our game and stand to attention.

We had a tennis court surfaced with crushed termite hill soil. There was no shortage of anthills at Moyale, which were the tallest I have ever seen with some at least 25 feet high. Naturally we had a club. All the NFD Bomas had a club and they all had nautical names such as the Whaling Club at

Garissa, the Curling Club at Mandera and the famous 'Royal' Wajir Yacht Club.

We had the Blue Turtle at Moyale. This name came from when the club was first created when a painter using blue paint on the club door decided to also paint the shell of a large tortoise, which lived in the vicinity, trundled by.

Despite the remoteness we all got on well and it was a happy Boma. There were inconveniences of course. We had no electricity and relied upon paraffin driven 'Tilley' pressure lamps and inefficient paraffin fridges.

We had no piped water. Untreated well water, usually slightly muddy, was delivered by bowser two or three times a week. Drinking water had to be first boiled and then passed through a large earthenware filter. All cooking, including making our own bread was done on firewood burning 'Dover' stoves.

There were no telephones, televisions or newspapers and of course we had never heard of home computers. We all had a battery-operated wireless, not the new transistor models but those with valves and we did not call them radios then. On these we tried to pick up news of the outside world from the BBC overseas service.

Reception was intermittent and accompanied by much static. Good reception appeared to be controlled by the weather, the time of day and even seemed to vary with the time of the year. A colleague owned a gramophone and it was a real treat to be invited to his place to listen to music.

Finally, we had no such luxuries as flush toilets and relied on outside bucket latrines that were emptied daily in the dead of night by the jokingly nicknamed 'Churas', the Swahili word for frogs. Life was Spartan but there was no whinging.

Fresh foods, especially fruit and vegetables, were what we missed most of all. During the rainy season and in the cooler weather, which followed, some sad looking spinach, a few tomatoes, and an occasional small lemon were produced from the D.C's vegetable plot.

There was no shortage of good meat however, and weekly I would buy a black- headed fat tailed Persian sheep on the hoof for ten Kenya shillings and have it slaughtered by my cook and his assistant. We sold the skin for two shillings. This supplied sufficient meat for my two staff, my dog and me for the week. That would be for a cost of about fifty pence at today's rate of exchange.

Fresh milk was no problem either for we each rented a lactating milk cow from the local Boran chief for five shillings a month which was kept in the so called DC's herd. This produced two bottles of milk daily, which was enough for my staff and me, and any left over accumulated to be turned into somewhat rancid butter by the cook. If the cow went dry the chief simply supplied a replacement.

Potatoes were often in short supply and lots of rice was eaten. Pasta was not fashionable in those days. Skinny little tough chickens could be bought locally as could eggs, the size of bantam eggs and always with a fertile blood spot in them and sometimes even a partly developed chick.

There were huge flocks of Vulturine Guinea fowl not far from the Boma and shoots were often organised. These made excellent curries but only the really young birds could be roasted. Generally, we relied a great deal on tinned foods. The greatest treat occurred during the long rains when for weeks the roads were impassable and our only contact with civilization was through the fortnightly visit by a Police Air Wing plane, the prime purpose of which was to deliver and collect mail.

The pilot had a standing order to bring masses of bacon and sausages and other odd luxuries such as cheese and fresh butter. Nowadays it would be difficult for most people to imagine just how much such simple treats were appreciated.

The usual drill on Sundays was tennis in the morning, followed by lots of beer and a curry lunch at the club, then more beer.

At about five the horses would appear at the club all saddled up, by which time, had we been behind a steering wheel we would have been in trouble with the law. But according to the District Commissioner who was also the local magistrate, there was no such offence as being drunk in charge of a horse. So off we would all go on a cross-country gallop.

Someone, usually the DC, would point out a particular tree or rocky outcrop in the distance with a cry of, 'Last one there buys the beer' and off we would race in a manner most reckless for both man and beast.

Occasionally somebody took a tumble but I never remember anyone being really hurt.

Sometimes I took an old bugle along and blew it like a hunting horn as we charged over the rough border country. What the locals thought I cannot imagine, though they must have believed us slightly crazy, but then all who served in the remote NFD for any period of time were considered by the down country people to be slightly 'Round the Bend'. Perhaps, they were right!

Our mounts were small Boran ponies, which we usually tried to purchase locally from the Southern Ethiopian Boran tribesmen. Some of them were proud owners of large herds of ponies, which were considered a sign of wealth and they were most reluctant to sell. They would certainly never agree to part with their better animals so we experienced constant difficulty in finding suitable replacements for our mounted section.

Very occasionally a Boran elder would appear with a pony for sale with its clumsy wooden saddle, cruel restricting bit and odd small stirrups in which only the big toe fitted!

The pony would be put through its paces and if it seemed up to scratch the bargaining began. This could take as many as three or four days and was conducted by the section sergeant without urgency by either party.

Haggling was a game and such was the unrushed pace of life in those days and in that part of the world. We would expect to pay the equivalent of ten to fifteen pounds for what seemed a reasonable mount. These Boran ponies were tough little beasts and seldom over fourteen hands.

My favourite was called 'Dera', which is Boran for tall, and he was fourteen-point-two hands. They were all geldings, unshod and surefooted. Ideal for Police patrols along the rugged rocky border hill country. They could go all day without watering and seemed to thrive on the sparse dry grass. On patrol we always carried a bag of horse cubes on one of the pack mules and these, for the ponies, were an absolute delicacy.

The border was patrolled to prevent friction and possible fighting between the different nomadic tribal groups encroaching, stealing (in their language) the other tribes' grazing and water rights. The situation was most tense during the 'Jilaal', the so-called very hot long dry season, November to March, when there was fierce competition over limited resources.

Another problem was constant pressure from nomadic Somali herdsmen who had for many years been migrating south and westward pushing out the Boran, Sakuye and Gabbra from their traditional grazing areas.

The Colonial Government had demarcated on the map of the NFD, a so-called 'Somali Line', running north to south from the Ethiopian border down to the Tana River beyond which the Somalis were not allowed to move with their camel herds. We had to enforce this line that ran right through the middle of the Moyale district and had been created to protect the less aggressive tribes from the more warlike Muslim Somalis.

Pony-mounted Boran raiders from Southern Ethiopia were a further problem. They crossed into Kenya to steal stock and murder lone herdsmen, whom they emasculated, taking the victims testicles back home to show they had killed a man as proof of their warrior-hood. It was said a man could not marry until he had killed either a dangerous wild animal such as a lion or a man. A few of the older Boran men quite openly wore a thick ivory bangle around the right upper arm to advertise the fact they had killed a man.

Poaching giraffe and the odd elephant was another pastime of these raiders mounted on their swift ponies. The wildlife in Ethiopia had by this time been virtually wiped out but quite a lot remained in northern Kenya.

The giraffe was especially important to the Boran; their hides used to manufacture sandals and whips and even more importantly to make hand sewn leather buckets used for bailing water from their deep wells. Giraffe tails were also highly prized for making bracelets and necklaces by the womenfolk. A tribesman was once arrested on the border with a bag containing no less than thirty giraffe tails that he was attempting to smuggle into Ethiopia.

Infrequently, some of these raiders were intercepted and with luck a pony or two captured. Naturally the Boran used their best animals for these raids and usually outpaced the police mounted patrol and made good their escape back into Ethiopia. They were excellent and courageous horsemen and being slim, small boned and lightweight their small ponies could easily carry them.

The origin of their ponies is obscure and debatable but from appearance they seemed to have a strong strain of Arab in them. The Boran pony is intelligent with a good temperament and is brave. They were trained to hunt and without the rider having to guide them they would gallop, without hesitation full pelt through thick thorn bush and across lava rock in pursuit of giraffe. Rather than use their ancient and unreliable Italian rifles the Boran preferred to get in close to spear or even hamstring the unfortunate selected beast.

Then, in early 1959, we received the good news that a Police mounted camel patrol, called a "Rakhoub", in the neighbouring district of Marsabit to the west, had captured fifteen ponies from Ethiopian Boran raiders at Kalacha.

The circumstance of their capture is interesting. The Rakhoub section had come across a large number of pony tracks and guessed they must be Ethiopian raiders as very few of the local Kenya tribesmen kept horses.

The patrol Sergeant-in-Charge realized the mounted raiders were heading for the only water available in that huge arid area – the nearby water wells at Kalacha, and knew that horses could easily outpace a camel. He therefore adopted the strategy of waiting until dusk before launching his attack. After following the tracks towards Kalacha the Rakhoub camels were left some distance from the wells and led his patrol in on foot.

He knew by that time the raiders would have unsaddled and hobbled their mounts so unable to mount and flee. Unfortunately a lookout spotted the Police Patrol at the last moment and following a short exchange of rifle fire, with no casualties on either side due to poor light, the raiders escaped, abandoning their ponies and equipment. They were then faced with a seventy-mile walk through very inhospitable terrain back home to Ethiopia.

When first told of this seizure we were delighted to hear the Moyale mounted section had been promised all fifteen ponies. However, after being herded over a hundred miles to the District headquarters at Marsabit through hot desolate country they were in a very poor and emaciated condition.

Their trek took five days with very little water and virtually no grazing. Strangely, camels and horses do not like each other and driving them would have been a difficult task for the men of the Rakhoub.

This group of ponies now needed to be transferred from Marsabit to Moyale and our horse section close by at Hiellu.

The only way to do this was by riding and herding them overland.

A Veterinary Officer inspected them shortly after arrival and recommended they needed at least a month to recover, grazing on the misty, cool green slopes of Mount Marsabit before attempting the one-hundred-and-seventy mile journey to Moyale across the Diida Galgallo desert.

Alec Abell – Police Officer

A Ride From Marsabit To Moyale – The Journey

Some six weeks later I arrived in Marsabit by police lorry with a Corporal and four men of the Moyale Mounted Section together with all the necessary tack and equipment. We were greeted with the very disappointing news that five of the fifteen had already been earmarked.

The District Commissioner, Marsabit, took two for his two young children. The other three had been purloined by the Veterinary Department to patrol their Cattle Quarantine Area at Provincial H.Q. at Isiolo. Naturally the five best ponies had been selected and I was pretty annoyed feeling that as they were Police 'booty', we should have had first choice.

The manes and tails of the three ponies selected by the Veterinary Department had been trimmed short to distinguish them from the remaining ten. They were to be trucked to Isiolo at a later date.

We now had to clean up and groom our ten Police ponies. They were looking better and appeared to have largely recovered from their earlier ordeal. We de-ticked and washed them down with "Coopertox" and gave them a thorough combing and brushing. Then, to really smarten them up trimmed their tails and manes.

This caused some confusion as they all now looked the same and it became impossible to distinguish between the Veterinary Department three and our ten.

We then gave them their first meal of horse cubes. This must certainly have been their first taste of such luxury food and they took to it instantly.

Now we spent time getting these semi-broken Boran ponies accustomed to our type of saddles and bridles as well as our different riding style. A couple were very skittish and could hardly be restrained by the more gentle

European bit, but after a couple of days we felt ready to start the long ride to Moyale.

We had a tight deadline as the time was just before Easter when the Moyale Open Tennis Tournament began and I was the No. 2 seed, so I had to be back in time.

I was the only European on the ride and looking back sixty years I simply cannot remember the names of the Askaris who rode with me. They would most likely have been Somali or Boran who were by far the majority in the horse section.

The Boran in particular were traditionally horse owners and riders. My Corporal wore glasses; unusual in those days so was nicknamed "Macho Enne!" by the Askaris. This means "Four Eyes" and we all called him that, but he did not seem to mind too much.

We started before dawn and followed the rough motor track leading northeast towards our target night-stop Lug Bubisa, or "The Seasonal Watercourse of High Winds", some thirty miles away. We knew there would be some suitable acacia thorn shade trees under which to camp.

The lorry carrying our gear, water and horse fodder went ahead. Very soon we left the cool greenness of volcanic Marsabit behind and passed several huge volcanic craters as the road descended to the hot plains some three-thousand-feet below.

Four of the men and myself rode five of the ponies whilst the other five ponies followed without actually having to be tied and led. We passed a small herd of Greater Kudu and noted that people on horseback do not spook wild animals.

We also saw several giraffe as did our ponies and a couple of them needed holding back else they would have been off in pursuit.

By mid-morning it started to get hot so after a cool drink from our water bottles we saddled up the five fresh ponies and pushed on.

The First Day

We got into a routine of walking for five minutes and then trotting for ten as being easier on both man and beast. We estimated to reach Lug Bubisa a little after mid-day by which time it would be really hot.

On arrival we unsaddled, hobbled and watered the ponies and gave them a close inspection and were happy to find them in good order with no apparent saddle sores; a possibility that had concerned us. Shortly a huge saucepan of African Safari Style tea was bubbling on the open wood fire.

The recipe: two gallons of water; bring to the boil; add two large handfuls of tea leaves; continue to boil; add at least one pound of sugar and finally add two large tins of condensed milk and boil for five minutes.

An alternative, when available would be two or three pints of fresh frothy camels milk instead of tinned milk. Absolutely nothing better than several chipped tin mugs of this as a thirst quencher - far superior to fancy iced drinks.

Lions partial to horse meat roamed the area, so a strong thorn Boma had to be constructed to corral the ponies and a plentiful supply of wood collected to keep fires burning through-out the night. An additional supply of firewood was loaded into the lorry for our crossing of the treeless Diida Galgallo. Translated from the Boran language the name means "The Plains of Night or Darkness".

We retired early as we had a long day ahead of us and slept on soft sand under the wonderful starlit skies of the NFD. Counting stars is better than counting sheep to quickly lull one to sleep.

That night Lug Bubisa lived up to its name as the temperature dropped and the wind picked up into an unbelievable howling gale.

This probably had something to do with the varying temperatures of the cool mountain behind and the scorching hot desert country ahead. Regardless, we all slept soundly. The next two days crossing the Diida Galgallo would be the hardest part of our journey.

Stretching approximately 90 miles it is a flat featureless desert of black lava rock and boulders, which must have been spewed from the Marsabit volcanoes thousand of years previously. There is no water and not a single shade tree. It is a completely sterile place.

Needless to say it is uninhabited, though the local Gabbra are known to occasionally cross it with one of their camel trains. At a guess the mid-day temperature there must be well in excess of fifty degrees centigrade.

With this prospect we were up well before daybreak to be on the move whilst still cool as here, as in most deserts, the nights are surprisingly chill.

After two large mugs of the inimitable boiling hot sweet milky African tea, we trotted off leaving our lorry driver and his single escort to break camp. It was still dark when we left, but all too soon the sun made its unwelcome appearance ahead towards the East above the flat horizon.

We pushed the ponies and covered a good distance for the first two hours. The lorry caught up and passed us. The driver having been briefed to measure about forty miles on the speedometer from the previous night's camp and find a suitable spot to spend that night. We estimated this would take six to seven hours on the ponies and get us there by mid-day.

Throughout the ride we rotated and all took it in turn ride with the driver in the lorry.

We continued to make good progress, changed mounts regularly and pushed on. The heat now started to stoke up. The black lava rock shimmered in the sun and the horizon took on a double appearance with strange mirages shone across the desert like lakes of water.

The temperature had a numbing affect on the brain and one is lulled into a sort of torpor. Our tough little ponies did not let us down and on time we saw the lorry in the distance. Or was it a mirage?

After being unsaddled and rubbed down the ponies were given water from the built-in hundred-gallon tank with which all NFD Police lorries were equipped. They were hobbled and allowed to search for the odd blade of dry yellow grass amongst the lava rock. They could look forward to a good ration of horse cubes that evening.

Night Camp

With no danger of predators in the middle of the Diida Galgallo we needed no thorn tree corral. Not that we would have been able to construct one anyway in that totally treeless place. There seemed to be very few living creatures: no animals, no birds, a few lizards but plenty of insects; ants and those annoying flies which appear from nowhere in the most unlikely of places.

There was absolutely no shade so we rigged a tarpaulin up along the side of the lorry where we sought shelter, sipping more sweet milky tea and gnawing on Government issued hardtack biscuits.

Our one proper meal of the day would come in the evening; a corned beef stew with lots of curry powder, tinned vegetables and rice. We always ate together and cooking and tea making duties were shared.

The afternoon we spent playing cards, which the Askaris always played with great enthusiasm and noise. Cheating was expected if you could get away with it and was part of the game. By now the men were getting to know the ponies, their characters and temperament and had already started to choose their favourites, so we also had lengthy discussions selecting names for each one.

We had only one mare amongst in the herd – a pretty little pony – the smallest of them all. She was given the name "Tare", Boran for the tiny little Dik-Dik gazelle.

Another, though sturdy and gutsy, was blind in one eye. He later turned out to be one of the swiftest ponies in the section by winning the annual Boxing Day race. He received a name, now forgotten, meaning "One Eye" in either Somali or Boran. Sadly I cannot remember the names the others were given.

In addition to a name each pony eventually would be allocated a number branded on the hindquarter. A file would eventually have to be maintained on each pony, detailing health matters mainly; for they were all now members of the Kenya Police Force.

We spent a reasonably cool and comfortable night in the middle of the Diida Galgallo lava desert. At each camp our Askaris were always on duty throughout the night, usually two-hour spells, to stoke the fire and keep the ponies settled and guarded. We did not want the Boran raiders to come and steal back their animals.

Reveille was well before daylight, then after tea and biscuits we were on the move in very much a repeat of the previous day. Our target destination was about forty miles away at Lug Warabesa, which in both the Boran and Somali languages means "Hyena".

Situated on the edge of the lava and with no chance of finding water we knew of the possibility of some meagre grazing for the ponies. We were now in the middle of the long dry season called the "Jilaal" by the locals.

We reached Lug Warabesa shortly after mid-day and saw a small herd of Grant's gazelle in the distance. In the shimmering heat of mirage they appeared to be walking on stilts. We each carried .303-service rifles in scabbards on the ponies so an opportunity for some fresh meat could not to be missed.

Accompanied by a single Askari we rode slowly after them and got quite close, perhaps sixty or seventy yards away. We had no cover and fearing that they would run off if I dismounted I decided to have a crack at shooting from the saddle of my standing pony.

My aim was true and my little Boran pony did not panic, buck or bolt. My escort – a Muslim – immediately ran to cut the animal's throat and with a recitation from the Koran made the meat Halal.

Most Askaris in the horse section were Muslim, Boran or Somali, and the others were Samburu or Turkana who tended to be pagan or Christian. All were tough frontier tribesmen completely at home in that desolate country.

That night we grilled gazelle meat over coals for our supper. It was tasty, a bit on the tough side but that did not prevent the Askaris consuming huge amounts. It has always amazed me just how much meat the average African consumed in a sitting.

We all slept well that night

We started on our fourth day hoping now the worst part of our ride was over. In the distance we could see the pyramid shape of Mount Turbi where we hoped to find pools or streams.

Here we might meet tribesmen watering their stock and if so, amazingly, they would be the first people we had encountered since leaving Marsabit three days earlier. Nor had we seen a vehicle during that time even though we were following the only road from Marsabit to Moyale.

We had now developed a routine and were very soon trotting along the road towards our destination the small Sololo police post right on the Ethiopian border about thirty miles away. From there we would be able to radio Moyale to tell them all was well and that we were on time.

Soon we left the lava plain and entered an area of sandy soil, bush and acacia thorn trees. The going was better for the ponies and by then we were all safari hardened and we had an easier day.

Immediately to the north was Mt Farole exactly on the Ethiopian frontier, with a cement boundary pillar on the six thousand feet summit – the tallest peak in Moyale district. I had recently climbed it and near the top had been very surprised to spot a small herd of Greater Kudu.

Drawing closer to Turbi we came across some Boran children herding "shoats"; combined flocks of sheep & goats. Seeing us, they immediately and instinctively ran off to hide in the bush. Such are the dangers and uncertainties of survival in those parts. We eventually persuaded them we would do them no harm and they told us there was indeed a little water at nearby Turbi.

After watering at Turbi, catching up with the local gossip and drinking "anan ititu" – curdled cows milk – we were again on our way. We reached Sololo well before midday and reported our safe arrival by police radio to District H.Q. at Moyale. The end was in sight.

We camped that night by the bush airstrip a little away from the Sololo Police Post and small trading centre. I bought a goat for the Askaris to celebrate nearing the end of our safari. They loved goat meat and given the choice of filet of beef, pork chops, roast lamb, chicken or what-ever they would go for tough old goat every time.

We even found even a little grazing for the ponies and gave them an extra ration of horse cubes and as much water as they wanted. They were still in excellent condition and had proved their worth. By now they had all been named and their ages estimated. Some notes on their character and any idiosyncrasies had been made for their individual files.

After a night disturbed by nearby whooping Hyenas, we rose early, with our Askaris were in a jolly mood knowing they would be reunited with their families that day. The lorry would follow the motor road the long way round Funanyatta whilst we would ride the direct route along the so-called Clifford Boundary Line.

This had been cut by a combined Ethiopian and British survey team just after the Second World War but never ratified. Marked with large cement pillars every five miles or so, it had developed into a well-beaten footpath and stock trail that ran mainly in a straight line through the bush and was relatively easy going.

In addition to the Clifford Line there were the Maude and Gwynne lines, surveyed many years previously and also never ratified. These were all marked by different coloured pencil on our office maps and they generally followed the same line but diverged at some important watering hole or well, for in that area whoever controlled the water controlled the people.

To add further complication a fourth line called the De

Facto line was the one we generally used. Periodically there would be a problem between the Kenya and Ethiopian administration, usually with each claiming the other's Police Patrols had strayed across the border. To help sort out border problems with the Ethiopian authorities a British Consul had been based at Mega some sixty miles north of Moyale, within Ethiopia.

We were now passing through an area populated by numerous Boran Manyatta; temporary villages, mainly built of grass huts wound over bent canes to form a shelter for Boran cattle herders with large flocks of shoats they use as currency.

The tribe kept donkeys as beasts of burden, but, unlike the despised Somalis living further to the East, Boran did not favour camels.

On this day we would travel the greatest distance; slightly over forty miles; but morale was high as we trotted along. Shortly after midday we reached the foot of the Moyale escarpment and the going became rough, steep and rocky.

In places we had to dismount and lead our ponies for three or four miles, climbing through quite dense bush – hot, hard going and we had become unused to 'shanks-pony'.

At the top we had an easy ride of two miles into Moyale Boma. We were back home after completing a tough and challenging journey, with most of the credit going to our tough and reliable little Boran ponies. The only problem I immediately faced was to decide whether after a period of five days without either, would I take a bath or drink a beer first?

In the end I had a beer in my bath.

The day after our return was Good Friday and the day of the Moyale 'Open' Tennis Tournament with a total entry of seven players. I ended up the surprise winner and the prize was a Concise Oxford English Dictionary. I still have it to this day, though now slightly worn and referred to whilst writing this account.

Subsequently, as we half expected, the Chief Veterinary Officer, Isiolo, complained in writing to the Assistant Commissioner of Police in charge of the Northern Frontier District that their three selected ponies had been 'wrongly taken' from Marsabit to Moyale. The A.C.P's letter of reply, a copy of which was sent to me and another copy placed on my Personal File, took the form of an apology for the 'misunderstanding' and severely reprimanded me for my 'carelessness' and demanded a written explanation. A letter stating how the confusion had occurred was sent to him but nothing further was said.

Some months later the A.C.P. made an inspection visit to Moyale. The Mounted Section turned out on some of their new smart Boran ponies, with lances and pennons as part of the parade. The A.C.P. took a particular interest in the new ponies and was duly impressed.

Later that evening at a drinks party he drew me to one side and told me in the strictest confidence not to worry about the letter of reprimand and that it had been removed from my file. He explained it had been necessary for him to go through the formality of offering an apology and appearing to discipline me for the sake of good inter-departmental relationships in the Isiolo Boma.

He laughed and complimented me for using my initiative saying he would have done the same in my place.

Warren Martin – Police Officer

The Highest Police Station in the British Empire

I was seconded from Eldoret to Timboroa Police Station, reputed, at 11,000 feet above sea level, to be the highest Police Station in the British Empire.

It was on the edge of the Nandi Reserve and there had been a spate of cattle thefts. A few confrontations leading to a few arrests and the seizure of a hundred or so cattle saw the crisis pass.

Because we had done a good job in recovering cattle, we received an invitation to the Wedding of a Sub Chief's son. This was an honour and an interesting occasion. From the several Police Stations involved in following and returning the cattle, we took three European Officers and about fifty Askaris.

The Wedding Party went on for three days but we found were not really there to enjoy ourselves. The Sub Chief had invited us to make sure that the young Morani did not get out of hand. These youthful warriors could become excited and aggressive on such occasions, especially after drinking too much native beer.

A few days before my return to Eldoret the local Forest Officer asked if I would baby-sit his two small boys aged five and three while he and his wife went to the cinema in Eldoret.

Timboroa was a very lonely posting for the family and as well as being responsible for Government Plantations, he was also Magistrate for the area. My Police Commander was more than happy for me to stay overnight in the Forestry Boma.

Around half past ten, the little five-year-old boy walked into the living room, teddy bear in one hand, and dragging a blanket in the other.

'There's giants outside.'

‘What do you think I should do about the giants?’ I asked.

‘Shoo them away with your gun.’

My little Patchett light machine gun in hand, I made for the bedroom to look out his window.

‘No, no, there,’ he said, pointing to the front door.

I changed direction and said, ‘You go and hide in your bed while I shoo the giants away.’

He seemed to think this a good idea. I tucked him safely in, but he seemed slightly nervous waiting to see how I would deal with the giants.

My heart racing and stomach churning, I opened the door and heard movements in the cattle pens.

Cocking my Patchett and quietly closing the door after me, I slid out into the darkness and felt great relief in hearing a strong voice calling in Swahili.

‘Hapana, hapana, effendi. Askari ya Forestry.’

Reaching back and pushing the door open to give a shaft of light from the hurricane lamp in the hall, I saw a well-built Nandi in the Green Jersey of the Forestry Department, Sergeant’s stripes on his arms.

He seemed to know all about me and said that they had just seized some thirty head of stolen cattle, put them in the cattle pens and asked if I would I sure they were fed in the morning?

Then he saluted smartly and disappeared into the night.

Mike White – Police Officer

Cattle and African Magic

While I stationed at Kapenguria, West Suk, the Administration decided that the Wasuk tribesmen had too many cattle for the grazing area available. A de-stocking campaign was decided on where the Watu would bring in ten per cent of their individual herds to be auctioned in several locations throughout the district with buyers being brought in by truck.

Heaven knows how the tribal herders were expected to get their cattle to the railhead at Kitale, up and through the Chepararia escarpment, a very narrow gorge with very steep, deep sides. It may be imagined that the Wasuk were not very pleased with the idea. 'What use is money they often asked?' Some even asked, 'What IS money?'

To say that co-operation was non-existent is an understatement. One of the reason was Chepusia, a blind woman Laibon who drummed up a lot of anti-government feeling through the Dini ya Msambwa (or was it the Dini ya Mariam? Time has taken its toll on memory.) Anyway, delay after delay occurred and then the rains came so nobody could bring in their cattle and nobody would come to the auctions.

A decision was made that the cattle for auction would now be slaughtered by the owner and as proof that the deed had been done he would bring in the end of the tail of each beast as proof that he had indeed slaughtered them.

After the rains, when we were able to get out again on safari, we noticed that many cattle had no tail ends.

As a tail end of this story, (sorry), a mobile eye hospital in the area, operated, I believe, by the Seventh Day Adventists Church were in the very early days of doing eye cataract operations. I think they were practising on

Africans to improve the procedure before taking it out into the wide world

As a demonstration that the White Man`s Magic could be stronger than Chepusia's, the Laibon, they operated to remove her cataracts and she was able to see again.

African Magic. Is there such a thing? The Africans certainly think so, for during our cattle culling campaign we often found stick barriers laid across the tracks. Special Branch enquiries discovered that the sticks were to warn us off and put a curse on the Administration and Kenya Police in the area. The curse said that we would all be forced out by Magic within a short time period.

Within a week or ten days the District Commissioner was kicked in the chest by his horse and suffered several broken ribs and flown out to Kitale. Then two European Police Officers leading a General Service Unit team both of went down with the severe runs and had to go for treatment. And I contracted what I believe was sand-fly fever and went back to Kitale Hospital for a jab or two, leaving only the District Officer to mind the camp.

So, does African Magic really exist?

Perhaps.

Graham Clark – Police Officer

My First Eventful Year

Bored with being a Policeman in Glasgow I joined The Kenya Police in July 1951.

I flew to Nairobi, the only policeman on a BOAC Hermes, and on arrival found that the New Recruit three-month Training Course had started two weeks previously.

With the next Course not for six months, the Senior Officer sent me to Kisumu to fill in the time. On arrival I met the Provincial Commander transferred me immediately by pickup truck to Divisional Headquarters at Kakamega, thirty miles away, still carrying my sixty yard bolt of Khaki Drill cloth.

My first stop in Kakamega was to an Indian tailor for my cloth made to be up into uniforms. After a quick lunch I was back in the pickup truck heading for Bungoma. After a long day I arrived in the dark to be greeted by an Inspector delighted to meet me.

He said, 'This place is driving me mad and I can't wait to get away.'

Five days later he had packed and departed to Kakamega.

Ten days earlier I had been in Glasgow and now here I am as Station Commander of an upcountry Police Station in Kenya, still in my town clothes and responsible for thirty African Police, only two of whom could speak any English. I had no telephone, no electricity and only rainwater stored in one thousand gallon tanks.

My predecessor been five years a Policeman, two years in Palestine and three in Kenya, so I spent the next five days before he left, trying to gain as much background as possible on the area and my duties.

It didn't sound at all encouraging. Bungoma was the focal point of an illegal quasi-religious cult, proscribed a couple of years ago. This newly established Police Station, still being constructed, owed its existence to the cult and a serious confrontation three years earlier at an eight-man Police Post about ten miles away.

The Police Superintendent from Kakamega had been on a visit and found an exited and threatening mob, estimated about one thousand, demanding the release of three prisoners. They refused to disperse and tried to seize the Superintendent's revolver. They then started attacking the Police with missiles, which led to the Police opening fire and killing eleven and wounding sixteen.

This stopped further disturbances locally, but the cult remained active in another province. Only fifteen months earlier a major affray took place involving more than forty armed Police that led to the death of a Police Inspector, a District Officer and a Tribal Police Constable.

That operation had gone badly wrong, but brought out the fundamental issue of who is responsible for ordering lethal force in defence of life and property? The District Commissioner, also present, had more than once countermanded the order to shoot, given by the Senior Police Officer present.

Eventually the Police, forced to open fire, had killed more than twenty-eight rioters and wounded around twice that number. The District Commissioner escaped unharmed, having beaten a hasty retreat, when the Police ran out of ammunition and withdrew.

Because of this, in my first meeting with The District Officer, Bungoma, for his views on use of firearms, with the blunt and unequivocal reply, 'Your men; your firearms; your decision.'

Fortunately my few months at Bungoma passed with only a few thefts, a few traffic accidents and drunkenness, mainly among my own rank and file.

At the end of December I transferred to the Training School at Kiganjo, handing my Bungoma command over to an Inspector just passed out from the Course I had just missed.

In January 1952 twenty-four of us started our training at Kiganjo for what we hoped would be an auspicious beginning to our chosen careers. Within a few days we were briefed on the Kikuyu Insurgency and the probability of being engaged in assisting the Police in that area.

Instead, on 21st January the School Commandant called me in with the news of my transfer to Marsabit Division in The Northern Frontier District.

Cattle raiders from Ethiopia had attacked a Rendille Boma about ninety miles inside Kenya, killing eighty women and children and making off with several hundred head of livestock.

Next morning I set off by lorry to Isiolo and after a night stop went on the 180 miles to Marsabit, nearly three-hundred miles from the Ethiopian Border, where I spent the month of February running the Police Station and supervising the daily duties of the men and families based there.

The Police Constables were put through daily training and small arms drill, including skirmishing order and other infantry skills, such as organised withdrawal under fire.

The men operated in Platoons of thirty-five and were regularly rotated to outstation duty at two main Border Posts.

On 1st March I went with my Platoon to Fort Banya, some three hundred miles distant, on the shores of Lake Rudolf and about six miles from the Ethiopian frontier.

We travelled with two Ford V8 three-ton lorries loaded with supplies for six weeks. Our main duties in this area of nomadic tribes allocated individual grazing and watering sections, were foot patrols lasting six to nine days, with pack camels belonging to a local cameleer, carrying water and supplies.

We were expected to cover twenty miles a day in ambient temperatures of 35C. In that vast expanse of desert, many days passed without seeing a soul.

So that month of March 1952 that started quietly, ended on 31st with an armed engagement against some two hundred and fifty cattle raiders in a running battle that lasted six hours.

Therein lies another story.

Sara Wright – Police Wife

Government House, Mau Mau And a Baby Grand Piano

I arrived in Kenya in September 1952, with the then Governor Sir Evelyn Baring, his wife Lady Mary and daughter Katharine.

Just down from Oxford I had no idea what I wanted to do. Katherine had just left school so I joined her as companion and close friend. We were supposed to do some earnest and improving reading together for a few months until she went to Art College in the spring. We had too many distractions to worry about the reading, but she is now a very good artist.

I think I fell in love with Kenya on the aeroplane steps. I had never seen such an immense brilliant blue sky, nor smelt that hot dusty exciting smell, nor seen flowers and birds so wonderfully coloured everywhere one looked.

It was however a sad time for Kenya: the Mau Mau insurrection was nearly out of hand throughout the central Kikuyu Province. There had been violent and horrible incidents and within a month of his arrival the Governor had to declare a State of Emergency.

Life in Government House went on as I imagine it always does, with an enormous number of visiting and local dignitaries, all full of advice, some of which was helpful, some idiotic. Katharine and I acquired a large Alsatian guard dog from an RAF family who had been posted back to England.

The Police guard around The House and in the grounds was increased and very visible, and various regiments of the British Army came out to join the Police, the King's African Rifles and the locally raised Kenya Regiment in the fight against the terrorist gangs.

Government House would have been instantly recognised by generations of Imperial and Colonial officials.

It was a large grand house with a ballroom and a billiard room, a big drawing room, a large dining room and innumerable house servants. There were smaller rooms, where we lived when not on duty.

It was very comfortable and furnished quite thoroughly, although the Barings brought pictures, more furniture and books from England or their previous Government Houses. It felt like an English country house, but much more comfortable, no icy cold passages, constant hot water and no washing up.

Katharine and I had our own small flat, a bedroom and bathroom each and a sitting room, and our own servant Njeroge, who taught us a little Kikuyu. All I can now remember is "niwega Muno" thank you.

Dr Leakey, the famous anthropologist, came and taught Lady Mary, Katharine and me Swahili and Kenyan history and pre-history. He was fascinating, though unwashed. We went to the museum to learn about the different tribes and their appearance, botany, birds and animals and went often to the Nairobi Game Park with the Game wardens. They seemed to know each individual lion and elephant and had given them names, such as Maude for an elephant, and Mabel for a lion.

We swam in the Government House swimming pool and Lady Mary set about transforming the gardens, with the help of an army of gardeners and a marvellous Hungarian called Rosie (so appropriate).

A team of African Police drivers drove us about Nairobi in large black cars with crowns on them. They very rapidly became our friends and teachers I think they probably taught us a slightly different but more useful kind of Swahili than Dr Leakey's.

We had comfortable life, but through it all felt the worry and anxiety of the Emergency and how to deal with it. One General after another would arrive for conferences, often bringing, to our delight as young girls, beautiful ADC's in exotic uniforms. They came from The Black Watch, The Green Jackets, The Parachute Regiment; you name it we danced with them all, whoever they were.

As well as the Generals, we had an unbroken stream of remarkable visitors. The Queen Mother refused to drive from Embakasi Airport to Nairobi in the large black car provided. 'No one will be able to see me, 'she insisted.

The only open topped vehicle at the airport was a rather small sports car. Into it squeezed the very tall Governor with feathers sprouting from his ceremonial hat and the rather stout Queen. Looking like cuckoos in a warbler's nest the pair drove triumphantly along, waving to the amazed crowds.

Princess Margaret came, very cross and sad about an unhappy love affair, and was rude to almost everyone.

Ava Gardner and Frank Sinatra arrived to make a film. She was beautiful but spilling out of her clothes. Sinatra was a huge disappointment, being much older and shorter than we imagined and only about five foot three inches tall.

Ernest Hemingway visited and told us we were all "Caking at the edges". We argued a bit about whether this was a compliment or not, and decided probably not.

Eminent botanists and earnest young scientists came and talked Latin with Sir Evelyn. Birdwatchers, sheep farmers, mountain climbers and old settlers all came – we learned a lot.

A few months after the Declaration of Emergency a young policeman came to an Investiture at Government House. He had been awarded the George Medal for bravery while fighting Shifta in the Northern Frontier Province. It was the first time Ernie Wright and I met. About four months later he was appointed ADC to the Governor.

Ernie settled in and very soon became one of the family. The breakthrough came during the Christmas holidays when the Barings' fifteen-year-old son, Charlie, came out from school.

There was a programme on the wireless called The Goon Show in which the actors did spoofs of spy films, heroic war films and the like and the like, all using silly voices.

We were all in the car going off to some grand function rather a long way from Nairobi. Charlie got bored and began doing an imitation of The Goon Show. Ernie, sitting in the front of the car in uniform, managed to retain correct official decorum for about ten minutes. He then burst out laughing with the rest of us, turned round and joined in the imitations and from then on he never looked back.

David Illing – Police Officer

Tsavo National Park

On completing my stint at the Police Training School at Kiganjo, I was sent by train to Voi, having no idea where the place was. Tim Trafford met me at the railway station and took me to the Assistant Superintendent of Police, Paddy Garland.

He informed me that I was going to assist the Parks Department in anti-poaching duties and told me not to unpack my kit.

Reporting to the Parks HQ I met David Sheldrick, the park warden and Roy Home, a hunter. They explained we would be following poaching trends and information gained to arrest as many poachers as possible, with the police providing custody.

David Sheldrick, wanting to know what sort of person had been foisted on him, gave me a grilling about my life before and after arriving in Kenya. He seemed quite content until he asked what I knew about elephants.

I replied that I had only seen them in a circus and they were big and grey.

He started my initial training that afternoon by taking me for a walk. I felt that every elephant we saw had its eye on me, but the knowledge and confidence I gained that afternoon were invaluable later on.

We took off in convoy going north from Mackinnon Road to the Galana River. We captured a motley collection of fifteen poachers from the Waliangulu and Wakamba peoples. The Waliangulu were a bush living people surviving on meat and berries. Since their poaching activities have been curtailed, their numbers have diminished and the survivors are living in poverty near Voi.

All poachers we caught in the National Park were jailed for thirty days in the district prison at Taita.

Having completed my anti-poaching duties I returned to Voi, where the new Police house complete with round windows made from the steel ends of the spun concrete pipes manufactured for the Mzima Springs water project and donated by Gumez and Bonner was ready.

The spun concrete pipes were there to carry water down to Mombasa and the steel ends gave us a set of large porthole windows with a wonderful view overlooking Voi Township and the hills beyond.

The water for Mzima Springs comes from the snows of Mount Kilimanjaro and travels almost a hundred miles underground through porous rock and springs into the world through a natural volcanic rock bank named Shaitani Rock.

This miracle of nature delivers perfectly fresh and clear spring water into the middle of the desert eighty miles down to the heavily populated coastal town of Mombasa.

Today Mzima Springs is seen by millions on the BBC news programmes link, with hippo apparently swimming in circles.

In those days a resident rhino lived on the hill behind the house. The loo was a wooden hut twenty yards up the hill and to ensure a safe journey from one to the other at night, a tin containing stones had to be thrown up the path. Our neighbour respected this and gave us safe passage.

My bush knowledge was tested soon after, when twenty-five Mau Mau detainees escaped from Manyani Prison near Tsavo.

Because of the likelihood of being captured on the main Nairobi-Mombasa road, they fled into the Tsavo West Park, towards Mount Kilimanjaro. With two vehicles, and fuel and food for a week. I was sent with six Constables into the area with the intention of making our presence known and to drive the escapees towards stop lines set up around the area.

What would one have to pay now for my experience that week and the counters with elephants, leopards, lions, hippos and rhinos? Plus to top that, sleeping under the stars.

The only untoward incident that week was when, early one morning, I accidentally got between a hippo and the springs at Mzima, when he was returning after a night out. Luckily I was near a tree and he definitely sensed my presence, but either didn't see me, or decided to ignore my presence.

Twenty-four of the escapees were caught that week. We are not sure if the twenty-fifth got away or was or killed by lion, buffalo or any of the other wildlife that abound in the very large Tsavo Park. Or of course, he could have died of thirst.

I later moved to Mackinnon Road just outside the park, where I was lucky enough to locate the most northerly point in that area that the German forces reached during World War One at a hill is Pika Pika.

I found the hilltop covered with thousands of .303 rifle cartridge cases. Its sister, the bigger hill Kilibasi, does not show any signs of being the site of any conflict.

Anthony Marx – Police Officer

Happy Days in Samburu

In 1959 I returned from U.K. leave and was re-posted a second time to Samburu Police Sub-Division in the Northern Frontier District of Kenya. The entire 10,000 square mile territory – I was told the size of Wales – and gazetted as a National Park was packed with wild animals including the "Big Five"; lion, leopard, elephant, buffalo and rhino

This wild semi-desert country is populated in the south by the Samburu tribe – a peaceful Nilotic people related to the Masai – and in the northern harsher country by isolated groups of the more aggressive Rendille who grazed their camels and goats and moved in continuous search for new fodder.

A few surviving remnants of the almost extinct El Molo people lived on the volcanic rock-strewn southern perimeter of Lake Rudolph, their diet almost entirely being lake fish as crops did not grow in the rocky ground. Some fell victim to the huge Nile crocodiles that waited off shore.

It is a stark and unforgiving environment, where the nomadic tribes exist from one brief rainy season to the next.

On police patrol, camping at night was an adventure often accompanied by the grunts and roars of lion and the likelihood of being joined by a passing herd of elephant.

I was a newly promoted Chief Inspector, assisted by one white Inspector at Maralal and another at Wamba Post and a hundred native Askaris. We wore a different uniform than the regions outside of the NFD. The men wore pale khaki shorts and shirts, with a round pillbox hat similar to the French Foreign Legion. On patrol, they carried the old .303 SMLE rifle and wore a bandolier across the shoulder.

European officers wore a pale grey short-sleeved woollen shirt and a lightweight khaki hat reminiscent of the German Africa Corps headgear, which had just been approved. It had a neck flap buttoned around the side, to be unfastened and rolled down to protect the ears and neck in the harsh sun.

For long-range patrols and transportation we used land rovers and a three-ton truck fitted with extra fuel tank and sand ladders bolted at the side. With no petrol available outside of three small settlements, we carried a forty-four gallon barrel of petrol fitted with a hand pump strapped in the back, together with another clean barrel of water.

Our armoury included a Bren light machine gun as well as Patchett sub machine guns and grenades as we functioned more like gendarmerie and peacekeepers than "Coppers".

Once a month I drove on a Patrol route taking a full week, which took me north to Baracoa and South Hour, then back diagonally south east on the Samba track to Samba township, then continued on south east to Archers Post which lies north of Isiolo, then back west along the Faso Nitro river to Salute and finally to Marital.

The Patrol purpose was to inspect each Police Post where the men paraded for kit and arms inspection and to replace worn kit. Additional duties included disciplinary hearings and meetings with the local chief or headman. The inventory included donkeys and camels used for transportation which was never short, as they naturally replaced any loss with newborn arrivals.

The inspection included a pay parade when the Askaris were paid their monthly salary in cash. I sat at a camp table with the money in a heavy cash box, together with a spreadsheet and the NCO Post Commander standing next to me.

The Askaris formed a line and each individual marched smartly forward when called by the NCO. The men would pick up their pay, sign for it and take one step back, salute and about turn to march away.

It was a simple but final ceremonial act before we left to continue to the next post, which had been radioed ahead.

On the northern leg I always camped overnight at Baragoi and sometimes spent the evening at the back of his trading store with Mohamed Ismail, the local trader and sort of mayor. He was a mine of information about local issues affecting law and order.

Incidentally, we both knew he was a member of the Somali Freedom Party whose mission was to secede the Northern border area from Kenya. Nevertheless we enjoyed a good relationship with politics kept out of it and I learned something of his Muslim beliefs, all discussed in Swahili.

Also at Baragoi was a long established Italian Catholic Mission, and I would sometimes dine with the priests and nuns in their comfortable stone-built surroundings, as the desert air was very cool at night. In return I brought them fresh vegetables I purchased, grown in the high elevation of Maralal.

Father Davoli and his staff lived amazingly well in that harsh environment and ran a free hospital dispensary for the locals. Tragically, his assistant priest was tortured and murdered by bandits at Lake Rudolph a few years after Independence. Father Davoli himself was shot and killed in 1981 when bandits ambushed him. The account can be found on Google.

On one inspection tour I arrived at Baragoi Post, just south of the Lake and was advised by the Sergeant Post commander that they were having trouble with a band of Rendille who had trespassed with their camels south from the Ethiopian border.

When warned off by the local Samburu Chief who threatened to call us they responded with the threat to kick us out.

This was too much. You don't threaten the British Colonial Police and get away with it.

So I packed an escort of four rifle-armed Askaris complete with bandoliers and extra ammunition into the back of my open Land Rover and with my driver Idi Uledi, a Muslim I managed to retain for many years, drove across country along goat tracks.

Eventually we encountered the large camel herd ahead of us in the camel thorn bush guarded by scattered group of tall fuzzy-wuzzy spear-armed and truculent Rendille who formed a defensive group, glaring in our direction.

I guess that when in Ethiopia they didn't have much respect for their local gendarmerie.

Next thing one young show-off started strutting towards us hefting a long spear and there we were, still packed inside the Land Rover, open without canopy.

Withdrawing my sidearm I quickly ordered the escort to load and aim from inside the vehicle, as he looked be intent on launching his spear in our direction.

He would certainly have got one of us.

At the last moment as he drew his arm back to throw, to avoid killing him and starting a violent exchange, I changed my mind and ordered three rapid volleys to be fired over the heads of the camel herd.

That did the trick. The camels took off in a huge cloud of dust back in the direction of Ethiopia, chased by all the herders including the young buck who had nearly met his end.

That was the last seen of them.

Relieved of the tension, my Askaris exploded in guffaws of laughter and repeatedly exchanged their version of what had transpired as we drove back to the post, and I'm sure related it to the local Samburu later.

John Hughes – Police Officer

The Murder Of Assistant Inspector Tom Mortimer

On the afternoon of Saturday, twentieth of December, nineteen forty seven, at a remote Reserve of Kenya Colony, Assistant Inspector Thomas Mortimer originally from Pietermaritzburg, South Africa, was murdered by members of a fanatical religious sect, originated and led by a Kikuyu named Reuben Kihiko.

He founded the sect amongst Kikuyu labourers living in the Rift Valley Province of Kenya during nineteen forty six on the basis of a return to the simple life, as opposed to the civilized way of life of the Europeans, whom he alleged were followers of Satan.

Reuben commanded his followers to wear skins, as the Bible related Adam and Eve had done when forced to leave the Garden of Eden. The sect was known in Kiswahili as the "Watu wa Mungu" Men of God or the "Dini ya Jesu Kristu" The Faith of Jesus Christ.

When a number of these Kikuyu squatter labourers refused to sign new agreements limiting the numbers of their stock and the land they could cultivate in The Rift, they returned to the Kikuyu Reserve.

In December nineteen forty seven the sect, led by Reuben, were living in a village near Gatundu, with his principal lieutenant, Ngugi Mungai and a large following of the new sect, mostly consisting of women and children. Reuben dressed himself and his lieutenants in red uniforms and paraded around the district with drums beating and flags flying

On that fatal Saturday morning Reuben went with some of his followers to a market close to Gatundu with a red flag, which had at some stage become torn. They went to the shop of a tailor named Stephen Mwenja and ordered him to repair the flag, which apparently he refused to do.

An argument developed which turned into a scuffle in which Stephen was badly slashed across the arm and body with a Simi, the razor sharp double-edged short sword of the Kikuyu. Stephen was then abducted by the gang who intended to take him back to their village to kill him in the presence of the women members of the sect.

A number of Kikuyu from the market then drove in a lorry to the Police Station at Gatundu to report what had happened to Stephen, the tailor. Assistant Inspector Peter Mwami commanded Gatundu Police Station with a staff of one Sergeant and six Constables.

Assistant Inspector Peter set off in the Kikuyu lorry with a Sergeant and three Constables armed with rifles to investigate. About three miles from Gatundu they met a group of about forty sect members, dressed in skins and armed with Simis and spears. They were singing loudly and were led by Reuben dressed in a white kanzu or Arab type robe and with two red banners.

In front held by two men was the blood-covered figure of the tailor. Assistant Inspector Peter stopped the lorry and the Police all got off, whilst the two men holding the tailor left him lying semi-conscious in the road and retired to join the main body. Peter could see that the man was badly injured and that his hand had almost been severed from the arm and there were deep slashes on his body.

Peter sent the injured tailor in the lorry to the Kiambu Hospital by a route that led through Ruiru, a village in the coffee growing district of Thika.

Assistant Inspector Peter then lined his men across the road facing the sect members and demanded to know who had assaulted the tailor Stephen. Reuben answered, 'He was cut by God's servants.'

The crowd now became very aggressive and threatening. At this point Reuben drew a line across the road with his Simi and shouted 'He whoever does not want to live should try to cross that line.'

After failing to calm sect members and faced by superior numbers, Assistant Inspector Peter withdrew down the road and the sect members turned off into the bush and followed a path to a group of huts some distance from the road, where they could be heard singing.

Assistant Inspector Peter then sent off a man by bicycle to the Police Station to get a message through to Divisional Headquarters at Kiambu. Inspector J.A. Lapage, the Officer-in-charge of Kiambu Police Station, temporarily commanded the Division. When he received a somewhat garbled message, Lapage was under the impression that Peter was reporting a drunken affray.

At that time I was an Assistant Inspector of Police, having arrived in Kenya in August nineteen forty seven, just two months after my 21st birthday and stationed at Kiambu Police Station as No. 2 to Lapage.

That Saturday afternoon I had gone to tea with my girlfriend, who lived on a smallholding in the district. Inspector Lapage later told me, that had I been in the Boma that afternoon, he would have sent me out to Gatundu and probably I would have been killed instead of Tom Mortimer.

When the lorry taking the injured tailor to Kiambu hospital passed through Ruiru, it stopped at the Police Station and Assistant Inspector T.D. Mortimer, when he saw the injuries to the tailor, realized that this case needed immediate action. He had not been in Kenya long, having come from Pietermaritzburg, South Africa and his attachment to his family was reflected in the fact that he carried a photograph of his Mother and Sister in the lining of his blue peaked service cap.

Although Ruiru fell under Thika Division and Gatundu was outside his area, Mortimer set off with a Sergeant and two Constables to drive the fifteen miles to Gatundu. In the meantime Assistant Inspector Peter finding that all was quiet in the direction of the huts decided to investigate.

He found the village deserted and all hut doors locked. This was now about five in the afternoon and whilst wondering where everyone had gone he saw Assistant Inspector Mortimer coming along the path through the bush with his Policemen.

Just as they joined the other Police in the centre of the village, there was a shout and the sect members rose from the surrounding long grass where they had hidden in ambush. They ran forward about fifteen yards, surrounding the Police party and as Mortimer turned to confront them he was stabbed with a spear.

He managed to draw his .45 Webley revolver and fired two shots at his attackers before being overwhelmed by men wielding Simis. He and a Police Constable were killed and Sergeant Samuel Kyule and two Constables wounded, one dying later that night in hospital at Thika.

By now the injured tailor, Stephen had arrived at Kiambu and Inspector Lapage having seen that matters were more serious than he previously thought, set off to drive to Gatundu not, of course, knowing what had happened to Mortimer.

I returned to the Boma at about 6 p.m. and reported in at the Police Station, where I met the District Commissioner, Edward Windley. He told me that there had been an attack at Gatundu and Assistant Inspector Mortimer was missing. He was concerned about ordering more reinforcements and, since darkness fell at around six-thirty, risking a night attack, but at the same time not knowing what had happened to Mortimer.

The news of the Gatundu attack now reached Police Headquarters in Nairobi and reinforcements from the Police Depot were ordered to the scene. Later that night the Commissioner of Police, C.H. Ward reached Gatundu himself and declared that he was not leaving one of his Inspectors possibly lying out wounded all night. He personally led a party of Police to the village to look for Mortimer.

When they found his body and that of the Police constable, but no members of the sect, the Commissioner ordered the village burnt to the ground. This subsequently caused more concern at the Colonial Office in London, than the deaths of the three Policemen.

The following morning I received a message from Inspector Lapage who had spent the night at Gatundu to join him there. I missed Lapage who was returning by a different route, so arrived at Gatundu with no orders and no idea of what I was supposed to do.

Anyway I met Assistant Inspector Peter at the Police Station and he said that I was to round up the sect members. I found that all the senior officers had returned to Nairobi leaving behind about a hundred Police constables from the Police Depot as reinforcements, who were now under my command.

The main body of the sect was reported to be in a valley close to Gatundu, so I ordered the Police into a sweep line and we proceeded to move through the bush in extended order.

Very soon I came across a skin-clad man hiding under a bush. He presented a pretty horrible sight as Mortimer had shot him in the face and one side had been blown open with a great flap of skin hanging down. He thrust a Simi at me and I cocked my revolver, but thought that unless he made a move to attack me, I could not just shoot him in cold blood.

He came out from the bush and I handed him over to be taken away for treatment. We continued on through the bush and gradually began finding women and children and a few old men and taking them in.

By now it was well after six o'clock and getting dark as we reached the road to Gatundu and got news that the main body of the men were ahead of us. I wanted to press on and attack them, but the senior District Officer from Kiambu, Leslie Pritchard now arrived and advised that we had better return to Gatundu for the night as it was too risky to chance a night action with untrained Police Constables.

Back at Gatundu the Provincial Superintendent of Police from Headquarters Central Province, Nyeri, Senior Superintendent A.W. Riggs, M.B.E joined us. We now received word that the main body of the men were coming to attack us as I had arrested all their women and children.

We put all the prisoners in the ground floor of the stone built Court House and laagered the Police vehicles around it in defensive positions. We three Europeans then spent the night on the flat roof of the Court House waiting for an attack that never came.

Next morning Senior Superintendent Riggs set off in pursuit with a party of Police as Reuben and the remaining members of his sect were headed for Mount Kenya, which they regarded as Mount Sinai. They actually reached the Mount Kenya snow line and planted a red banner there before they were tracked down and arrested.

Reuben and Njugi Mungai, the man I had arrested, were later charged with murder along with fifteen others of the sect.

The Kenya justice system required that before a murder case could be heard in the Supreme Court a Preliminary Enquiry was held before a Magistrate. Accordingly at the Preliminary Enquiry hearing when I was giving evidence, I was asked if I recognised anyone in Court. As the person I had arrested Njugi Mungai was sitting in the dock with his head swathed in bandages I found him easy to identify.

Later in June nineteen forty eight when the same question was asked of me in the Supreme Court trial, I was taken aback as by then the doctors had repaired Njugi's face so well that I had difficulty in deciding which of the accused he was. He solved my dilemma however, as he recognized me and obligingly stood up.

Reuben, Njugi and two others were sentenced to death and later hanged whilst two juveniles were sentenced to detention during the Governor's pleasure. Eleven of the accused were acquitted. Forty-five other members of the sect being unable to furnish securities for their good behaviour were committed to prison.

This story is dedicated to the memory of Assistant Inspector Thomas Mortimer, a promising young South African who gave his life in the execution of his duty and but for the chance of circumstances, might well have been murdered.

John Ross – Police Officer

Up Whitehouse Hill

One evening in late 1951 or early 1952, there was a traffic accident in Whitehouse Road. Police were in attendance and an ambulance (at that time operated by the police) had been called for a badly injured African pedestrian. As was normal, it took about forty minutes to arrive.

A European gentleman who declared himself to be a witness to the accident was beside himself with anger over the non-appearance of the ambulance. When it did arrive, the injured man was fully strapped to a stretcher and loaded on to the ambulance - the stretcher was on four small metal wheels and was put into the ambulance on two steel runners. The agitated man said (shouted) that he was going to follow the ambulance to ensure the injured man arrived at hospital safely.

All three vehicles – the ambulance, the witness's vehicle and the police car – set off for King George's Hospital, up Whitehouse Hill. This particular hill was rather steep, with two sharp 90-degree bends.

About half way up the hill, the ambulance's rear door flew open and out trundled the stretcher. Frantic and panic-stricken action by the vehicles following behind narrowly avoided our patient being injured any further, as the stretcher on its four wheels thundered off down the hill.

Thankfully there was no damage to patient or stretcher, but bear in mind that if the agitated witness of the original incident wished for something to complain about, we certainly gave him plenty of scope for his remarks.

Paddy Kearney – Police Officer

Three Short Stories

At the Nairobi Police Mess Toby Norman (R.I.P.) looked after ALL of us like a Mother would do. Great food, cleanliness, wonderful Buffets, Special Dinners, Wedding Receptions – Olga and I had our Reception had there some sixty-three years ago – and putting up with we rowdy Policemen at all hours. A wonderful lady.

We had a ritual in the Mess on Stag Nights. With the Party in full swing, we debagged unfortunate Groom, and covered his rear – both cheeks – with fingerprint ink.

We then raised him on high and printed the image of his backside to show on the Bar wall.

To save embarrassment the imprints were then covered with a picture frame. Needless to say the Bar walls were covered with many picture frames and were often removed, mainly by Ladies, to view what was behind.

I wonder how many of the "unfortunates"" are still with us to tell the story? I had my stag night at a friend's home and avoided the fingerprint ink.

At Torrs Hotel, Nairobi, that famous landmark on Delamere Avenue, near to the famous Settlers' Leader's statue on the roundabout with the New Stanley Hotel.

Ray Morgan (R.I.P.) and I were Traffic Motor Cycle cops, known as the Terrible Twins because of the many traffic cases we processed for Court where the renowned "Bugs" Emery (R.I.P.) was Court Prosecutor.

We had a call to the Mess from the 999 Control Room, reporting a domestic argument outside the Torrs Hotel. We agreed to go and went by motorcycle to the scene.

On arrival a Police Ford Blue V8 also arrived with Assistant Inspector Maurice Silcock (R.I.P.) with another Assistant Inspector in support. Maurice had served with us in The Palestine Police, so we decided to stand back and leave the domestic, to him and his colleague.

Maurice went to break up the argument. The lady was screaming and on the ground. Maurice was a little rough in pulling her assailant away and, being drunk, he lost his balance and fell.

His Lady friend – in floods of tears – rushed to check on him and seeing him more or less unconscious, grabbed her umbrella and lashed out at Maurice, hitting him with such force she broke his defensive upraised arm.

Needless to say both the man and woman spent time in Kingsway Police Station before a Court Hearing and two guilty pleas for assault.

As a very new Assistant Inspector I was sent for duties in Mombasa, where Ernie Wright (R.I.P) was Station Commander and then, I believe, a Chief Inspector.

Once, I was on Traffic Duty at the always-crowded main Market, when a fight broke out between two of the stallholders and knives were drawn. It was a very heated argument and, to be honest, I was at a loss, at the time, as to what to do in the situation.

Someone must have called the Station and, to my great relief, Ernie arrived in quick time with several Constables. Ernie approached the fight and one of the culprits raised his knife and proceeded to cut his own hands.

He seemed obviously under the influence of some drink or drug. Ernie spoke to both men and to the people gathered to watch. The crowd dispersed with help from some Police Constables and Ernie coolly arrested both culprits and away they went to the Station.

The way Ernie dealt with what could have developed into a nasty situation made a lasting impression on me as a lesson on how to address similar difficult occasions, of which I experienced many during my Police career in Kenya.

John Clark – Police Officer

My time in the Kenya Police

I flew to Kenya in 1954 on a two-year Kenya Police contract.

Previously I had served in the Special Investigation Branch of the Royal Military Police in Germany.

What impressed me on arrival in Nairobi was the wide variety of police experience shared among my newly arrived colleagues. Several ex Palestine, South African and Malayan Police Forces, among them experts in firearms, explosives, radio communications – you name it.

Even two chaps I remember who could fly aeroplanes.

During training at Kiganjo I recall many happy evenings at The Outspan Hotel, at Nyeri, a few miles away from the Police Training School based at Kiganjo. I also recall how entertaining I found the range of subjects taught at PTS and the chance to meet and work closely with African and Asian colleagues.

What many do not appreciate these days is their wonderful sense of humour, amongst other attributes.

Senior Superintendent Ken Akker, when in charge of Southern Province, decided on a Special Branch anti terrorist operation in a hilly-forested area south of Narok.

To carry this out he dispatched several Tracker Groups on a far-reaching intelligence gathering operation in and around The Province.

Based on Narok, I set off in pouring rain to patrol the hills and forests of the Masai and Mara River area

My Group consisted of a very good Masai Assistant Inspector named Augustino and four ex Mau Mau terrorists, plus a Kikuyu tracker who knew the territory well.

My four ex-terrorists, now cleansed of their Mau Mau Oaths and turned, had been in gangs in this section and we hoped would lead me to the terrorist message drop sites and, perhaps hidden weapons stores.

We walked through intermittent rain for about three days with my tracker leading the way. It's always pretty uncomfortable patrolling through the forest in heavy rain and it is even worse having to sleep on wet ground when it's bucketing down during the night.

Especially with four ex Mau Mau, a Masai Inspector and a Kikuyu tracker; all of us huddled together under a zebra skin.

In the small hours of our third night my tracker went out to check around and came back with news.

'I've found a hide. They're there.'

Just before dawn we crept up and waited. At daybreak one guy came out for a pee. I fired a short burst with my Patchet and winged him.

This raised the alarm and two other men rushed from the hide. All three took off like bats out of hell and we sent a hail of bullets after them, but they got away.

At The Hide With My Tracker

I decided to follow and with my tracker twenty yards ahead following their trail, it took us a day and a half before the tracker found one of them lying in the bush injured. I had hit him in the leg during his escape from and he now wanted to surrender.

I think he must have been happy that we found him and probably hoped his tracks would lead us to where he lay.

We found no sign of the other two, now probably long gone and we found no tracks to follow. We never saw them again.

But in the end it turned out to be a fairly successful operation in capturing one terrorist, despite the discomfort and rain and mud and not finding any message drop sites or arms store.

During this and several other operations I had the good fortune to work with my Masai Assistant Inspector, Augustino. He became a close friend. Whilst in the Mara River area he asked if we could divert about twenty miles and visit his Manyatta, to see his father, a respected Headman and Elder.

We did – and what an experience.

Being an Officer in the Kenya Police the people of his village greeted Augustino as somewhat of a hero, sweeping out of the Manyata to give us a fantastic welcome; almost a mini-ceremony in itself.

The young Morani leapt up and down in that unique Masai dance, bobbing their heads with a musical grunt.

The women giggled and laughed, pointing at us in great excitement. They pushed their young children forward and a group stood with their heads bowed in front of me.

I looked at Augustino in query and he said, 'They are giving you respect and want you to touch their heads briefly.'

I patted the head of each child, acknowledging the respect and they trotted away happy, giggling and skipping.

Augustino and I were then ushered towards the entrance of one of the long mud-and-wattle huts to sit on rocks and wooden seating and were offered a thick gruel-like very potent beer with the consistency of diluted porridge and a bitter taste.

After the beer we were plied with pieces of very tasty roasted meat, probably young goat. After this ceremonial feasting and drinking to welcome Augustino, a large bull was led into the compound.

He strolled in completely unconcerned, stood quite still, looking bored with it all and not perturbed in any way. It seemed almost as though he knew the drill and had done it all before.

I became worried about what might be about to happen to the animal and that he may be slaughtered in front of us. I asked Augustino, who reassured me that nothing drastic would happen to the bull and to wait and watch.

A young Masai Moran fired a plugged arrow a few inches into the animal's neck and withdrew the arrow, leaving a sort of tap made from the plug. Blood gushed out to be caught in a wooden kalash and mixed with goat's milk. The young Moran then slapped a dollop of mud and dung onto the small wound and the bull went happily strolling back to join the herd, having apparently noticed nothing.

The kalash was then handed round for the senior tribe members and Augustino and I to drink the mixture.

Wow! Give me a Tusker beer any day but, apparently, by this drinking of blood and milk they were honouring us as important visitors to Augustino's birthplace and, for me, an absolutely unique experience.

The mixture tasted pretty awful, but well worth the few sips I managed to keep down, watched closely by the group of Elders.

We spent three days at the Manyatta and I recall sleeping on the floor amongst several very young goats, brought inside as a safety precaution in case hyenas and other predators leapt over the Boma surrounding the area.

Another memory I have is about the time it was decided by HQ at Ngong that the few Mau Mau residing around the Mara area may be persuaded to surrender if promised safe conduct, food, blankets etc. by way of leaflets dropped from a Kenya Airways plane.

The plane was piloted by a good friend of mine, Paul Harroway, known to us all as Bushy, because of the enormous moustache covering most of the lower half of his face and extending up to his ears.

Augustino and I flew over the designated area dropping handfuls of printed leaflets However, the exercise was exciting as it gave Bushy licence to fly several aerobatics, flying low, with sweeping turns, giving us the thrill of a lifetime.

Eventually we tired of throwing handfuls of leaflets and, now it can be told, threw out several sealed and unopened containers.

Needless to say the idea yielded NIL results.

Overall, my time in Kenya forms the happiest part of my life. I married a wonderful girl named Shirley in 1958 in Mombasa. We had our honeymoon at the Sindbad Hotel, Malindi, costing me a whole month's salary, and Shirley subsequently flew as cabin crew with East Africa Airways.

John Standring – Police Officer

Filmi Filmi

In about 1956, when I was Second In Charge of Nyeri Division, I received an instruction to get up to Nanyuki on the slopes of Mount Kenya and to report to a film crew based at the Mawingo Hotel.

They were making a film called Something of Value, based on the book by American author, Robert Ruark. My instructions were to give the crew local help, especially regarding any work up the slopes of the Mountain as remnants of Mau Mau gangs were still using it as a base.

The film, being directed for MGM by the famed Richard Brooks (famed as much for his flaring temper as for his skill with film-making) starred Rock Hudson and Sidney Poitier.

Kenya was regarded in Hollywood as still being too dangerous for the actresses, Dana Wynter and Wendy Hiller, who also starred, but remained in Hollywood.

It was, quite literally, a fabulous two weeks. I had little to do on the Police and minding side, but plenty of other things to do in helping find local sources such as a rough looking crowd; tree hyrax calls and a typical farm in which to film and so on.

The typical farm produced an amusing occurrence during a scene when Rock Hudson was to embrace the heroine, who in this case was a local stand-in: a quite stunning young Italian woman who, alas, spoke no English.

Richard Brooks found she could speak Swahili and asked me to translate his directions, using Swahili. This gave me no problem, except whatever I said she almost immediately forgot when she was in Rock Hudson's arms.

That was when I experienced Brook's famous temper as of course it was my fault she didn't behave like a professional actress.

There were umpteen retakes until finally she looked into

Rock Hudson's eyes in the manner wanted and that was that.

What I never told Richard Brooks was that in the small crowd of onlookers was the Italian girl's glowering husband right in her line of sight, which I think put her off as much as her six-foot-five handsome Hollywood star.

Towards the end of filming Richard Brooks relented and let the cast off for a Sunday break and asked me to find some to entertainment for them.

Sidney Poitier played golf so I had no trouble in approaching Nanyuki Golf Club to let him have a round. For Rock Hudson I asked a well-known local resident, Logan Hook if we could visit and see one of his half-tamed cheetahs.

Both requests were happily accepted and having delivered Sidney Poitier to the golf club I took others up Mount Kenya to Logan Hook's home. Logan was very well known in Nanyuki and Kenya history and had long developed a safe method of catching and taming cheetah.

Once before the war he took some cheetah to the UK to race against greyhounds, a venture that stopped immediately hostilities started and was never going to amount to much anyway as the cheetah were just too fast. I think they caught up with the mechanical hare and swatted it.

We were a small party; Rock Hudson, the producer who was, I think, Pandro Berman and one or two from the film team. Logan made us very welcome and showed off a beautiful cheetah in an enclosure. After a few moments he arranged for one of his garden staff to race past the enclosure with the remains of a dead rabbit on a long string and then let the cheetah loose.

We have all seen many nature films and this scene was no exception. The cheetah leapt out of his pen and just bounded until he was running alongside the meat, whereupon he smacked at it with both paws.

The chase stopped and the magnificent animal crouched some twenty feet away and ate his meal. When finished he turned very gently and still crouched licked his lips and stared right at Rock Hudson.

As fast as the cheetah could move he was not a patch on the producer who, in a split second bundled up a startled Rock Hudson and stuffed him unceremoniously into the back of the car and stood guard at the door.

Later we were chatting and he told me that MGM would put up with some mistakes but never ever would they have let him have their famous star chewed on by a wild animal.

After the film party left for the hotel I stayed and thanked Logan Hook, who brought up the cheetah. Although only half tame he stayed quite happy alongside me to be and patted and stroked. I think he had stared at Hudson as simply another if bigger star in the film business.

Rock Hudson

The photo of Rock Hudson is one I took myself during a break in filming on a farm near Nanyuki. It would have been unthinkable to try and take a snap while shooting was going on, especially with the fiery director. I took the opportunity while things were quiet and the assistants had the lighting etc. set up. The film star was watching a Kikuyu dancer who was to take part when filming recommenced and gave this relaxed and un-posed picture.

Rock Hudson was an impressive man, six foot six inches tall and very handsome.

One evening I spent an hour or so with him outside in Nanyuki trying to hear a tree hyrax so that he could imitate it in the film.

No luck with the hyrax, but he was interesting to talk with – mainly about Elizabeth Taylor and his recent film Giant – and I left with no idea he was gay. I thought him a better actor than some made him out to be.

When they were filming in Nairobi, Tom Lawson did the minder job and he told me that after a session filming in the rougher part of Nairobi the crew hurried back to The New Stanley where they were staying and Sidney Poitier, still dressed as a Mau Mau terrorist, was smartly refused entry to the Grill Room.

It took only a minute to put things straight but I would have liked to have seen the face of the maitre'd who on a much later occasion wouldn't let me in until I put on a tie.

The crew completed their work and returned to the USA, where I think the film didn't gain the name and kudos for which they had worked so hard, although meticulously produced with two giant stars

I think times had gone forward to where the story about Kenya just wasn’t of interest.

Whatever, the reason those few weeks were unforgettable for me as was the kindness and ace professionalism of the many people involved.

Mrs Susan Mansfield – Police Wife
As told to me by my Husband Derek Mansfield

Not Livingstone It Is To Be Presumed

Imagine the scene, somewhere in the Rift Valley. A marvellous morning, crystal clear and delightfully cool.

On the road near the local Police Station two young men in their mid twenties approach each other. One, a good looking tall young man with blue eyes dressed in a crisply starched Police uniform, new in Post, driving a Land Rover. The other also very correctly dressed in riding clothes, astride a chestnut gelding.

They draw level with one another to exchange pleasantries.

Not having met before and it being long ago when there was a right way to do things; both wish to be very correct.

The Policeman announces, 'Good morning, my name is Mansfield'.

'Now, that's a funny thing, so is mine,' replies the Rider.

The horseman, David, as it transpired, was also in the Police force and on local leave.

I expect some of you will remember him.

And also, I very much hope, you will remember the blue eyed Policeman, my husband, Derek Mansfield who served in Sotik, NFD, Bechuanaland, Naivasha, Nakuru and others, during ten years service, returning to UK late 1958.

Here is a rather strange story Derek told me a bout something that happened one night far out in the Northern Frontier District.

At a Police Post whose name I cannot recall there was a considerable rumpus in the Lines, ended only by the removal from the scene of a very annoyed old woman who had been shouting some very stern words at her dismayed Askari son-in-law.

The next morning, when the Constables were called on Parade, the numbers were seen to be one short.

The Sergeant explained to his Inspector-in-Charge that the young Constable in question was not willing to come out of his hut as his mother-in-law had last night put a Curse upon him.

The Curse decreed that a hyena would bite him within a short period of time and he would only have himself to blame.

As can be imagined, words along the line of 'Stuff and Nonsense' and 'Get him on Parade at once' from the Inspector-in-Charge and similar, though possibly stronger phrases in his own vernacular from the Sergeant, soon had the reluctant young chap in line, standing at one end of the back row and looking very much as if he wished that he was not.

Make of the above information what you will, but some halfway through the proceedings, a very mangy hyena was seen to stalk cross the parade ground, pausing only to sink teeth into the trembling calf muscle of a certain Son-in-Law, at one end of the furthermost rank.

I am ready to believe that the kudos of Mothers-in-Law in general in that part of the Northern Frontier District was greatly enhanced by these events and that very possibly there were fewer intergenerational domestic arguments for many miles around. Certainly, one young man had cause to regret raising his voice to his beloved's Mother.

I do not imagine that he ever did so again!

Though this story sounds extraordinarily far-fetched I can vouch for the truth of it, my husband Derek Mansfield being on an Inspection Visit and observing the Parade in question.

David Hewson – Police Officer

A Mountain Recovery Operation

Mount Kenya is over 17,000 feet above sea level. After the Majestic mount Kilimanjaro, Mount Kenya is Africa's second highest mountain.

To the Kikuyu and the Masai tribes it is the Mountain of God. To the early explorers it was an extraordinary sight, a snow-capped mountain virtually straddling the equator. When the German Missionary and Explorer, Johann Ludwig Krapf included this amazing fact in his report to Europe, both The Royal Geographical Society in London and it's German equivalent, The Berlin Geographical Society, they refused to believe him and ridiculed it as a tall tale.

Mount Kenya's two highest peaks, Batian and Nelion, named after two Masai Chiefs, are divided by a gap known as the Gate of the Mists. Off to the right of these peaks, when looked at from Kiganjo, is the wide sweep of the Lewis-Lenana Glacier. The peaks tower above the moorlands and are a beautiful and breath-taking sight.

The Police Training School nestles in the foothills between the mountain and Nyeri, the main town and seat of government for Kenya's central province. Because of the permanent presence of over one thousand fit young men, and because of its disciplined life, the Police College linked with the Mountain National Parks for mountain rescue. At the drop of a hat, sufficient fit young constables, their NCOs and officers would assemble to help in the rescue of those injured, lost or in trouble on the mountain.

I was involved in two rescues on Mount Kenya; the first occasion, in 1965, when stationed at the Provincial Police Headquarters as Deputy Provincial Police Officer, Central Province.

At around 5pm we received a telephone call. A young British soldier, a trooper from the Royal Artillery, had just arrived at Naro-Moro Police Station at the foot of the mountain. He reported a concern for the safety of three companions who had failed to return to Top Hut after an attempt to climb the peaks.

He told us that he and his three companions were from an elite regiment of the Royal Artillery and that they had come to Kenya on a voluntary training and leadership expedition. Their leader – a young officer and experienced climber and a member of the Alpine Club – took them up the mountain.

On the morning of their fourth day, the soldier's three friends had risen well before dawn and set out on their assault of the main peaks, expecting, with luck to be back in camp by around three in the afternoon. Each man took warm clothing, a supply of food and water and glucose tablets.

The young soldier had prepared himself some food and waited for sight and sound of his returning companions. By four o'clock he began to feel anxious as he looked and listened but saw and heard nothing. From the camp he studied the glacier for signs of their return but saw no sign of movement.

He thought he detected something on the glacier; perhaps one climber had dropped a piece of equipment on the way up, but he found it impossible to tell.

Was he really seeing something or was it a shadow, or his imagination?

He didn't know what to think.

The next morning, at first light, he again began to search the peaks and the glacier, but saw nothing and saw no one.

In his mind he knew that something must have happened. Just what, he had no way of knowing.

Searching For His Comrades

He decided to go for help.

Packing his haversack as taught in the Army, checking he had enough food and water to see him through the sixty odd mile walk back to Naro-Moro, he reached our Police Station around four o'clock the next afternoon.

We debriefed him in our house in Nyeri and concluded that an accident must have occurred on the mountain. How serious, we did not, of course, know, so we planned to take action at once.

Charles Moore, our most experienced mountaineer, would lead a team of National Parks Rangers on to the mountain that night. They would drive to road-head at ten thousand feet and walk from there, climbing as far as they could a short rest, then continuing through the night.

In fact, they walked all night and I was able to speak to Charles by radio from his position on the Darwin Glacier at eight the following morning. He had only left our house at eleven the night before.

Charles told us they had found three bodies on the glacier, still roped together. It appeared they had fallen from a considerable height. He reported that two of the bodies had lost their boots and were bare footed, a phenomenon related to falls from great heights. In addition, they lay among a mass of rotten rock strewn across the glacier.

His appraisal of the situation was that they had been climbing and, unfortunately, carried away by a substantial fall of rock and plummeted to their deaths.

From his evidence it seemed clear that a small avalanche came down, hitting the climbers on their heads, shoulders, arms and hands, knocking them off the mountain onto the hard ice below. He reported that not only were boots torn off, but also helmets and rucksacks as well as ropes and climbing equipment were scattered across the glacier.

Death appeared to have been instantaneous.

Charles suggested that the bodies be buried temporarily at the edge of the glacier until everyone had been consulted. I advised the British High Commission that such a burial would take place while the wishes of the next of kin were explored.

Charles and his party placed the three climbers in a shallow grave and marked spot. Some weeks later, after everyone concerned had been consulted, we arranged for a party of National Parks Rangers and a Police Bugler to climb up and recover the bodies from the glacier. In accordance with their families' wishes, the three soldiers were placed in a proper grave on the mountain and a cairn of stones placed over the spot.

The Royal Air Force arranged for a Beverley transport plane to circle overhead carrying a suitably surpliced Padre. He read a service for burial of the dead, relayed by radio to the mountain graveside party. At the correct time during the service and instructed by the Padre, the Police Bugler sounded the Last Post.

I was on board the aircraft to point out the exact spot to circle during the service. Charles and his party later made another trip up the mountain to place a plaque on the cairn, engraved with the names of those who died and their date of death.

I do not know what happened to the young survivor over the years. He impressed me with his behaviour under what must have been extreme stress.

I hope that this remarkable young man stayed on as a soldier, undoubtedly endowed with leadership potential.

In dreadful circumstances and completely alone, he acted calmly and with great dignity and fortitude.

Bryan Coleman – Police Officer

My Father J. C. Coleman

My Father arrived in Kenya in 1923, having already served in the British Army in India and then the Palestine Police.

He lied about his age to get in, but was shipped back to England when The Army discovered his true age of seventeen made him too young to be a soldier, so he returned to England and at the age of eighteen joined the Police in Palestine then later transferred to The Kenya Police.

After five years, serving in Kenya my Father went on leave to England and married my Mother. Their first home was at the police post in Kabete about ten miles outside Nairobi.

My Mother, of course, experienced a cultural shock. She had only been in Kabete a week when my Father had to attend a court case in Nairobi. My Mother said that she would like to go too and do some shopping.

In those days the roads were made of red cotton soil and the only available transport – a couple of mules pulling an ox cart ruined my Mother's dress. My Mother wore her best white dress, so by the time they arrived in Nairobi she, of course, wore a red dress and looked like a Masai woman covered in red ochre.

By tradition the Kenya expatriates used to hold sundowner parties followed by dinner. One evening, my Mother's kitchen staff had forgotten to bring the toast to the table with the soup. My Mother went to the kitchen to investigate and could not believe her eyes on seeing the cook sitting on the floor with his back against the wall, toasting a piece of bread held between his toes over the wood stove.

One wonders how he did not burn his feet doing this, but in those days, the locals rarely wore shoes so the bottoms of his feet were like seasoned leather. Needless to say, no one ate the toast, but he told my Mother that is how he always made toast. She made sure after this incident that toast was made by using a fork instead of a foot.

My Father gained the nickname of Kamukwa, given to him by the Africans during his time stationed at Kabete Police Station, the reason being that when he went out on patrol and made an arrest, he tied his prisoners up with the rawhide straps that Kikuyu women used on their heads to carry loads on their back.

These straps are called Mukwa. The nickname Kamukwa stayed with my Father for the rest of his life in Kenya and he became well known amongst the Kikuyu.

During my career with the Kenya Police I obtained the name Muruwa Kamukwa, which meant, "Son of Kamukwa". This too remained with me even after I quit the Police and throughout my career as a hunter.

When based at Karen Police Station during the early days of World War Two, my Father had the task of keeping an eye on Karen von Blixen's house whilst she was away.

To save going out there he decided to call the house staff by telephone to find out if all was well, but he got no reply. That evening he went out to check and found one of the house staff ironing on the back veranda.

When asked where he had been, the servant replied that he had gone nowhere and had been there all day long. My Father asked why he had not answered the phone?

The answer – 'Bwana, if you had a parrot like that one in the cage who made a noise like a phone all day long, you too would not answer the phone.'

So that answered the question.

In Nairobi, the old Kenya Police Inspector's Mess and Police Lines were situated at the top of Government Road opposite the Norfolk Hotel and used by off-duty Police

Officers to be found in the Mess at the bar or playing snooker.

On a weekend many of them spent the whole day at the mess, not wanting to leave. When the wives called up to ask for their husbands, the answer would always be, 'He's just left'. The husbands would usually have a few more drinks before leaving.

On one occasion my Father and Bob Christian, both stationed down at the Police Depot, went up to the mess on a motorcycle one Sunday during daytime and my Mother called up to find out where my Father was.

Bob happened to answer the phone and told her that they would be leaving at once. So they went outside and Bob got on the motorcycle ready to leave whilst my Father had not yet mounted and Bob, not noticing, left without him.

Not realising, he talked to my Father all the way back and pitched up at the house without him. Worried that my Father might have fallen off, Bob decided to go back to look for him and, at the same time my Mother called the Mess again, asking after my Father.

Needless to say, she got the old answer, 'Oh, he's just leaving now,' and after another couple of drinks he made it home.

When my Father was transferred to Kingsway Police Station we moved into an ancient corrugated iron house between the Norfolk Hotel and the old Hospital.

As with most houses in in those days had an outside toilet, serviced, like most dwellings in and about Nairobi, by the honeysuckle cart consisting of two oxen and a large tank on wheels collecting during the night hours.

One night my Mother went out to use the toilet, which consisted of a wooden seat with a five-gallon bucket underneath and a trap door at the back to remove the bucket.

She had the shock of her life when suddenly the trap door opened and a hand reached in to remove the bucket to be carried out to the waiting honeysuckle cart. Five minutes later reappeared and my Mother never used the toilet again at night.

Incidentally, one always knew when they were near the honeysuckle cart at night. The smell was the giveaway and oxen patties strewn along the road as evidence.

Mike White – Police Officer

Perjury

Rawson Macharia was a Kikuyu and Crown Prosecution witness during the Kenyatta trial in nineteen fifty-three. He told the court he had 'heard a choir singing Mau Mau songs' in Gicheha village while he was in the Gatundu market. Kenyatta lived in Gicheha, about half a mile across the valley from the market.

Shortly after I arrived at Gatundu the Officer was Chief Inspector Ken Price. Rawson Macharia was a fairly frequent visitor to the station and spent some time chatting to Ken in the office during each visit.

One day, while looking through a pile of Bail Bonds and Distress warrants I came across Macharia's name on several documents. I asked Ken if this was the same Macharia and said 'Yes.'

The warrants had not been served because Macharia was one of his informants and always brought in accurate and useful information. The reason for not serving the warrants was that this being near the time of Kenyatta's release from jail, any news of possible unrest was vital.

When Kenyatta's release was eventually announced, Macharia, expecting to be in real trouble after Kenyatta arrived at Gicheha, withdrew his trial evidence saying that he had lied. The Director of Public Prosecutions now started legal action against Maracharia and we were asked to check if singing from Gicheha could be heard at Gatundu Market. A really big case was now started by the DPP part of the outcome of which was that we, at Gatundu, should check to see if singing could be heard coming from Gicheha at Gatundu Market. By this time Ken had been posted to Nakuru and Van had taken over.

If memory serves me well it was the Special Branch officer, Jacky Miller, who arranged for a small group of singers to be at Gicheha and we would be at the Market to listen at the target time was eight pm.

Jacky, Van, the District Officer, Village Headman Gachui and I were in position before time as we had agreed to get there early and barbecue a goat to be downed with a few Whitecap beers.

I think that it was at about 2200 hours that Jacky said, 'We forgot to listen out for the singing.'

We stopped chatting and sure enough we could hear the poor choir singing away. They'd been at it for over two hours since beginning and, by now, were getting a little hoarse I imagine.

Shortly afterwards my Police service ended and I left for the UK to train as a commercial pilot for East African Airways. On my return Van told me that Macharia's evidence at the Kenyatta trial was not perjury and proven to be legal.

I always wondered what happened to Macharia and later discovered that Van was wrong.

In nineteen fifty nine Macharia swore an affidavit that he had committed perjury at Kenyatta's trial, was taken to court and received a prison sentence of twenty-one months. He died in 2008 at the age of 96, knocked down by a motorbike whilst crossing the Thika Road.

Wendy Smith – Settler's Wife, Policeman's Wife and KPR Policewoman

A Typical Kenya Story

In the mid twentieth century, when I was nineteen, because of the famous Happy Valley scandals, people used to think it amusing to ask, 'Are you married or do you live in Kenya?'

In my case, a few years later, I could answer, 'Yes' to both questions.

Because in time honoured Kenya fashion I left my farmer husband and bolted with the local Policeman, Bill Smith and Inspector at Soy Police Station. Not just because I loathed farming - to prove it we have been married for over 60 years.

Having been evacuated to the States in 1942 on the last ship carrying children before the sinking of the *City of Benares*, I spent the war years in America and did not appreciate how deeply English people felt about class.

I foolishly married a Coldstream Guards officer and was deemed unacceptable by his family. Although handsome he was thicker than two short planks so when a less well-born Policeman looking for stolen cattle came on to the farm but had a brain I fell in love and took the chance for a better more interesting life.

Our wedding ceremony, at the height of the Mau Mau emergency was typically an odd Kenya one in the Registry Office in Nairobi. The officiating District Officer appeared ineffably bored by the occasion so mumbled his way through the protocol.

All I can remember the D.O. saying was, 'If either of you gets married again without a divorce, you will be committing bigamy.'

Despite such an inauspicious beginning our life together when finally I joined William in Fort Hall, centre of anti-

Mau Mau police operations, was busy, happy and interesting.

While waiting for an official house to become available in Fort Hall I stayed in Nairobi, working at Kingsway Police Station. As a member of the Kenya Police Reserve I went occasionally with other KPR officers for odd field duties outside the city.

On one occasion we found ourselves in a disused abattoir searching African women for the rounds of ammunition used as currency, with which they had been paid by UK troops for services rendered, the bullets being destined for transfer by the women to the Mau Mau terrorists.

It was not a pleasant experience, made even less so one day by hearing shots being fired nearby. Some of our Askaris dropped to the ground but we KPR women just looked around to see where the shooting came from. Luckily Mau Mau homemade rifles held together with string or wire tended to be less than accurate.

When finally I got to Fort Hall my job was in the VHF Room where radio traffic was not always by the book. One senior officer was known as 'Vulture Black'.

Woe betides any officer in the field caught not adhering to Vulture Black's meticulous standards. At least he didn't always insist on regular and frequent whitewashing of the stones placed around police posts, as did another senior officer known to all but himself as 'Gorgeous George.'

One of the drawbacks to being a Kenya policeman's wife was sudden change in one's circumstances. We were due to go by train on a much needed holiday in Malindi on a certain day when my husband was ordered to cement a safe to the floor at a police post on the forest edge, miles away.

At another time I had just bought kerosene operated fridge for our house in Embu when we were ordered to go to Nairobi where everything was electric.

So much for dreams of gleaming white Foreign Legion-type forts fringed by palm trees, desert oases and camels. The nearest either of us got to that were nightmares of can after can of whitewash.

Anonymous – A Police Officer

So Many Years

We who were born and bred in Kenya grew up devoted to King George and the Empire upon which the sun would never set.

Or would it ?

We saw our future either on the farms or following our fathers or elder brothers in serving in the Army or in the Civil Service of our land. Thus after five years of Public School, medically unfit for the Army and against the wishes of my parents who already had a son-in-law in the Police, I joined the Kenya Police as a Cadet, then styled Assistant Inspector (Learner).

Until the age of twenty we locally recruited Cadets were paid half the salary of those who enlisted in Britain. And we A.I. Learners were to be closely mentored by a senior rank and as far as possible to live at home.

This did not happen.

Stony broke we were left to find our own way.

So to the Training School at Nyeri Station to join the other learners in a Mess shared with some good fellows, including a bright young man, Rajinder Singh, who would have a fine career in the Force.

We had drill instruction and endless weeks of riot drill including learning how to form a square, a military manoeuvre last seen at the 1898 Battle of Omdurman in The Sudan.

We spent many days with African recruits, keen as mustard, but mostly knowing only their own tribal dialects.

The School Commandant, SSP Jim Sweeney – a splendid man – originally came north from The Cape Mounted Police. One day he ordered a route march for we Cadet Inspectors to and from Naru Moru along with more than eight hundred Askaris who covered the thirty-six miles barefoot and singing all the way. I grew to like in particular the Kalenjin and the Northern tribes.

We were joined by a group of twenty recruits taken on in Britain. They were paid much more than we locally engaged trainees. Some of these fellows tried to take over our Mess and caused trouble and barred, so they formed their own.

Following an argument with one of them I proposed settling it in the boxing ring although the other fellow was some years older than I and a good three stone heavier.

Chief Inspector Bert Ednie refereed and set up the ring with my corner facing the evening sun. The odds sere too heavy and I was knocked down and counted out, but from this we locals achieved respect and made a number of friends from the recruits from Britain.

Not long out of school we rather fancied ourselves as athletic, a view cut down by Senior Sergeant Kipsang, who asked to have a crack at throwing our javelin.

Handing his tarbush to a Constable he cocked the javelin over his shoulder and launched in near twenty yards further than we could.

Lesson learnt.

After passing out my first job found me with a Norton motorbike and a lorry, but not yet knowing how to drive either. With the lorry came First Grade Constable Kipkoske of eighteen years service. And well known, when faced with a sticky situation, might bring his great fist out to flatten the opposition.

When a young man he had been a proud tractor driver until the day a Police Sergeant demanded he get down to answer some questions. He only complied when told to get down and fight. After a sound thrashing he asked the Sergeant's name and how could he join the Police?

Sergeant M'rindari, the man who taught him the lesson, later became Senior Sergeant of the Force and for many years taught drill to new Officers, including Cadet Assistant Superintendents.

During the First World War M'rindari had served with General von Lettow Vorbeck's forces in German East Africa. After that war he moved to the King's African Rifles and then to The Kenya Police.

Once in my Police career I recall taking a violent individual from the mental hospital to court and keep him handcuffed at all times. This prisoner eventually became Vice President of Kenya. He had a keen memory and in later years made life extra difficult for me when I worked in the Government Secretariat.

Another prisoner I took to court – a respected local farmer charged with unlawful wounding – had the KC doyen of the legal profession as defence lawyer.

The farmer, clearly over confident in gaining sympathy from the court, concluded his evidence by saying, 'And if that bastard ever comes back I'll shoot him again.'

Instead of walking free, those words earned him a six-month sentence.

In Kabarnet District a new religion, The Dini Ya Msambwa, arose among the Suk tribe, complete with prophet and followers attacked the Tribal Police.

A small Kenya Police contingent commanded by Superintendent Swayne, accompanied the District Commissioner to meet the sect at Kolloa and were charged by an armed war party of the religious fanatics.

Swayne prepared to shoot in self-defence, but the DC ordered him not to shoot without his authority and Swayne, while arguing, held back from opening fire, unsure of his seniority over the DC.

The delay caused by the disagreement allowed the fast closing fanatics overran the Government party, killing Superintendent Swayne and a number of his Police. The District Commissioner managed to hide and escaped injury.

This tragedy caused a Government ruling that the Police are always senior and in control in such circumstances of danger.

The Suk tribe was ordered to pay the costs of an African Levy Force for the next four years. I visited the place in 1967 and found the bronze commemoration plaque scarred and dented by spear thrusts.

A lesson forgotten.

During 1950 the Police Reservists were called in to help we Regulars deal with three weeks of strikes and riots in Nairobi, with men also brought in from up-country Police Stations.

Now seemed a good time to test the riot drill remembered from our Police Training School days.

For almost three weeks baton parties with steel helmets and shields gleefully wielded pickaxe handles against mobs in Shauri Moyo Township.

Elsewhere other mobile units went round the city dealing with Kikuyu gangs attacking other tribes, particularly the Luo, shaving their heads with broken bottles.

Attached to Special Branch with two other Officers, I worked cutting out and arresting ringleaders in the crowds.

This three-week affair gave grim warning of what was to come. Around this time the Malayan Emergency called for more manpower and Kenya Police Officers were invited to go to Malaya.

A number accepted, resulting in a Force Order from our new Commissioner thanking us for offering to go, but saying that if we all went he would be left with only some elderly gentlemen and Police dogs.

A few went off to Malaya, but, in truth, The Kenya Police now needed every man and 1952 saw a huge increase in numbers of both Officers and Other Ranks to cope with the Mau Mau Emergency.

We had some excellent African colleagues, including a Charge Office Literate, Corporal Henry, a badly scarred man who had been the sole survivor of the Gatundu Mau Mau ambush that wiped out A.I. Tommy Mortimer's patrol.

Mortimer came from the British South Africa Police, in Rhodesia and worked by the book and never carried a loaded gun. So when the attack came his pistol ammunition was in his pouch while the men each had their rifle magazines loaded with five rounds each, but still in their pouches.

I was happy to find Henry in Garissa in nineteen sixty nine, now a Chief Inspector now more concerned with Somali Shifta crossing into Kenya to kill and steal.

Another early memory is of a Kipsigis recruit not much over sixteen years old who passed out at the same time as we did. Sadly his name is lost to me.

His first posting was to Railway Police and soon after that he was riding guard in a goods wagon when he tackled a gang of four trying to force entry.

A grim fight followed ending in defeat for villainy and Force Orders later published a Commendation for his bravery.

In the same year, now posted to Royal Naval Armaments Depot, Ntongwe and supervising a lighter off-loading ammunition from a supply ship, he saw smoke among highly explosive cordite charges.

He jumped into the barge and began throwing overboard the charges, which were now taking fire. By this brave action he successfully saved the barge and its cargo.

He certainly deserved much more than another commendation and I think he was indeed awarded a medal.

David Hewson – Police Officer

Sergeant Kipsoi Arap Sang – Stock Theft Investigator

I first met Sergeant Kipsoi Arap Sang while stationed at Rumuruti in the heart of Kenya's Ranching country in nineteen fifty-two.

The word Rumuruti, I was told is Masai for the place of the swamp. There was certainly a swamp along one edge of the tiny township.

Sergeant Kipsoi taught me more about stock theft and stock thieves than anyone else I encountered during my years as a Policeman.

Kipsoi himself looked nothing like a Policeman. I later learned he had the looks of a stock thief, or perhaps a trader in stolen cattle or hides and skins. Or, at first sight, he could have been butcher.

Not a big man; slight, with a lean face and a wispy moustache on the upper lip of his finely chiseled features. His ear lobes sliced and stretched and then either double looped over the top of his ears in typical Kalenjin fashion, or with a copper weight hanging at the bottom of each loop.

When he turned his penetrating eyes on you and searched your face he seemed to look into your very soul.

I never saw him in uniform.

He invariably wore a pair of old khaki shorts and a white singlet with an old blanket draped Kalenjin fashion and tied in a knot on his right shoulder with a battered pork pie hat of indiscriminate age and colour and sandals made from old car tyres.

On a belt under the blanket he carried an extremely sharp two-edged native sword known as a Simi.

Like so many Africans he was a linguist, and in addition to Swahili and his native Kipsigis he could converse in all the Kalenjin dialects, Nandi, Elgeyo, Marakwet and others. He could talk in Masai and its kin dialect Samburu as well as understand Turkana and Suk.

He was a formidable adversary for stock thieves. It was said, perhaps with considerable truth and not a little awe, that he was a Kipsigis Laibon or witch doctor, and attributed by some Africans with supernatural powers.

Stock theft was the "raison d'etre" of Rumuruti Police Station. The Ranchers believed that the Police were useless at investigating stock theft and the Police thought the Ranchers put too much trust in their herd boys and failed to personally count their stock at the weekly dipping against East Coast Fever and Rinderpest.

Six head of cattle would be found missing from a mob of cattle the night before they were due to be dipped. They had probably been stolen immediately after their last dipping by thieves who paid off the herd boy living with the herd.

With the stock long disappeared into the adjacent Samburu or Suk African Reserves I would drop Sergeant Kipsoi and his squad off at the Ranch. The Rancher would batter my ear for an hour about general Police inefficiency and my lack of competence in particular. After a cup of tea or a beer I would return to the Police Station to await results.

While questioning the herd boy and the nyapara or head stock man, Sergeant Kipsoi would send off two of his experienced trackers to examine the scene of the theft and look for any indications of tracks or the direction the thieves may have taken.

In the case of collusion between thieves and herd boy, the remaining main herd would be driven over the tracks and round in circles in an attempt to cause as much confusion as possible.

A lesser man than Kipsoi would have been put off.

If the theft was within three days, and there had been no rain, Kipsoi would find the tracks and off he and his team would go, taking the herd boy with them, ostensibly to identify the stolen cattle, but in reality to keep him on edge and prevent him communicating with any accomplices.

Good stock thieves will easily cover 50 miles in a night. All they do is catch hold of the steer's tail and twist it. The pain causes the steer to run while the thief hangs on and runs behind pulled along by the unwilling steer. Stock theft takes place at the full moon.

Out in the African bush, you read a newspaper in the light of the full moon. One can see for miles and stock thieves can be into their Reserve and merging stolen stock with their own cattle in a matter of hours.

All cattle must be branded with the owner's brand. Unbranded calves are kept separate by herd boys for replacement at a later date when a better animal is to be stolen for breeding purposes at home in the Reserve.

The brands of stolen cattle can be mutilated or over printed or just burnt off. The colour of animals can be change with vegetable dyes or by simply burying the animal in the ground, with only its head showing, for a couple of weeks.

Kipsoi knew every dodge and avenue in stock thieving and had an uncanny knack in his assessment of a case and was seldom wrong. His greatest coup was to return from an enquiry with sixty head of prime cattle that the Rancher had no idea had been stolen.

He and his team had camped on a series of tracks they had been following for two days. In the early hours of the morning their sentry heard a mob of cattle moving at speed in their direction. A quick deployment and they had six thieves and sixty head of stolen stock.

Kipsoi handed over thieves and stock to the astonished farmer and continued following the original tracks to another successful conclusion.

As I said he taught me all I know about stock theft, information that stood me in good stead in the future.

The real lesson he taught me was patience. He would

bring in his prisoners. He would book them in the Occurrence Book, charge them with the appropriate section of the Penal Code, and place them in cells.

He would then take them out one by one and sit under a tree in the Station Compound and talk with them; going over and over the evidence and their involvement until he was satisfied he had everything.

He and I would then record their statements and they would agree to the accuracy and sign each page with their thumbprint.

Sergeant Kipsoi was totally illiterate and could neither read or write. Nevertheless as an expert at his job, he never bore malice and would not bend the evidence for anyone.

If Kipsoi said not guilty there was no prisoner. The case would be placed on one side but, in his mind, never closed.

By the time I left Rumuruti he had been promoted to Inspector and was, literally, worth his weight in gold.

We last met in nineteen sixty-two at Bomet, his home district, where he lived in retirement.

While driving in the area I noticed this solitary figure, wearing blanket, pork pie hat and tyre sandals walking along the road.

My driver pulled over.

I got out and called 'Inspector Kipsoi.'

We greeted each other as long lost friends.

He told me of his retirement and that although happy to be at home, missed the life of an investigator.

Without doubt he was one of the very best.

I am grateful to have learned so much from such a humble man.

Kwaheri na enda na Mungu, Kipsoi.

Warren Martin – Police Officer

Kerugoya

Soon after passing out of PTS I was posted to Kerugoya, and before long before found myself leading patrols in the High Forest on Mount Kenya.

In order to make progress through thick bush that covered the forest floor, we often used game tracks so close encounters with elephant, buffalo and rhino were frequent. Coming across a steaming pile of elephant dung concentrated the mind and raised the pulse.

Later I had to shoot a rogue male elephant raiding tea shambas. This duty was carried out at the request of the Game Warden, whose area responsibilities were far greater than mine.

We frequently helped out with game control and were responsible for most of the enforcement of poaching by ambush, resulting in arrest and conviction. Because of our success and methods, Alan Childs went to Voi and set up and operated the first anti-poaching unit in the Kenya Police. As time went on I took more and more responsibility for the keeping of records, the enforcement of legislation and investigation of crime.

Appearing at the local Kiama (Court of Tribal Elders) and the Magistrate's Court at Embu became less and less of a trial for me because of increasing fluency in Swahili and increasing confidence in the legal niceties. I gave my evidence in Swahili without a stumble and often I prosecuted a case in its entirety as I took the role of Prosecutor. Eventually I became Station Commander.

I a very intense and busy period had time in Kerugoya and have a wealth of still very clear memories. Back in Wales, when my mother met Bob Johnson, a Chief Inspector and good friend I worked with in Kerugoya, he told her I had saved his life twice.

Once when a Mau Mau gang attacked our Police Station, Bob went outside our perimeter wire as a diversion and got in a very difficult situation. I could see he was likely to be overrun and led four Askaris in a charge to chase the terrorists away.

We were together in several other desperate situations and close quarter engagements with terrorists in the forest, near the end of the Emergency and we did not expect to be attacked.

Not all our dangerous problems were terrorist incidents. Facing up to a group of drunken Askaris on pay night was very similar to a night out in the Army in Barnard Castle and demanded the same kind of skills in talking the heat out of a situation.

A tribesman running amok with a Panga and probably high on Banghi, the local drug, was a stern test of decision-making.

Facing up to hundred women who decided that a fellow villager, an old woman, was a witch and should be drowned was very intimidating. The woman, they said, had been casting spells on people and causing problems such as miscarriages. They dragged her down to the river and we arrived just as they were about to drown her.

With my two Askaris I jumped in the water and dragged them away from the crowd. We pulled her across the river and stood on the other bank and, shouting across the water, calmed them down and stopped them killing the woman.

Even in the most difficult of times we found humour.

Whenever we needed to go to Embu town with our five-ton lorry, we always tried to take a number of off-duty constables and a few of the wives for a day out. My corporal drove and I sat in the passenger seat.

Late one dark evening on a return trip, as we turned off the main Nyeri road onto a bush road towards Kerugoya, we heard banging on the cab roof and shouts of, 'Njeroge has fallen off the lorry.'

Placing the lorry in a good position and deploying the Bren gun we always carried at its most advantageous point on a slight hill. I set off with two constables to find Njeroge.

We walked and walked for several miles until his lumbering form appeared out of the darkness, explaining, 'I needed to pee Effendi over the side of the lorry while we were driving and fell off.'

Reaching the lorry some two hours later, we were properly challenged but it did not make me any happier. 'Why did you not stop us sooner?'

'We were laughing too much. At Njeroge trying to pee and falling off.'

We were soon on our way with the whole crowd singing their hearts out, telling the story of how Njeroge had fallen off the lorry and the Effendi had gone to look for him.

That sound of Askaris telling a story in song as they went along will stay with me forever.

The singing as we returned to the Station after attending a large fire told how the Effendi could not run down the slope to the river to get water in his bucket, so slid down on his backside instead.

After parade, if Sergeant Major Matua was having trouble with his children the following day would be a torment in Hell, for the poor man, because of the clever instantly devised lyrics about his family problems.

How did they know that Cpl Maina's wife was withholding her favours and turn it into a wicked and accurate song?

Everything became an impromptu song, telling a story in great detail

Whenever a group of men were returning from an incident, one would begin to chant and the story would grow into a really true story of what happened, including unrealised little quirks in my own character.

These songs and chants were and still are haunting in my memory.

Mike Smart – Police Officer

Introduction to the Kenya Police

I joined the Kenya Police in January 1954 and went straight to the Gilgil training school.

On leaving Gilgil after two or three weeks on posting to Thompsons Falls Police Station, I was left with the following impressions: -

Being issued with a revolver but no ammunition.

The lack of food hygiene, the majority of us having suffered stomach upset.

The Chief Inspector who had been in a Mental Institution, so had written evidence stating he was sane that he occasionally showed around.

From Thompsons Falls I was posted on to Kowop, a Detention Camp in the desert area between Lake Rudolf and Baragoi, with two hundred suspected Mau Mau Detainees supervised by two Europeans and about eighteen Askaris.

We Europeans lived in a small wooden hut each, with the Askaris and Detainees living under canvas.

On my arrival I found the other Inspector had no interest in being there, not liking the heat, the desert or the whole setup. So he just hung around and did little or nothing, leaving our African Police Sergeant to run the camp.

So I began to reorganise the place. I got to know the local people and local Chief at Tuum, a village eight or nine miles to the north from where we obtained clean drinking water. I made friends with the Chief and took various photographs that I still have, including one of him with his two-year son.

I sussed out a supply of palms to thatch a roof and moved the huts together so I could build a veranda with shelter from the sun and a kitchen area at the rear. Whilst collecting the palm I thought I decided to climb and see the top of Mt. Nyiru. So with three Askaris and five Detainees set off on the three thousand foot climb.

Arriving at the top I found myself with only my five Detainees. The three Askaris had all fallen by the wayside, but I was not worried. If the detainees had done a runner they had little likelihood of making it to civilization.

My Detainees and I had a wander round the summit. We all found it amazing to climb out of a desert to a fertile area of three feet high grass and tall trees, waving in a gentle breeze. On the way down we collected the three exhausted lads, still recovering from the climb they had made and set off back to camp.

In August I received orders to close the camp because the prisoners were being sent down to a large Detainee Centre at Hola, near the Coast. Everything moveable had to be transferred to Maralal, including a box of unstable and sweating dynamite, probably used to blast long drop toilets, left by the Works Department.

I drove down on my own in the Land Rover and handed the dynamite over to the very nervous personnel at Maralal Works Depot.

Thus ended a very enjoyable six months for me. I felt satisfied that I am the type of person who could make the best of whatever circumstances in which I landed.

Returning to Thompsons Falls I became a real Policeman again, after being a form of prison warder.

I took over Police Post 41 for a year, then formed

Tracker Team No.7 and based myself on an abandoned wooden shack, by a river, in which I lived, slept and ate. My seven African companions slept under canvas.

After a couple of months I was posted to the Kiganjo Training school, much to my annoyance, where they tried to teach me law and other important Police techniques I had not previously needed.

I then built and opened a Police Station at Lanet which I ran until I left the Police in 1957.

I returned to Kenya several times and managed to get to Tuum where I discovered that my friend the Chief had been killed by cattle rustlers, but his family were all still there. I discovered that the two year old boy I had photographed, those years ago had inherited the Chiefdom from his father. He now works with the Government Fisheries Department, at Marsabit.

I wrote him a letter and he replied with a picture of himself as he is now. We are now hoping to meet in three months time when I return to Lake Rudolf in June for the 2015 Turkana Cultural Festival.

Ann Silcock – Police Wife

Driving Lessons

About 1949 I had bought my first car, a Ford Anglia, my pride and joy. I was not at that time in the police.

To my horror, soon afterwards, I was told to report to Central Police Station Traffic Division. There a white haired Assistant Inspector, lolling in his chair called Silcock, young, but prematurely grey interviewed me.

He did not have even the courtesy to stand up as I entered the room, but kept me standing while he berated me for five minutes for what he called my fast, careless and dangerous driving.

I felt incandescent but did not dare to show it before being ushered out.

Soon after I received a phone call from an unknown certain Assistant Inspector Derek Mansfield, always known as Bertie, who asked me out.

I fear dear Bertie got a flea in his ear that said 'Thank you, BUT I do NOT go to Police Stations to arrange a rendezvous.'

Skip forward about nine months, by which time I had been "introduced" again to A.I. Maurice Silcock, my erstwhile interviewer and we had become friends.

One day I was giving him a lift when I decided to ask him a favour.

'Could you please give my darling Father a little word of caution because *he really drives too fast, carelessly and dangerously* for his age.'

I thought Maurice was going to pass out laughing, and laughing and laughing.

Eventually he managed to control himself and speak.

'Ann, who do you think asked me to speak to you about *your* driving that day in the Police Station'

Six months later Maurice proposed and we got married.

John Standring – Police Officer

Wajir Scorpion

In 1958/59 I was posted to Wajir to take over command of the division from my very good friend Peter Hughes, who was going on long leave.

In those days Wajir, was far different from the large town it is now; then inhabited only by a few shopkeepers and used as a base by two or three Somali clan chiefs for wells that were the only source of water for livestock grazing the area.

Also based in Wajir, were the District Commissioner, we Police and a doctor, Jimmy Clearkin.

With duties that took us away for days and weeks, we were rarely there together, but when we did manage to meet we celebrated at the noted Royal Wajir Yacht Club, so named although the Indian Ocean – the nearest sizeable body of water – was hundreds of miles to the East.

On one occasion a small brown Scorpion stung me. Luckily Jimmy the doctor happened to be in town and treated me by injecting anti-snake bite venom all around the sting and handing me a couple of aspirin.

End of incident except that when my orderly heard about it, he came to me and said that as a young man in the isolated desert area of Turkana he had been initiated into his age group, that year named the Scorpion group. As a result, he told me, he was now permanently at one with Scorpions and they would never harm him etc. etc.

I mentioned this in passing to the doctor who asked if my orderly would allow him to photograph him handling a Scorpion. The response from my orderly was a prompt, 'but of course.'

Two evenings later Jimmy came to me with a shoebox containing a skittering and very angry Black Desert Scorpion. These things are fearsomely large and menacing although, curiously, not as venomous as the smaller brown ones.

My orderly smartly picked up the Scorpion and plopped it onto his bare arm. Amazingly the insect lost its aggression, lowered his tail and simply relaxed.

We pondered this and discussed things in Swahili so my orderly could join in. Had he breathed on it and stunned it?

My orderly moved his arm and hand close to Jimmy, whereupon the Scorpion ran instantly to the orderly's wrist with its sting in a very menacing position.

We moved slightly away and the Scorpion relaxed again.

Ah. Perhaps it could not sting beyond 180 degrees i.e. on a flat surface such as the arm, so keeping my orderly safe?

My orderly immediately cupped the insect with his other hand. Now surely, we thought, with this change of angle, he must be vulnerable.

I later saw Jimmy's 8mm film and the sight of the Scorpion's appearing from under my orderly's fingers, thrusting out his head and claws seemed the stuff of horror movies.

We tried all sorts of arrangements but no matter what we did, the Scorpion remained aggressive to us but quite relaxed with the orderly so in the end Jimmy thanked him and asked it if was all right for him to get rid of the damned thing.

My orderly said fine but not in his presence as it was a friend.

I discussed this episode in detail with Jimmy, a fully trained doctor and always scientific in his work and approach to everything medical.

But neither he nor I could ever work out what had occurred except, possibly, that the orderly believed so utterly in his immunity that perhaps his vibrations passed this on to the insect, which reacted accordingly.

As a post script: some months later on a trip back to Wajir from Isiolo – a long boring dusty drive in those days –

we stopped for a cup of tea and a break by a thorn tree.

My orderly pointed to the branches and said, 'Oh look, here is some of the plant that they used in my age initiation. It is so easy I just need to make a couple of small cuts on the back of your hand and squeeze some of the sap into them. Then you too will be a friend of Scorpions and never be stung'.

I hesitated and confess to passing the moment by without having the treatment.

I didn't think I could ever really believe that, if I'd been inoculated, I would never again be stung.

I am quite sure my orderly would quite soon have come along with a bruiser of a Scorpion friend to test his theory.

And who knows what would have happened?

David Reeve – Policeman's Son

Return to Kenya And Some Fading Recollections

Inspector Bill Reeve, my late father, joined the Kenya Police in 1955 and returned to the UK in 1963, just before Independence. He came away with a wealth of fascinating memories, having experienced the dying elements of Empire and British involvement in Africa.

I was born in Kenya in 1960 and managed to return for a visit the first time since 1963 with an expedition organised by the Army Cadet Force Association to work at Thangathi Primary School in Sagana, a couple of hours north of Nairobi.

The generational connection with Kenya continues as my daughter Jennifer is an editor of this book and her brother William has completed his Infantry Officer initial training, which culminated in a gruelling exercise in the forest around Mount Kenya. He is now serving in Nepal with one of the last vestiges of the Military Colonial connections, the Royal Gurkha Rifles.

As a two year Contract Officer, my father trained for three months at the Gilgil Training School before being posted to Dundori Police Station where the routines of Colonial Policing included one of his dogs being poisoned and among his Police duties, having to administer corporal punishment with a light cane.

And he had to, sadly, shoot a leopard caught in a snare. He collected the beautiful hide and brought it home. I still have it on the wall in my lounge. Other jobs included tracking and shooting a wild buffalo that was destroying the local crops and helping with the rescue of an elephant caught in a mud hole. I have a black and white film of that saga, involving a lot of the locals and Askaris attempting to get the poor beast out, I think unsuccessfully.

I have a surviving series of photographs of a very neat Police station and local village, with white washed huts, smart security fence and fearsome ditch.

On the subject of Police stations, I recall being in a Kowloon Police station in Hong Kong during the 1980s, whilst serving with the Gurkhas. The smartly dressed station sergeant, reception desk, colonial Police regulations and riot shields and sticks, all carefully lined up on the wall, looked spookily familiar at the time – presumably from a few old Kenya Police snaps.

In the 1950s, my father was involved in the protection and escort operation for the visit of the late Princess Margaret, which apparently went very well according to his archived letters.

He obviously met a number of other interesting characters during this time. He spoke of the ex-Palestine Police who had transferred to Kenya in particular. An especially tough bunch he told me.

My father's previous military and airborne training probably led to him to being given the job of commanding a Police Tracker Team. He told me many stories of hunting and engaging with various Mau Mau gangs. These fights, he said, were brutal and unforgiving in the bush and forest.

Some of his stories from this time included a Mau Mau homemade shotgun blast to his inner thigh during one forest contact. Not a serious wound so he carried on chasing the gang. In another story he told me of a fleeting sight of a terrorist on a jungle track. The man instantly disappeared into thick bush. My father's Alsatian leapt from the Land Rover in chase and didn't return for several days.

On transfer from Short Contract to the Regular List my father went to Nyeri to complete his Police training. I found my recent trip to Nyeri very strange having read a lot of history of the Mau Mau Emergency and actually drove past the Police Training School, still at Kiganjo.

A visit to the local Colonial cemetery in Nyeri revealed a number of British Police graves along with the European farmers and traders. One poor soul must have left his mark with some of the locals, as the cross on his grave had taken an obvious battering.

While at the Cemetery an apparent supporter of long lost freedom fighters appeared. He claimed to be renovating the various historic stones. As an alleged member of the local boy scouts, he also proudly briefed us on Lord Baden-Powell, who is curiously also buried with his wife in the only really well kept grave there.

We saw that the other local church in Nyeri – built by Italian prisoners of war – remains in excellent order – as does, thankfully, the Commonwealth War Cemetery, containing the graves of a wide variety of Colonial troops.

The War Cemetery has an exceptional view over a local valley and hills. It must have been the same in my father's time at Nyeri.

Inspector Reeve also went to the Northern Frontier District for mainly infantry operations. I know he did not really enjoy the NFD and even applied to leave early. Curiously he appears to have recorded little of his time there.

In his albums are a few surviving and very small black and white photographs of whitewashed stone buildings in a very arid landscape; presumably Police buildings in the desert. Again, I recall his stories of patrolling on horses and camels in the desert, allegedly whilst responsible for 2,000 square miles.

Commanding only a hundred African regular and reserve Police, he must have been very busy on the Somali border. During my trip back to Kenya we were unable to visit this area, due to the current terrorist threat.

In the late 1950s he moved to Prosecutions Branch in Nairobi, his final posting. He found this nearly as interesting as his time on the Tracker Team. In addition to a variety of criminal cases, he was often on duty for 999 calls in the City Centre and was involved in pre-Independence riots.

I do believe that he heard the fatal shot when a Kenya Police Reservist killed his houseboy and caused a national commotion when sentenced to death. Apparently this man became the first white man to kill an African and then be executed for the crime.

My Mother recalls, rather bizarrely, actually going on one late night 999 call with him. There was also an incident involving a bar brawl involving a Scottish regiment where the first Inspector to arrive was struck with a bottle causing significant facial damage.

My mother also recounts an attempted mugging by three armed Africans, whilst she and my father were parked watching a polo match at Mitchell Park. The robbers found they had picked on an armed Policeman. Not a good idea.

My father jumped up and chased them off then followed up with some local officers and Police dogs to assist in a final arrest.

Meanwhile, during one of the early 1960s riots in Nairobi, a tear gas grenade struck in the back of his neck, leaving an unpleasant carbuncle and scar.

On another occasion, after a possibly over-enthusiastic day of crowd control, he anxiously checked the evening Television News for incriminating evidence of a cameraman being accidentally struck by his Police baton.

In filming the melee the media came too close to his swinging riot stick and a promising Police career could have been adversely affected, but happily no pictures appeared and no complaint made.

I also have a newspaper article that reports him and an Askari, rolling around the floor of a public court trying to control a violent defendant who had refused to follow proper court protocol.

My mother's recollections are getting a little faded now, but she was a nurse at the Princess Elizabeth European Hospital in Nairobi when she met my father. She had gone to Kenya oblivious of any problems of any kind, let alone the Mau Mau Emergency.

Sister Evelyn Reeve was instructed not to walk out from the hospital when she first arrived, as it was not safe, but inevitably did so for shopping and a bit of social life in the city clubs.

As a nurse she seems to have looked after a number of characters, several of who were in hospital courtesy of their pets. This included one man who had been shredded by his pet leopard and whose main concern was that the animal had not been destroyed.

Her favourite memories are still of the game parks, safaris and wild animals, heavy rain, the immediate fall of night darkness, noisy insects and Police Doberman Pinschers, one of which we brought back to UK.

She also still speaks fondly of beach holidays at Malindi and Mombasa, long leave back to the home country on meandering cruise ships, via the Suez Canal and rather quicker journeys on BOAC.

Once married, she did still walk out, with the Doberman offering her, my brother and myself, then aged two and one, more than adequate protection. We apparently lived in a bungalow in Northampton Road and also in Jacaranda Flats at one stage, whilst she specifically remembers the Police Mess and the New Stanley Hotel.

The outside cinema drive-ins were also popular. Finally, she recalls the death of one poor rabbit, eaten by a marching column of soldier ants one night. Only the gleaming bones survived.

Concerns over the family's safety led to our final departure for Northamptonshire in 1963 and a return to where the then Mr Bill Reeve had begun. His addiction to strong Rhodesian cigarettes imported into Kenya and a very high blood pressure problem eventually killed him. He did however stay in the security world initially, with the job of running security for Weetabix.

I suspect he had been living on borrowed time anyway, as my Mother had already nearly shot him twice whilst in Nairobi, through a couple of negligent discharges of a Police revolver. It seems she had woken up to the terrorist threat by then.

My father's eight years as a Policeman in Kenya left a huge impression on him, and made him the man we all knew.

Tarsem Rumpal – Police Officer

A Career To Remember

When I told my father I wanted to join the Kenya Police he was totally against the idea, wanting me to find a more "respectable" career. After a lot of cajoling and persuasion he relented, but only after I promised never in any way to tarnish his good name in society by my actions as a policeman.

Thus I joined The Police in 1955 and a budding police career was born.

During the period of my initial training at the Kiganjo Police Training School the Mau Insurgency was very active. As part of our training we were supposed to guard a railway line that passed through a nearby forest. Each evening two Cadets were sent out to do the job. I was paired with another Indian recruit, both carrying a Sten gun and magazine full of ammunition.

In the forest, I must admit, I found the quiet in the dead of night extremely frightening. The only sound was of wind disturbing trees around. All of a sudden we heard a very loud rustling of the leaves. My colleague, thinking that Mau Mau was around, let off the whole magazine of ammunition into the trees. We learnt later that a monkey must have jumped between branches. I must say that it was embarrassing to explain the whole saga to our superiors in the morning.

At Eastleigh Police Station in Nairobi I was attached to the crime branch and had to be stand-by for twenty-four hours from 8 am to 8 am the following day. And that following day you spent in dealing with all the previous night's influx of criminals and the remaining time in court. So the total time I would be on duty for almost thirty-six hours at a stretch. I wish I had been paid overtime.

I remember that often when on stand-by I would be

called out at around four in the morning to attend, for instance, to someone's kitchen having been broken into during the night. Most Indians, except me, are early risers.

I went once to the house of a totally blind Sikh lady who, to my total amazement, looked after her household in a way one could not make out that she was without sight. In fact on the occasion that I went to deal with her kitchen break-in she served us with tea, moving around the kitchen with total confidence, knowing where everything was by touch. Even when pouring the tea from the teapot, she touched the cup with her fingertips and got the tea into the cup without spilling a drop. Absolutely amazing.

In another incident we were called out in the dead of night to deal with a shop break-in. On arrival we found two youths who had tied up their loot into a bundle and were lying next to it on the floor. They could not resist the lure of liquor, which was in plenty in the shop. We collected them both out of their mind with drinks. I have to say that it was the easiest of crimes that I ever dealt with and brought to such quick solution.

I remember in 1959 the Liwali of Mombasa passed away. Police were asked to honour him with an escort on foot, wearing ceremonial uniforms with collar and tie. My place was to lead the procession from in front of the coffin, which was being carried on peoples' shoulders. My small squad marched behind the coffin.

The problem was that the pallbearers changed with such frequency that the coffin swayed from side to side and, in fact all over the place. And my quandary was to determine where the Liwali was so that I stayed in front of him and his coffin. We went through the narrow streets and lanes of Mombasa Old Town and I did the best I could and fortunately it all ended to everyone's satisfaction.

But what I remember the most was the stifling midday heat, which was just unbearable, although the occasion was so interesting and exciting, I did not really take it in until afterwards when I reach home and thought about the day.

I was Deputy Divisional Commander in Kitale in the west of Kenya and Wednesday used to be market day. All the local European farmers would come to town with a shopping list, which included a visit to the Police Divisional Headquarters.

So I had to be available to deal with them, or, should I say, pander to all their wishes. For instance, they were indeed a law unto themselves and insisted on me giving them a list of all crimes in their area, which they then spent time discussing in detail with me.

Tarsem Rumpal Drawn By Granddaughter Rhea

My next posting to Kericho was, to me, heaven on earth, with lush green tea estates covering the rolling hills and valleys all around. Afternoon tea at the Tea Hotel with a splendid array of cakes and cucumber sandwiches was a must. That is if I got the chance.

Everyday day around one in the afternoon there would be a heavenly threat of hailstones that were not good for the tea growing bushes. This was around one in the afternoons. So the tea estates' Wallas used to fire rockets into the skies to make the hailstones come down as rain. Clever stuff.

Of all the places I served in the police I found Kajiado an enigma. The terrain and the soil were different, to my previous experience, being a dry and dusty plain and vey hot. Dress code for the Masai was non-existent; being only a red blanket tied over one shoulder and flapping in the wind. Modesty was also non-existent.

The seven-bedroom house allocated to me in Kajiado and my wife and three-year-old son was on stone-built stilts. In the mornings we could see spoors of all sorts of wild animals, including the big cats, leopard and lion all around the house. They were obviously on the prowl for prey.

All in all not a bad neighbourhood to see and enjoy, with so many different animals in their true natural state.

When 1966 I arrived in Kajiado as deputy divisional commander on transfer from Nandi Hills. I travelled in civilian clothes, with my uniform packed in the luggage that accompanied me.

A report awaiting immediate action said that two Masai clans, the Matapato and the Katangere, were gathering in big numbers and spoiling for a fight in the forest.

So I gathered some Constables and Tribal Police – I think a total of eight - and set off in a Land Rover to resolve the dispute, the nature of which as yet I did not know. I was without uniform, still in my luggage. We caught up with the offending parties late into the evening.

We learnt that the cause of this dispute was one dead cow. No one we spoke to could tell us to which group the cow belonged and who had killed it. Just because someone told someone else that a fight was on the cards and was imminent, all came along for the fun of it.

When we arrived and started talking to the Masai, their numbers multiplied like mushrooms, forming themselves into fighting lines approximately ten deep.

During this time I tried to talk some sense into them but to no avail, as they were concentrating on moving along to find a place to have their battle.

Eventually we arrived at a place with two hills and a valley in the middle. The adversaries occupied a hill each. In order to keep them apart I deployed my meagre force of Askaris along the valley. By this time I estimated about a thousand Masai on one of the hills and approximately fifteen hundred on the other.

The way we were deployed, I thought, we would be massacred without much of an effort on the part of the Masai. Fearing for our safety I decided to withdraw my Police to one side and we became spectators.

All of a sudden spears and arrows started flying between the two opponents. I saw one person standing when a spear went clean through him. He stood there for a while not knowing, I imagine, what had hit him. He slumped to the ground. This carnage lasted for about two to three minutes before the two clans dispersed as quickly as they had gathered. They left behind eighteen dead and approximately twenty injured.

Upon my return to divisional headquarters I reported the incident to provincial headquarters in Nakuru. Our current chairman, Paddy Kearney was the Deputy Provincial Police Officer. I must put on record my appreciation for the support and encouragement he gave me at this time and in subsequent events. Thank you Paddy.

President Kenyatta set up an Enquiry under the chairmanship of Mwai Kibaki, which exonerated the Police of any wrongdoing. Upon hearing the result of the Enquiry I treated myself to a hefty meal after what seemed, for me, a long time of stress, wondering what would happen to me if the result had been different.

My last post in 1969 was at CID HQ as a staff officer – a

glorified pen pusher, I suppose – until I left The Kenya Police as a Chief Inspector in 1971 after a sixteen-year career of great interest and variety.

Talking of nostalgia. Yes I am nostalgic about Kenya in general. The weather and the people were so fascinating. But I am nostalgic about the Police Force in particular; the sudden rush of adrenalin when faced with what the mind perceived a dangerous situation; the variety with never two days alike; and the feeling of oneness with people at work.

I still miss it all, even after so many years in England.

However, as compensation we ended up in this country that, despite the cold, is not bad at all.

Philip Wood – Police Officer

Don't Sleep On The Job, A Strange Gun And Singing In The Dark

When in Nairobi 999 during 1956, we started our midnight to eight patrol shift with two patrol cars newly serviced at the Transport Department.

The shift went well without any incidents and we all went off duty as normal. The next night we were all called into the boss' office before starting duty. One patrol car driver was asked what he had done on the previous night's shift. He said that it had been a quiet night without incident and had nothing to report.

A circular piece of paper was then produced and the Inspector who drove that car was asked to look at the disc and explain what he saw. Puzzled, he examined the disc and passed it round to the rest of us without comment.

We had never seen or heard of such a thing and were told it was a tachograph chart installed in the two newly serviced cars. This new device had been fitted to both cars during the weekend service to track every movement of the car during use.

A second chart from the other car showed normal standard use, but the first car's chart showed twenty minutes normal use, five minutes of sixty mph driving, then six hours of the car being stationary before a further five minutes of sixty mph followed by an hour of normal use.

The rest of us were sent out to commence normal duty. The Inspector who had driven the car stayed behind to explain what he had done.

It turned out that he had started patrol and driven normally for twenty minutes. He then drove as fast as he dared to his new home at the North side of Kileleshwa Estate and gone to bed.

He had fixed up a pulley system between the car and his bedroom window, with a tin box on the pulley end for his Askari to warn him of any contact from the Control Room.

After a good night's sleep the officer was woken up by his Askari and returned to duty in the normal manner.

Needless to say we all learnt a lesson from this incident.

The officer concerned left the Kenya Police soon after.

In early 1956 I was Control Officer for 999 Nairobi.

On one shift, Frank Abrahams, Chief Inspector in charge of 999 entered the Control Room and said, 'I'll take over. You report immediately to Senior Superintendent Eric Lindsay's office.'

I went, nervous and wondering what offence I'd committed to warrant this possible looming disaster.

SSP Lindsay said, 'Your record shows you are a good shot, so for the next five days you are to act as escort and bodyguard to Vice President of India, here on an official visit. Go and collect your firearm. Get back immediately as we are late.'

I was taken next door to the Assistant Superintendent of Police and handed a Berretta Sub-Machine Gun and magazine belt, the worst weapon I have ever seen. It weighed more than twenty pounds and looked like an ancient square version of a Bren gun, all levers and catches.

SSP Lindsay ran past shouting, 'Come on, we're late.'

Carrying gun and bullet belt I ran after him to a waiting police car driven by a very nice Sikh policeman to overcome any translation problems.

For four days we travelled to various Asian communities with the VIP. On the last day of his visit we went to four or five settlements in the Kiambu area.

All went okay without problems until the very last place. The VIP was to visit a Temple, but when we arrived we found the whole place filled with thousands of people.

The VIP's car finally stopped about fifty yards from the Temple. He jumped out and was immediately lost in a melee of hundreds of Asian families all trying to touch him and give him flowers.

We all jumped from out car and struggled through the crowd, eventually reaching our VIP, who was staggering under the weight and lack of vision from the hundreds of flower garlands that had been put around his neck.

His head had disappeared into the flowers, but when we reached him he was laughing, so all was okay. He went into the Temple and performed what he came to do.

Apparently, as leader of a particular Religious Sect in India he came here because this is the main Temple for the Sect. Asian devotees came from all over East Africa to see him.

My escort duties ended, I went to hand the ancient Berretta machine-gun back in. I took to the ASP's office and on the side of the table, after much pushing and twisting, finally managed to strip the gun down to prove it was unloaded.

I saw immediately that it had no firing pin. I pointed this omission out to the ASP and he made a telephone call. A few minutes later a European armourer in overalls appeared.

He examined the gun and agreed the lack of a firing pin.

After a moment's thought he said, 'That must be what I found it on the floor last week. I wondered where it came from and put it in my drawer'.

I left the ASP to deal with the matter and never heard anything else about it, nor did I see the armourer again.

I have often thought about how the lives of several VIP Officers would have changed if there had been reason to use the gun.

In 1957 I took a patrol of seven Constables and one Corporal in a small lorry with the task of stopping Wakamba tribesmen coming up the river valley to gather honey from the bees nests that abound in the trees.

Their method – to follow bee-eating birds – took them to the bee's nests and the honey, which they collected by setting fires and driving the bees away.

One man climbed the tree and pushed burning grass into the nests. With the bees gone he stripped the honeycombs and dropped his harvest to the men below. When finished, they left the area without bothering to douse their grass fires, which then set the surrounding bush alight.

We left Makuyu and drove along the south side of the Tana River, from the Tana River Bridge on Nyeri/Nairobi Road, turned eastwards downriver past the Tana Ranch and into the bush.

We passed the tiny Our Lady of Mercy Mission comprising four huts with three resident Nuns, all European but speaking no English.

The Tana is very wide in this area with large papyrus swamps. We kept at least a mile inland from the river to avoid the numerous and vicious crocodiles.

About five miles past the Mission we could not get the vehicle through the trackless bush any further, so in the late afternoon made camp on a hill further inland.

We settled there for three nights, and carried out two days of foot patrols around the area. We did not catch any Wakamba, but the word went round that we were there and looking for them, so they probably took the hint and went home.

After our evening meal I got my prized possession out of the vehicle – a new battery driven record player for which I had about four records – and set it going at full volume with music from Last Night of the Proms.

This fascinated my Constables. They crowded round amazed by the large orchestra and the audience singing along. I joined in with the record and sang all the way through Rule Britannia, Jerusalem and various other tunes.

They shouted, clapped and were delighted with my performance and asked that I do it all again.

For three days we carried out foot patrols eastward, southwards and all around the locality, finding many isolated settlements of Kikuyu, Wakamba, and Embu, all living off the land on small plots they had cleared. Many of the children had never seen a white man before and none of them had ever been to Nairobi or to the Coast.

On our return to camp each night from quite exhausting patrols, my Constables asked me to play the records again and again and had many questions about the music. With my poor Swahili I had no real idea how to describe The Royal Albert Hall or the audience to them.

On the final night we had a large group of local villagers standing in the shadows listening to the Mad White Police Officer singing away in the dark.

Everyone – me, Constables and local villagers – all had a good time.

The next morning we returned normal duties and came back in the evening for another concert.

David Hewson – Police Officer

Sergeant Kitele's Goat

I was to learn that Sergeant Kitele was typical of his tribe. He was tall and thin but well muscled, with a head of curly black hair mixed with a wash of grey that gave him a distinguished look. In the manner of the WaKamba, his top front teeth had been filed into sharp points. His face was marked with the scars that indicated his tribe and his clan within the tribe. He wore a thin straggly moustache that hung down on each side of his upper lip, in the manner of a Chinese mandarin.

Always immaculate in uniform, shorts neatly starched with razor sharp creases, his navy blue woollen jersey, with leather shoulder pads perfect, his lanyard fixed in regulation manner around his neck, with the whistle tucked neatly into his belt buckle.

His black leather belt shone like glass. Barefoot navy blue puttees evenly wrapped and tied off at regulation height just below the knee. On his head, the tall red fez with its black tassel, his Police number set at the regulation distance below his shining Police cap badge. He always looked a picture of alert authority.

He looked every bit the excellent instructor of raw Police recruits, who in the early nineteen-fifties were, on the whole, straight from upcountry villages and illiterate.

Off duty he became a different Kitele, dressed simply in an old shirt worn over a very old pair of uniform shorts and old boots with no laces.

As constant companion he had a goat. Where ever Sergeant Kitele went so did his goat. Not your average African goat. Sergeant Kitele's Goat was large and brown with a pair of bright yellow eyes below a pair of magnificent horns. A long and aristocratic beard, turning grey but as crisp and pointed as a Spanish grandee at the head end and an up-turned tail, proud and vigorous at the other.

There were occasions – Commandant's Parades, Passing Out Parades and other very Official Occasions when Sergeant Kitele's Goat had to be banished – but in the day - to-day business of the Training School, Kitele and his goat were inseparable.

On the drill square teaching recruits basic drill, teaching riot drill, or in the long fifty bed barracks, inspecting his Constables' personal kit laid out for inspection, Kitele's goat attended.

On the rifle range firing point at shooting instruction, the goat attended, standing neatly at Kitele's side. Even when Kitele was in the Sergeants Mess his goat was stationed outside the door loyally waiting. Kitele's goat was his shadow him everywhere. If you saw the goat, you knew that Sergeant Kitele would not be far away.

When Sergeant Kitele was Orderly Sergeant and responsible for mounting the Quarter Guard on the Main Gate of the Training School, the goat would fall-in beside Kitele and march off with him to post the sentries. We all believed that the goat understood the orders when Mounting the Guard and certainly knew all the various bugle calls that regulated the day for all of us at the School.

I cannot recall, nor did I hear of any misdemeanor attributed to Sergeant Kitele's goat, nor did I hear a name. The goat was always Sergeant Kitele's Goat.

When Kitele retired he and his goat went off by train to Machakos, and then on by bus to Kitui, Kitele's home district. For, I hope, a long and happy association in retirement.

Sergeant Kitele's Goat

Anonymous – A Police Officer

Ol Kalou and Happy Valley

Ol Kalou and the valleys leading up to the Aberdare Forest and to the Rift Valley Escarpment consisted of very fertile wheat, cattle and sheep country, and some very large farms.

Shortly before my arrival in Ol Kalou a Mau Mau gang entered a farmhouse at around seven in the evening and murdered two European farmers.

The two men, Ferguson and Bingley followed the European farmers' custom to bathe before dinner and to sit down to eat in their nightclothes, with their guns on the table beside them.

Ferguson and Bingley were overwhelmed and slashed to death, their guns and ammunition stolen, and the house ransacked. The house staff let the terrorists in and disappeared with the gang but were later caught and killed in Security Forces operations.

To say that some of the farmers were eccentric would be a reasonable statement. One farmer, named Morgan Grenville, claimed to be a direct descendant of Morgan the Pirate who died in 1688.

Another dinnertime attack in a different area two elderly ladies living alone on their farm, except for the house and farm staff suffered a similar attack but with a different result.

The two were relaxing after dinner with coffee when their servants unlocked the door to a Mau Mau gang and led them to the sitting room.

However, the two ladies reacted with great courage and speed. They both had pistols and opened fire and killed the first gangsters coming through the door.

At the same time, the ladies' two dogs raced into the kitchen and savaged some of the other gangsters, who fled.

The ladies then managed to barricade the door and radio for help

Hearing a noise in the kitchen cupboard the ladies put several bullets through the door.

When the door was eventually opened, the body of their cook fell out. It had been he who had led the gang into the living room.

Unfortunately, the ladies accidentally shot one of the dogs during their battle with the Mau Mau.

Both ladies received awards for their bravery and on one visit to the area Sir Evelyn Baring, The Governor, called to meet with them.

They continued to stay on their farm despite the risks and danger involved.

However, the Mau Mau terrorists stayed away from this doughty pair during the rest of the Emergency.

Mike White – Police Officer

Wild Animals and Me

I had quite a few experiences with wildlife during my time in the Kenya Police.

I had a Police Post up in the Suk at a place called Psigor. My accommodation, such as it was, consisted of an A-Frame tin shed with a concrete floor, two rooms and a stable type door at each end with a six-inch gap at the bottom.

One room housed my safari gear and tents. The other I used to sleep, eat, wash and read. My bed was the usual canvas fold up affair, hard as hell and not long enough, me being 6ft 2in.

Being near a river, mosquitoes were a problem and snakes in abundance and green scorpions nested under my folded tent in the other room. And on several occasions, while sitting outside under the stars, I saw leopard prowling around the Boma.

I had a double mosquito net around the bed, well tucked into the paillasse and I kept my Colt .45 hanging over my head, and, within easy reach, a Simi in its scabbard and a torch within easy reach.

One night I heard a swishing noise passing the bed, shone the torch and, to my surprise saw a green mamba, about six feet long, passing through my bedroom.

I didn`t say 'frightened', you notice. At 23 years old one is brave and, of course, immortal

Some nights later, covered in the usual sheet, I woke to feel something heavy crawling up my leg.

'That bloody mamba again', I thought and reached for the Colt, but, lying on my back, decided not to shoot its head off as I might miss and blow off one or two of my toes, or, possibly, my whole foot.

I decided that my best action was to shine the torch at it and whip its head off with the Simi before it got me.

I flashed my torch all I saw a nine-inch long millipede about three quarters of an inch across and – in my imagination - weighing several pounds.

Animals and insects are not the only upcountry danger. Long drops can also be a hazard.

Danger lies in the construction, where a metal cone sits across the hole with the wooden seat atop it. There is usually a small gap between the two items and therein rests the danger, very often in the form of a scorpion.

On one occasion I entered the earthy aroma inside the box, sat down and a few seconds later……POOOWWWW.

Not quite a bull's-eye but very close.

Looking down through watering eyes I saw a green scorpion scuttling back to its lair. I had no idea what to put on the wound but did have some Savlon that I rubbed in. I don`t think did any good as I felt a little off colour for a day or two.

My friend Boet van Rensburg – often known as Van – was a well-known and respected Kenya Police officer between the nineteen fifties and seventies. I had the pleasure of serving with him at Gatundu for a couple of years.

One day we received a report of a leopard trapped near one of the villages up near the forest edge and the Headman didn`t know what to do with it.

We went with a shotgun and, according to the description of the trap it seemed obvious that the animal had been caught in a mantrap spring device attached to an anchored chain.

As we neared the spot we could hear the animal straining and coughing in an effort to escape. As Van passed a dense bush area there was a rush and noise of a chain rattling and the leopard charged him, got to the end of the chain, pulled free and shot straight past him, missing him by inches, before disappearing into the bush.

Van didn't have a chance to get off a shot. We never saw or heard of the animal again. It probably had a severely damaged leg and, maybe, couldn`t hunt again and so starved in agony under a bush somewhere.

On investigating the device we saw that three teeth were missing from the steel jaws and it was, of course confiscated. Those of you who knew Van can imagine what a strip was torn off the Headman who had put out such a dangerous and cruel machine.

The surprise of this encounter was that the animal was very dark, almost black, and I'm sure that if seen at night it would have looked more like a black panther than an African Panthera Pardus Pardus.

Back at Kapenguria a report came in that a herd of Rothschild's Giraffe had wandered into the north farming area from the Suk and some were entangled in fencing. Rothschild's Giraffe, (Giraffa Camelopardalis Rothschild) is an endangered specie so, apart from any other reason, a group led by the District Commissioner, his wife, Chris Megson of Special Branch, Ted Baily from The Administration and me went to find and drive the herd back into the Suk. I had never seen this type of giraffe before and was surprised at the darkness of the areas within the surrounding light marks on the hide.

It is terrible to see the suffering of animals caught in fencing wire where the leg is swollen and suppurating. On two occasions we had to shoot giraffe unable to free themselves. It was an awful experience to see such graceful animals fall with a crash to the ground.

I will always remember the sound.

Van and I were fishing the Twiga Coffee Estate Dam, near Ruiru one day at a good spot for tilapia and black bass. We visited the dam early that morning on the way to a court hearing and ground-baited a spot in a pool surrounded by lily pads. The dam was quite big, being about four hundred yards long and two hundreds wide. We had a ten-foot boat moored there with an anchor made from an old small car wheel.

In the late afternoon, after court was finished, we returned and rowed out to the spot, dropped anchor and started to catch tilapia. The dam was also home to a very old hippo that often gave the workers cause for alarm when out of the water grazing. Today we could see it over on the other side, and in the water, so gave us no worries, yet.

After an hour or so a number of young African boys the local village or farm arrived on the opposite bank and started throwing stones at the hippo.

Not good.

We became a little concerned that it might move nearer our fishing spot so kept a good weather eye open for it. A hippo can stay underwater for about four to five minutes. I kept an eye on the kids, noted the nose of the hippo above the water, caught a fish and took it off the hook, turned to look over at the hippo and could no longer see him there.

A second later I saw his bow wave coming towards us. In shallow water hippo run along the bottom at speed, so now we had cause for alarm. I called to Van that we should leave and he started to row while I started to bring up the anchor and began to panic because as Van rowed one yard, I pulled at our car wheel anchor and dragged us back.

Another big heave.

The same scenario.

This happened three or four times with us both shouting at each other to get a move on.

In the end I cut the rope and we glided across the lake to safety just as the hippo, now only about ten yards away, ripped out of the water mouth agape, and large enough to swallow a Land Rover, right in the middle of the place we had, only seconds before, been caught up in the lily pads.

Sara Wright – Police Wife

Zanzibar, A Big Fish and Getting Married

My soon-to-be fiancé Ernie Wright came from Newcastle-upon-Tyne and the Barings lived in Northumberland, so they knew all the same places, which helped his relationship with us all.

He was a tremendous sportsman and played fierce and regular tennis with Sir Evelyn Baring, The Governor, who was also a keen rock climber, a sport that Ernie also enjoyed. They spent happy days together at Lukeniya near Machakos and at Hells Gate in The Rift Valley. Ernie was also an excellent fisherman both with rod and harpoon.

The Governor, Lady Mary, Katherine and me and the two ADCs, one of whom was, of course, Ernie, went to Zanzibar on a formal visit.

We were all staying at The Residency and on the evening we arrived were due to go to dine at the Sultan's Palace.

We went scuba diving in the afternoon and Ernie harpooned the most enormous fish. The Resident's wife was faintly horrified, as she had nothing large enough to cook it in.

'Why don't you present it to His Highness?' she said.

So of course Ernie did. It was cooked and served up on a huge gold plate as part of a very grand meal while the Sultan's band a medley of songs; Arabic, mostly, but also including "D'ye Ken John Peel," and, embarrassingly, "God Save The Queen."

Ernie was much congratulated.

It was during this period Ernie and I became close friends and began to discuss the prospect of getting engaged.

When Katherine went back to Art College in England the Barings decided I was quite useful in dealing with the immense numbers of visitors at The House, so I stayed on.

This, of course, suited Ernie and me very well

As the Queen's Coronation approached, practice parades became more frequent. The Sultana of Zanzibar arrived to buy clothes for the Coronation in London.

Lady Mary tried to persuade her to buy clothes more suitable for her age and figure – both considerable – and for the English climate, with no success. "The Sultan likes my knees" was all the answer Lady Mary got.

During The Sultana's stay there was a horrible murder in Nairobi and some of the Europeans marched on Government House. The Governor's Private Secretary drew his elegant but flimsy dress sword from its jewelled scabbard and stood guard outside the Sultana's bedroom. I hope it comforted her.

The Coronation parade was very splendid. We listened to the event being broadcast from London. Various ADCs ran backwards and forwards between wirelesses in Government House and the Parade Ground so the Royal Salute could be fired at the precise moment the Queen was crowned.

Ernie and I got married in my home village in England in Feb 1955 and, not surprisingly, came straight back to Kenya for our honeymoon. We went to Lamu and stayed in a house right on the beach. Lamu in those days was very quiet and unfashionable, a perfect honeymoon place.

It took us all day to drive there, and we arrived too late to go to our house on the beach, so we went to Petley's Hotel, an imposing 2-storey building. I was asked if I would like a shower and as I was hot and filthy I said "yes".

I was shown upstairs where there was a row of cubicles divided by not very high walls. I chose one with a door, but then found that a gentleman with shining gold teeth who leant on the top of the dividing wall with a watering can in his hand created the shower. I have never had such a quick shower in my life.

The long-drop lavatory was upstairs, possibly the longest long-drop in Kenya. We left as soon as possible after breakfast for the relative civilisation of the house at Shella.

Ernie was posted to Fort Hall as it was then called, now Muranga, where we lived in the small Boma. There was a DC, a DO, an Agricultural Officer, a doctor, and several other policemen living in the small mess. We had wonderful views of Mount Kenya from our veranda, Nelian and Batian peaks shining with what I was sure was snow, and a forest with huge trees. There was sun and warmth and friendliness, and Mau Mau.

Life in Fort Hall was a big change from Government House. We lived in a small PWD house in the Boma. I never felt frightened, as we had people all round us whom I knew and trusted.

There were just the two of us, newly married. We had domestic servants and Ernie had an orderly and we lived in a four-roomed bungalow. It was a very happy time. Ernie was out a great deal, sometimes at night dealing with violent gangs, but I felt well protected. People came to stay with us, and we went and stayed with our settler friends.

We entertained a lot of soldiers from England, including a boy doing his National Service from my home village who only wanted to have a bath and lie on the grass in the garden, talking about home and how he wished he was there, and how pleased he was to stay with us "just like the General". He was much easier to deal with.

It was very different for some of the settlers and the people who worked for them in isolated farms, reached by long, often muddy, tracks, some of whom we knew and visited. I was always glad to get back to Fort Hall, though I am not sure Ernie was.

He had brought a splendid manservant with him from the Northern Frontier Province – a Gellubba called Adan, who was a better cook than me; he at least could make caramel custard. I could barely boil an egg.

Luckily Ernie wasn't a greedy man, as we lived on a diet of caramel custard, cheese, crackers and marmalade – my contribution bought in the marvellous Goan shop in the Boma. Our diet did improve with time.

We had been there for about six weeks when our wedding presents arrived from England. These included a grand piano, admittedly a small one, elaborately packed in a tin case. There was very little room for a piano in our small house and it was always rather a worry. The tin case became an enormous success once cut up and used for roofs in the village. I saw them often on my walks, shining in the sun.

Warren Martin – Police Officer

From Wales to the Naivasha Swamp

With a party of twelve other recruits I arrived in Kenya by air in 1955.

We were taken in a Kenya Police lorry the Force Headquarters in Nairobi and told we were to spend a few months working from Police Stations around the Colony, before going to The Kenya Police Training School at Kiganjo, on the lower slopes of Mount Kenya.

In the late afternoon we were sent to the Queens Hotel, an informal Police watering hole we would get to know quite well during the next few years.

After an evening meal we sat in the bar and two of the old Middle East hands in our party introduced us to Ouzo.

Although I had not served in the Mediterranean, I knew enough to keep well away but one of my new friends, known as Scouse downed a few too many and had to be helped to bed.

At breakfast the next morning Scouse made the mistake of drinking several cups of coffee.

Fatal.

The coffee sent him back being just as drunk as last night.

Two of us had to support him while he took the Oath of Allegiance. Fortunately we had a distraction when a very large ex-Highland Policeman found it difficult to accept Queen Elizabeth the Second as the rightful Queen of Scotland and several swore they heard him say 'The First' just after 'The Second'.

We had a long day being measured for uniforms and listening to a lecture on the basic organisation of The Kenya Police and then spent a quiet evening without any more Ouzo.

The next day we collected our uniforms, personal side arms and warrant cards. The efficiency was impressive but a little alarming when Scouse and myself were told that we would be moving to an operations area on the morrow.

We already knew upcountry postings were planned for a short period before going to training school but some of the older ex UK Policemen thought this ridiculous, but I can't remember being particularly bothered.

The following day I boarded a train to Nakuru. After a long and interesting seven-hour journey, I arrived at dusk. An African corporal met me and we drove in a Police Land Rover to Naivasha.

He drove fast through the dark night in a way that made it obvious that we needed to be there as quickly as possible. On reaching the Naivasha Police lines I knocked loudly on the door of the European Inspectors' Mess, called my name and shouted that I needed a bed for the night.

To my surprise a voice from inside called back in Welsh, 'Where in Caernarvonshire do you come from?'

It was Bill Hughes from Pentraeth who had recognised my accent. We became friends, but within a week he moved to Eldoret, where, he taught me much about Police work when I later joined him at Eldoret.

The following day I was second in command of a patrol tasked to enter the Naivasha Swamp. Some Mau Mau leaders had been holding a meeting in the thicket.

The British Army surrounded the area while we Police went into the swamp to try to find the terrorists. By the time I got into position it was strongly rumoured that they had escaped through a gap in the line.

We were to rendezvous with an out-coming patrol and whom did I see but an old boy, Raymond Tucker, from my school, Friars Grammar School in Bangor.

He was leading a General Service Unit and was as amazed as I that we should meet again under such circumstances.

As he left he shouted, 'Don't worry, they've all gone.'

Three days later, very wet, very muddy and very tired, I had to agree.

We did not see a single terrorist the whole time we were in the swamp.

Mike Wade – Police Officer

A Will to Die For

(Adapted from a piece written for the *Police History Society Journal*)

One of the more interesting aspects of being a country copper is that one is often able to take a full part in a crime investigation, unlike our town or city colleagues who often deal only in particular areas of a crime. One such investigation occurred after the murder of Major Tom Mills.

In 1955 I commanded the Kenya Police Station at Rumuruti in the Laikipia District of the Rift Valley Province. Policing, now that the Mau Mau emergency was drawing to a close, was mainly to prevent cattle rustling of which there was a great deal.

A single white rancher assisted by Kenyan labourers occupied most of the ranches. One such rancher was Major Tom Mills who was single and had no local family. He also carried the rank of Chief Inspector in the Kenya Police Reserve, although he was not active at that time.

In May of that year, Major Mills mentioned to me that he had hired a trainee farm manager straight from England under the auspices of the Land Settlement Scheme. His name was Alan Edward Huxley.

Shortly after Huxley's arrival I met him at the Rumuruti Club, which formed the hub of the local social life. He was unaware that I was a police officer and we engaged in free-ranging conversation during the course of which I formed the definite impression that he had been very glad to leave England. I was also concerned that he seemed to be seeking information about his new employer's friends and family.

Having learned that he had come from Lewes in Sussex I wrote to the police office there asking if anything was known about the man. I was not surprised to learn that he had a previous conviction for theft and that a warrant had been issued for obtaining money by false pretences and others were pending.

Checking with the Land Settlement Board I learned that his application form declared no criminal convictions, one of the conditions of entry, had in fact been signed not by Huxley, but on his behalf by a clerk after Huxley stated he was unable to do so as his arm was broken.

I determined to have a word with Major Mills upon his return from a holiday South Africa.

One Sunday, my wife and I were just finishing Sunday lunch when a Land Rover skidded to a halt outside the bungalow and the driver ran on to the veranda thrusting a note into my hand that read "Come quickly. Tom's been taken."

The bearer of the note added that Huxley had written it and that when he left the ranch some fifteen miles away, Major Mills, who had returned overnight, was lying on the floor of his dining room apparently dead.

Accompanied by two Constables, I hurried to the scene and found Mills lying on the floor of his dining room with the remains of a meal upon the table. A cursory examination of the body led me to believe that not only was he dead but that he had died in agony, probably from strychnine which was a fairly common substance held on local farms, being used to poison vermin.

During the intervening five or six hours before the arrival of the doctor, who officially certified death, I sketched the scene – no camera – and took a witness statement from Huxley.

He was very calm and claimed he was astounded when Tom had collapsed. House staff stated that Mills had drunk a large gin and tonic, and one had prevented Huxley from removing bottles from the room. Securing the entire premises I left the two Constables on site and persuaded Huxley it would be in his best interest if he spent the night at the Club.

Following the post mortem examination I then changed to my administrative role and issued the burial certificate and arranged for a grave to be prepared in the local graveyard.

Whilst all this was going on, the evidence gatherers were covering a lot of ground. They discovered that the gin bottle recovered from the dining room contained traces of strychnine. It was also learned that Huxley has purchased a similar bottle a few days before Mills returned home.

Upon gaining access to the ranch safe, a will was discovered which purported to leave the entire ranch ('should he still be in my employment') to Huxley.

Wide-ranging enquiries found a Secretarial Agency in Nairobi where the will had been typed in accordance with a draft submitted by a man answering the description of Huxley. A returned cheque in Mills' office desk bore marks of having been traced and when matched with that on the will, proved to be identical.

Huxley was arrested and detained in the cells of Rumuruti Police Station. By this time we had an overwhelming amount of evidence linking him to the crime, including traces of strychnine found in the pocket of a pair of his shorts.

Huxley was interviewed at length by senior CID officers but consistently denied any involvement in the matter. However, the evidence was, as stated, overwhelming.

He was charged with murder and appeared in the Supreme Court, Nairobi, on 12th March 1956 before the Chief Justice, Sir Kenneth O'Connor. Thirty-seven witnesses appeared for the crown.

Huxley was found guilty of murder.

Following an appeal hearing on 12th May and subsequent consideration by the Governor, Sir Hugh Evelyn Baring and the Executive Council, Alan Edward Huxley, 25 years of age, was hanged on 2nd June 1956.

David Hewson – Police Officer

Thomson's Falls – The Emergency

The Governor, Sir Evelyn Baring, declared The Kenya Emergency on 20th October 1952. At that time I was Inspector-in-Charge of Rumuruti Police Station in the Laikipia Division of the Rift Valley Province.

Rumuruti was a large Police Station area with wide ranging cattle ranches as the main constituent with some wheat and maize farms along the Ol Arabel valley overlooking the edge of the actual Rift Valley.

The area population included Europeans and their African labour and a store owned and run by Jack and Erna Forester. Also in the area were a few Asian shopkeepers and mechanics, a Post Office and a couple of Bars in Rumuruti Township.

Prior to the Declaration of Emergency we experienced mainly crimes of stock theft and the occasional housebreaking of European and African dwellings.

During the dry season, in addition to stock theft we had the scourge of grass fires caused by Ndorobo honey hunters. Indeed on my first night in Rumuruti in February 1952 I watched helplessly as one Rancher lost twenty thousand acres of prime grazing. He had no stockpile of hay or other cattle foods, but in hard times all the farmers helped each other.

On my arrival at Rumuruti I was allocated the house, adjacent to the Police Station. It had been a family home for a married couple and their children in earlier times. Sparsely furnished with the standard issue of Public Works Department furniture, it was comfortable.

Pre-Emergency security problems were minimal and the house was rarely locked. I kept my service revolver, a Smith and Wesson forty-five, together and a few boxes of ammunition in a drawer, partially hidden by socks. The cookhouse boy knew where it was and my trust was implicit.

With permission from the Ranchers we sent regular foot patrols that toured the district at night, checking labour lines, picking up information and noting new arrivals in the district.

The patrols showed an obvious police presence and the resulting Patrol Register was a useful source of information. A full debriefing of the patrol commander was a worthwhile task. Not only did one learn what the African population was about, but also obtained an insight into the ways and habits of the Ranchers and their families.

The Station strength consisted of one Inspector, myself, one African Assistant Inspector, a Sergeant Major, a Sergeant, three Corporals and eighteen Constables and a Constable Driver.

The Police lines were a series of mud and wattle Rondavels with thick-thatched roofs. The inside had whitewashed walls and a compacted earth floor covered by slurry of cow-dung and water that dried to a hard, clean surface that acted as a disinfectant and kept the hut free from fleas and other bugs.

The outside was also whitewashed and black painted cow-dung slurry covered the raised base of the walls. No cooking fires were permitted in the huts and all cooking was done either in the open air outside the hut or in a separate structure set aside as a kitchen.

The area between huts was kept spotlessly clean the grass inside the Police compound cut regularly to a tidy length.

The Police Station was a cement block building with a cement floor. There were two offices, one for the Officer-in-Charge and an outer officer with a counter where the literate constable on duty kept the Occurrence Book and the Cell Register along with all the other official books and Patrol Register.

The Police had been aware, for some months prior to the Emergency, of the administration of Mau-Mau Oaths by travelling Oath Givers. We had difficulty in obtaining evidence, or indeed witnesses prepared to give evidence against the Oath Givers.

They worked in strict secrecy late at night and into the early hours with the powerful and ever present threat of a dreadful death for anyone breaking the Oath of silence.

The Oath itself was most repugnant and as the Emergency dragged on became more and more awful. With the Declaration of Emergency things began to change gradually.

But as murders increased, particularly against those Africans who, for a variety of reasons – religious, loyalty, education or family – refused to take the Oath tying them to the Mau-Mau.

At one stage my Police Station staff were investigating five serious murders of African loyalists at the same time. In a short time I had four newly appointed European Inspectors patrolling and investigating. In addition the Kenya Police Reserve were called up and two Ranchers' wives started work in the Station. They took over the radio and kept contact with outlying police posts and Ranchers' houses. The Police Station became a fortress.

Cattle were slashed; African huts were burnt down with the inhabitants locked inside. European houses were ransacked and food and firearms stolen. Every Rancher and his wife wore a gun.

One Rancher climbing into his bath slipped whilst wearing his gun belt. The revolver jerked from his holster and landed hammer first in the bath mortally wounding him.

Tempers became frayed and fear caused and outbreak of retaliation. Ranchers demanded action. Various factions formed their own little action groups that were finally brought under central control of a District Security

Committee set up by the District Commissioner with the Police Superintendent in command of all operations.

A Police mounted Section started operating along the edge of the Aberdare Forest chasing terrorists said to be responsible for Oathing ceremonies and raids on farm homesteads to steal food, blankets and firearms.

At that time I was investigating a particularly brutal Oathing murder. A young schoolteacher had gone missing and we heard rumours that he had refused to take the Oath.

As the Emergency proceeded and the Police and Army, along with the loyalist Kikuyu Home Guard, began to eliminate the forest gangs and their leaders, the Oathing and murders of Africans by their own kinsmen declined and the beautiful Thompson's Falls town and area eventually became peaceful again.

Avtar Matharu – Police Officer

Rookie Days, CID, Guns and a Deserter

After finishing my very nomadic schooling at age of seventeen in December 1952 I joined the Kenya Police in January 1953.

I say 'nomadic' because my father worked for the East African Railways & Harbours in the civil engineering department and prone to frequent transfers.

I first went to Nyeri in 1947 with my dad and stayed in his rest house. During a walk along Nanyuki – Nyeri road I went past what became the Police Training School one day. It seemed deserted and, of course, I never thought that in this place I would later commence to learn the ropes of life.

I later learnt it had been be an Italian Prisoner-of-War camp and converted to PTS Nyeri during the late 1940s, a fact confirmed when in January 1953 I saw some documents in the Training School clerk's office rubber stamped "Italian POW Camp".

During the war period our family lived in Kisumu, Eldoret, Kampala and Nairobi.

In Kisumu we suffered to blackouts at night. We also had petrol rationing at about four gallons a month for my dad's Baby Austin. And because Kisumu was a potential war target because of the Lake Victoria seaplane and shipping ports we had air raid shelters in our railways housing estate as well.

In Eldoret on one occasion a rumour went round that all railway houses would be searched for hoarded food and other goods.

My mother had a substantial stock of matchboxes and hid them in the kitchen Dover stove. She used the Dover stove only for baking bread with improvised yeast from potatoes.

Mother cleverly hid her hoard of matches behind the stove firebox. The search did not materialise, and she forgot all about them.

Several days later she lit the stove and chain reaction of explosions ensued. Mother's fire fighting with a bucket of water was totally in vain. Luckily the kitchen had been built separate from the house in case of fire, so our main dwelling survived.

In Nairobi in 1944/45 Italian POWs marked by a prominent blue diamond mark on their backs, used to sell clandestine items of army clothing such as sweaters and woollen stockings.

They would wear several layers of clothes, which they used to peel off one by one. Such was the dearth of wool in those days that my mother and her contemporaries used to buy them. The Italians were also given refreshments, which they cherished.

The ladies promptly picked apart the adult size sweaters for re-knitting into required size sweaters for their children. The Italians also sold very finely made wooden jewellery boxes. This activity showed the lack of security in the POW Camps.

The war ended to great celebrations in Nairobi in the form of victory parades and marches. My two uncles, who had served in the British Army Engineer Corps, were amongst the proud marching squads.

My father took my brother and I to see the march-pasts, which were quite a sight to witness as young Totos. I was only 10 years old, but the memory remains vivid. We also enjoyed the occasional supply of NAAFI chocolates and chewing gums, which were hard to get in the market.

By the age of fifteen my career choice of Policeman clearly defined itself in my mind. I had already been an imaginary pilot, a railway engine driver and even a train guard. Such was my early interest in the railways that during my school holidays, when I went back home to

Karatina, I used to play with the Morse Code signalling at the railway station. Only two trains passed in twenty-four hours so the stationmaster did not mind. I became fairly proficient in transmission, but receiving was hard.

Thereafter, anything police – a policeman, a police vehicle, a police station etc. captivated my attention.

By the time I joined the Force straight from school I had become conversant with the ranks. The sight of a police motorcyclist was absolutely thrilling. In spite of my nomadic schooling, I managed to achieve Cambridge School Certificate educational level in 1952, the maximum available in Kenya in those days.

In January 1953 I entered the Police Training School with my kit box, packed with boots, putties etc. and a long length of Stockport khaki drill material to be tailored into uniforms by a tailor in Nyeri town.

At last I had a Police rank: Asian Police Constable. I joined the other Asian rookies who had arrived before me. Such was the enlisting need and process then. There seemed to be no formal start or finish of squad training, at least for our section. Those who had undergone a stay of three months were passed out in small batches. It was exciting to travel back to Nairobi in uniform.

When I later attended a PTS training course in the 1960s, I learnt that during the early 1940s two Italian POWs escaped from the then POW Camp and remained missing for many days. When they returned they disclosed they had climbed Mt Kenya. They wrote a story of their climb, which was available in the PTS library.

In the book they described how keenly they used to watch the snowcap from the Camp, which enthused them run away and undertake the adventure and face the consequences later. They knew that otherwise their climb would have never been allowed.

Although they carried equipment hardly ideal for their trip up the mountain, given their clandestine circumstances, I gained many useful tips from their book for my preparation to climb Mt Kenya up to Point Lenana, the third highest peak; an essential component of my training course.

I only just about made it as I suffered badly from altitude sickness that caused dehydration and weakness. Thanks to Phil Oddie (RIP) who gave me an orange that gave me a brief burst of energy and did the trick, enabling me to walk the last hundred yards or so to where our course team hoisted the Union Jack.

From our Peak, we called the PTS on our walkie-talkie radio to let them know of our triumph.

Avtar On Lenana Point, Mount Kenya

Posted to CID Headquarters, Nairobi I was initially attached to the Investigating Branch. I found this exciting and did not feel the loss of uniform, which I cherished to wear.

About a month later I moved to another Department – Supervisees Section – within the Criminal Records/Scenes of Crime Department. In the wisdom of a Superintendent I was considered a 'vulnerable Toto' and much deflated.

It was a period to bide my time. For next two years I concentrated on my desk job under the tutelage of an experienced Chief Inspector who was a very good mentor.

His conversations and experience of case histories were something to learn from. On the quiet, behind his back I used to acquire old crime investigation files and read them thoroughly. It was good exercise. I used to keep the subject document in an open desk drawer and when interrupted would push the drawer gently shut.

Amongst these files was the "Great Train Robbery" of Kenya in 1950, near Nakuru. Interestingly enough, I knew some of the cast in this act; two were Railway employees and were already under suspicion for relatively minor criminal activities on the trains. Obviously, they graduated to higher performance. Before long all four were arrested and charged, convicted and jailed. This kind of learning through the experience of the others gave me good insight of statement and report writing.

From 1953 onwards came an influx of Contract Inspectors from the UK into Kenya Police. One such Contractor was posted to our department in CID headquarters.

Completely disinterested in his work, he did the minimum, spending a lot of time reading the newspaper and smoking. His work experience in Ireland had been in steel girders assembly at building sites; which explained his lack of interest in deskwork and his inefficiency.

He had been in CID for about four months when he decided to go on short leave. He asked me if I could take care of his revolver in his absence, which I foolishly agreed to, as at my parent's home there was a secure storage place. So I went home carrying two guns like a cowboy.

Our Contract Inspector did not return on due date. Several days passed when I had to report to my Department Head about the man's revolver being in my possession.

My boss was initially annoyed and then gave me some advice. He put my participation in this episode to immaturity and lack of experience. But I had to accompany him when the matter was reported to the Assistant Commissioner of Police, who duly gave me further advice.

So I learnt a lesson.

After some enquiries our Contract Inspector was published in Force Orders regarded a deserter.

It is an acknowledged fact that the calibre of some Contract Inspectors, who were rushed to the Colony in the nineteen-fifties, left much to be desired. During my later career I came across some of them whose suitability to have become good policemen was questionable.

After over two years I applied for transfer to uniform branch and posted to Nairobi Area Traffic. It was like emerging from the shadow into bright light.

My various experiences with guns ran from achievement to failure and fright.

I had been in Traffic Department Accident Investigation Section only for a few months attached with an experienced officer, accompanying him to all scenes of accidents.

One late evening we went to the scene of an accident in Landhies Road. After the initial crash both cars ended up far apart from each other as they had been travelling in opposite directions.

Whilst Tony, my mentor, was taking details of one the car drivers, the offending vehicle, a dark box body, drove off. On noticing this I reacted to prevent it escaping. In the excitement the only action that occurred to me was to commandeer an approaching car to hike a lift and follow the offender.

Luckily, a Ford Prefect, with two occupants in the front stopped. The driver, a very compliant Sikh, dutifully complied. I jumped into the back seat and we followed the quickly vanishing vehicle. It was getting dark and visibility was diminishing as it drove down Racecourse Road.

Several efforts to draw the driver's attention were in vain, by which time I had decided to shoot at the tyres. This was difficult from the rear passenger seat behind the driver, although I tried it by opening the door and keeping my right foot of the foot board and holding the off side door pillar.

It was risky business, both for my own safety and others. The tyres really had to be shot at from the side almost at a perpendicular. The escaping car eventually arrived at the roundabout of Ngara Road and Park Road. I asked my Ford Prefect driver to slow down and hoped the offending car would go round the roundabout and turn left into Park Road, which he fortunately did, offering me a perfect straight line to aim along.

I shot twice at the rear offside tyre. We continued to follow. After about a hundred yards the offending car lost speed and came to a stand still. With the help of my adopted crew I managed to arrest the two occupants of the immobilised car.

With due respect to these fellows, I must admit, they did not resist. It was evident that one bullet had hit and flattened the tyre and the other the rim of the mudguard. Both men were wanted for breech of the Emergency Regulations, and they were duly processed.

My side arm was a .38 revolver. The after effect was some concern to me for use of a firearm.

The following day before reporting off duty my Officer Commanding debriefed me.

Coincidently, the site of this incident is opposite where The Brilliant Restaurant was located on Ngara Road in Nairobi.

The pleasant surprise of this episode came when the Commissioner's commendation awarded to me was published in the Force Orders in 1955.

My earlier experience with a pistol was disappointing. On arrival in CID Headquarters as a rookie from PTS I was issued with an Italian .32 pistol. I carried it dutifully in shoulder holster for many months, day and night. There was an urge to use it in right circumstances, not that I was trigger hungry. It was the simple desire for thrill of a young lad.

Once over a weekend I decided to have a go and explain it later. I went to a remote place. I fired in the air. Nothing happened. I tried again after some adjustment to the magazine, but no shot could be fired. I felt embarrassed and disappointed, but happy I was not in a real time dangerous situation.

A gunsmith examined the pistol and reported that the pin was not striking the point of percussion of the bullet. The dummy pistol, which gave me false sense of security for many months, was quickly replaced.

The third episode with a stock of guns nearly gave me a heart attack, and could have ended my police career and possibly sent me to prison.

As second in command of Nairobi Area Traffic I was responsible for a stock of fifteen revolvers and about one hundred rounds of ammunition. These were kept in a safe mounted in the wall in the office and I carried its key in my wallet, which always lived in the back pocket.

Additionally, the safe was used for storage of monthly pay cash for the rank and file pay parade. On this heartrending occasion, after the pay parade, I stored the remaining cash in the safe and reported off.

The following day I returned to duty and about mid-morning, whilst enjoying my cup of tea, I noticed that the key of the safe still in the keyhole. I was shocked, and froze, almost trembling.

I did not have the courage to check the safe. I locked my office from inside and summoned a trusted colleague of mine and showed him what had happened. He was also shocked, but less so than me.

I regained my composure and we counted the revolvers and ammunition many times, individually and jointly. Likewise the cash was also counted. Fortunately nothing had disappeared.

It took some days before I stopped visualising a court case, dismissal and the prison gate. Thereafter the safe key always lived tied to my lanyard with the whistle and it underwent a daily check. I swore my trusted colleague to conspiracy of silence.

The positive irony of this event is that the office peon-cum-cleaner was always victim of my criticism for not doing his job properly. He had terrible body odour, which I could not stand and was lazy to the extreme. Had he been a policeman and not a civilian, it could have been dealt with.

I had tried to shunt him on transfer, but he had established himself as unacceptable, having been around some other formations. No other department would have him. Just as well that on this nerve wracking and fateful day for me he did not clean my office thoroughly; otherwise not only would he have cleaned the office, but also cleared it as well.

Bryan Coleman – Police Officer

My Father and the Poison Arrows

A book called *The Kenya Police 1887 to 1960*, written by Robert Foran, tells the story of when my father was shot by poison arrows by a religious sect called Dini Ya Watu Wa Mungu – The People of God.

Members were brainwashed into believing that anything they did was something God wanted them to do and they had committed several robberies and murders – including, in 1934, robbing The Patel Store on the Kabete road.

They killed the owner Mr Patel during the robbery. On the day of my first birthday, my father told my mother that he had come home to get his revolver.

He did not tell her the reason, but she knew something was not right, as he did not normally carry his weapon. On that same evening she heard that my father had been shot with a poison arrow and was in a serious condition in the European Hospital.

Doctor Brainbridge operated on him to remove an arrow that had penetrated his lung – perhaps the first ever operation like it. The Doctor removed the arrowhead and gave it to my mother, with the poison still on the shaft. I am told that after my father passed away my mother donated it to the British Museum.

Before the incident, my father had entered a hut whilst his colleagues, Bob Christian, three Askaris and a Sergeant Major, stayed outside. This is contrary to what is written in the aforementioned book.

Inside the hut an older woman sat by a fire cooking a fresh batch of poison made from the wild coffee tree root, and mixed with any other poisons available, such as those from scorpions and snakes.

At this point my father heard a commotion along with the sounds of shots being fired. He went to the hut door and noticed that Bob and the others had taken cover. He tried to join them but as he left the hut he saw three men with their bows drawn.

They immediately shot at my father as he was trying to reach the others. Three arrows hit him in the back and he collapsed. Bob and the others kept shooting and managed to kill two of the attackers. The remaining one, having run out of arrows, started an attack towards my father with a Simi.

The Sergeant Major shot this man between the eyes with a .303 rifle before he could do any damage. A total of 52 arrows had been let loose.

Men in the Police Party were able to pull two of the arrows out of my father's back, but the third came apart, leading to the operation by Dr Brainbridge. One of the reasons my father survived was that the poison from the arrows that hit him was old and less potent. His colleagues also sucked the poison from his wounds on the way to hospital.

My father was awarded the MBE by King George the sixth.

Around the age of seven or eight, I asked about the arrowhead my Mother had kept and she told me never to touch it.

When I asked why, she told me the story that nearly left me fatherless.

The Royal Wajir Yacht Club

John Newton says

The Royal Wajir Yacht Club, parked firmly in the Northern Frontier Desert many hundreds of miles from any water, is one of those beautifully eccentric places that seem part of being an Englishmen Abroad. Especially in deserts where the heat, sand and wide lonely horizons send the imagination off into sometimes hilarious fantasies. The RWYC has many stories about its origins and practices. The two explanations below may clarify that dear place. Or they may not.

Mike Fogg-Elliot – Police Officer

The Royal Wajir Yacht Club

There are several versions of the Royal Wajir Yacht Club and mine's the best.

The Royal Wajir Yacht Club was founded after the First World War, half a crown for life membership. It was a hut with a bar - a long, long bar, with the ends of the bar signified by the Admiral's epaulets. In the middle of the bar Admiral's fore-and-aft hat, which was placed crossways when the bar was open and long ways when the bar was shut.

The story goes the after the First World War when there were lots of Admirals and Generals milling around, they got dispatched to the far corners of the British Empire.

When this particular Admiral was sent off to Wajir he promptly wrote back to his dear friend Bunny who was Secretary of The Royal Thames Yacht Club requesting affiliation to The Royal Thames and would that be acceptable?

A letter came back from The Secretary, saying, 'My dear Admiral, we'd be delighted to reciprocate with you. We've had a meeting and by agreement you may call yourselves The Royal Wajir Yacht Club.

This carried on until almost the end of the Second World War, when in those days the RAF and other personnel we coming down from Ethiopia and other places on the way to Mombasa for a bit of R&R.

They all had to stop at Wajir to get a drink and stay for a longish time, and, one happy day, a Corporal who'd done the trip found himself in London with nothing to do and nowhere to go and he saw this sign and he saw this sign saying "Royal Wajir Club, reciprocating with Royal Thames."

So he takes himself in.

The barman says, 'What do you want, Corporal?'

'I'd like a pint of bitter please, mate.'

'Are you a Member?' asks the barman.

The Corporal shows his card.

'Yes, Sir, take a seat please and we'll see what we can do for you.' says the barman and sends for the Secretary.

'Ah, Corporal', says the Secretary. 'How nice to see you. What will you have to drink?'

'A pint of bitter please, like I told your Oppo.'

'Certainly. A pint of bitter please barman, on me, and tell me, Corporal, what's the sailing like in Wajir?'

'Sailing, mate? We're a thousand miles from the bleedin' seaside.'

So that was the end of the reciprocating rights with The Royal Thames Yacht Club.

I found it in 1957 or 1958, still with the Admiral's epaulettes still the Admiral's fore-and-aft cap, so the Admiral has to be a true story.

Three or four years ago there was an article in the Field Magazine about Funny Clubs and I wrote up this story about this reciprocating Royal Thames and Royal Wajir.

The Field received a very sniffy letter from a Colonel saying 'Absolute nonsense. The reason it is called "The Royal Wajir" is because Edward, Prince of Wales went up there before becoming King in 1936 and gave permission for it to be called Royal.'

Then someone else wrote in, saying, 'Absolute stuff and nonsense. The reason it is called "The Royal Wajir" is because during the Second World War we captured an Italian Duke. He said he had only one absolute right in his life and that was to give the annotation of Royalty to anything he happened to be going through.'

But, if those two stories are true, where do the Admiral's epaulettes and hat come from?

The Royal Wajir Yacht Club In All Its Glory

Alec Abell – Police Officer

The Royal Wajir Yacht Club

Below are Ten Facts About The Royal Wajir Yacht Club, put together by the Late Bob Stanyon. He served as a Chief Inspector at Wajir in the early sixties and was "Chief Purser" of the RWYC. I´m certain Bob would have no objection to me passing this on to you. Incidentally, the RWYC has its own tie of which I am a proud possessor.

1. The Club´s First Commodore in 1932 was the then District Commissioner, Freddie Jennings. The club provided him with a measure of self-defence against the plundering of his hospitality by safari parties wishing to experience the Beau Geste magic of the remote NFD – which was mostly a Closed District at the time.

2. The Commodore's regalia came from various Royal Naval sources, including a sword donated by Lt Cdr Maurice Vernon. Vernon had joined the KAR in 1936 or 1937 and died in 1993 aged 97.

3. Visitors were expected to donate a hat to the club. Occasionally they resisted and more than one visitor left irritated that his headgear had somehow gone missing for it to reappear in the Club´s collection later. It was the purser's job to label and display these trophies. They included three or four Governors hats, a couple of GOC´s, about four from Members of Parliament and one from Kermit Roosevelt. Valerie Hobson donated an extravagant Ascot hat when she visited with her husband John Profumo.

4. Permanent European residents in Wajir rarely exceeded six; one District Commissioner, one District Officer, two Kenya Police Officers and two Kings African Rifles Officers; occasionally supplemented by a doctor or vet. The number of residents rose during World War Two and during the Somali Shifta Campaign in the nineteen-sixties. During the Shifta Campaign a semi-permanent RAF

detachment of up to three Twin Pioneer aircraft detached from RAF Eastleigh were posted to Wajir.

5. From inception the club never operated a colour bar.

6. Qualification for the club tie was six months continuous residence in Wajir either in the boa or in the KAR camp. Qualified members were therefore few, numbering only forty-four by the mid-sixties.

7. The club had a boat in 1961 when the long and short rains merged and the Commodore's fundi made a small flat-bottomed boat that could be rowed or punted. Big lakes lasted six weeks or so. The northern Uaso Nyiru river burst through the Lorian Swamp and spread into Somalia south of Dif. Normally the nearest surface water to Wajir was 250 miles away.

8. The Prince of Wales, later King Edward VIII, was due to visit Wajir in 1934 but his father's illness cut short his Kenya tour. The Prince's equerry sent a letter of regret and authorised the "Royal" in the club´s title.

9. At least two Commodores were teetotal.

10. And in case you think sport was neglected; In 1963 The World Series Liar Dice Championships were held at the Club. The winner by a mile was the Irish entrant, Ship´s Surgeon Jimmy Clearkin, The NFD Provincial Medical Officer.

As far as I am aware none of the above has ever been published previously and is little known.

Warren Martin – Police Officer

Police Training School at Kiganjo

After about five months in different areas, helping with the Emergency, the group I came to Kenya with were all posted at the same time to PTS Kiganjo, where we reassembled as recruits.

We came together in Nairobi and went by train to Nyeri, then on to Kiganjo by lorry, arriving in the late afternoon.

We were shown to our sleeping quarters, which were large oblong canvas tents with twelve beds, six on each side. We were then taken to the canteen to relax and eat.

A very warm interlude with much conversation about or journey came to an end when we were told to parade in uniform at eight the next morning to be shown around the camp, introduced to our class instructors and learn the routine that would control our lives for the next sixteen weeks.

I slept soundly that night.

The next morning we divided into two classes and marched off to our placement classrooms in old Nissen huts. While crossing the main Nyeri road we saw groups of Europeans and Africans and one mixed group being chased around a very large open space that turned out to be the parade ground.

Some of the older lads in our group shouted out in some distress, 'Oh my God, do we have to do that?' and, 'I told them that all I wanted was to be a Policeman.'

The Chief Inspector marching us to class yelled, 'Stop talking.'

Up to that point he had seemed quite pleasant and the sudden change to harsh drill instructor shocked us all.

Our classroom instructor, an Assistant Superintendent, introduced himself and outlined an intensive training programme that included a test every week with a longer test every fourth week and a final examination in week sixteen.

The timetable included lectures, practical work and drill ground parades along with guard and ambush duties.

In reply to a question, our instructor told us that the mixed squad we had seen being harried round the open space was a refresher course of all ranks from all over Kenya.

He told us that once we had learned the Kenya Police drill system each of us would take command of a squad of African recruits and learn with them how to interact with a group of African Constables.

'We won't have time to breathe, let alone eat,' muttered someone in the back.

During our time at PTS we had many interesting and difficult things to do and learn including how to get round a very demanding Obstacle Course.

This Obstacle Course had been built as a particularly refined kind of torture. In retrospect, the amount of mud involved meant that the Kenya Police were probably some forty years ahead of the Foreign Legion in trial and tribulation.

The most frightening test in this Course was the rope slide. First you climbed a steep hundred and thirty feet slope through thick forest to a high cliff that formed one side of an almost vertical river gorge.

On the cliff edge you looked down over the river to a shingle beach on the opposite bank, alongside rushing water flowing from the Mount Kenya snowfield.

Your test – to cross from cliff top to shingle beach – could only be accomplished by hanging on to metal handles in the form of an upturned U and sliding a hundred yards over the river down a hemp rope.

And, of course, dropping the hundred and thirty feet from cliff top to shingle beach.

This had been set up as the first obstacle before running the whole course.

Our drill instructor, known as Screaming Skull, stood in front of Scouse and myself and said, 'Right. You two old soldiers can show the way.'

I was just about to cry, 'But I'm too young to die,' when I realised that Scouse had gone.

He'd taken the plunge without waiting.

I grabbed one of several iron slides and launched myself into space after him.

Absolute exhilaration.

I loved it.

In a few seconds the pebbles were rushing up to meet me.

Just in time, sliding my heels into the depth of stones and letting go of the iron, I rolled over to gaze into Scouse's boots.

'Get up and look at that Taff,' said, pointing at the sheer cliff of mud we had just flown over and now had to climb back up.

We could see hardly any handholds so ran downstream to a easier slope where crossed the stream and pull ourselves up on roots and branches of small trees and bush.

Ignoring the shouting coming from the start point we ran over the top of the gorge and re-joined our squad, expecting to see the ranks depleted. But not one other of our group had moved.

Screaming Skull told us in no uncertain manner that the whole point of the exercise was to climb the cliff we'd come down and that we would have to do it again. When we again reached the top we were to stay there and help the others.

This crossing the river experience terrified many, especially amongst the African recruits. Their instructor would demonstrate, then climb back up to supervise them one by one down the slide and then make a final run himself.

Knowing that Screaming Skull had another course on the slide in a few minutes, the moment our lesson was over Scouse and myself went down to the camp and found a fire axe.

We returned to the top of the cliff and hid for five minutes in the bushes, waiting for Screaming Skull to make his last run and when he disappeared down the slide, we drove the axe right through the rope.

The splash of him hitting the water echoed through the gorge as we ran back down to the canteen.

We replaced the axe and nobody ever knew what we had done.

Screaming Skull just assumed that the rope had broken, so we got away with our little prank.

David Illing – Police Officer

A Drunken Elephant, A Black Leopard And A *Very* Long Snake

Most officers from upcountry when holidaying at the coast were content with the sun, sand and sea and the marine creatures therein. They didn't have the time or inclination to search out or come across the wildlife.

I had not been posted to Diani very long when my initiation began. Driving one day from the main South Coast road through the scrub, my companion pointed and said 'Simama. Tchui' and pointed at what appeared to be a Black Leopard.

On further examination its spots were twice the normal size and its main background colour was a dark orange. It wandered completely unconcerned some fifteen feet in front of us, looking over its shoulder a couple of times before turning into the scrub.

Later, talking to some of the local residents, it emerged that it had been seen before. They were aware of its presence but kept quiet, fearing someone may want to make a trophy of it.

Whilst talking to an employee of the Jardini Hotel about local wildlife, he mentioned that elephants from the Shimba Hills often came down to the coastal scrub to visit a cashew nut tree when it was fruiting. I suggested that a few Shillingi would be available if they told me when the elephants arrived and guided me to them.

It seems that the elephants were attracted by the smell of rotting fruit carried some five miles to the hills by an onshore breeze.

Sure enough, after a bit of financial bargaining, I was guided to the said fruiting tree. Most elephants had left, but one remained. It was so intoxicated that it could only lean against the tree and appeared oblivious to our presence.

It had gorged on the ripe fruit, which resembled a large yellow apple. This fruit had fermented in its innards, causing astounding sounds.

The long snake made its presence known when I took my new bride on honeymoon to the Twiga Hotel. We drove to the Tiwi River one day and then on to the Tiwi Mosque, which is believed to be a thousand years old.

It is simple in construction, resembling a small Nissan hut made from coral blocks that, over the centuries, have weathered worn, grey and covered in lichen. We drove up quietly as the building is used daily. As we stopped a snake some ten feet long rose four feet and took off into the overhanging trees.

Finally, for those of a more enquiring nature, the Shimba Hills to the east of Diani are the home of elephant, buffalo, colobus monkeys – the black and white variety – and sable antelope. The real surprise is that the male sable antelope are usually brown, but when sexually mature the alpha male of the herd turns turn jet black.

With their long tapering horns they are a magnificent sight. The high point of the reserve gives a wonderful panoramic view of some twenty miles of coastline and seascape.

David Hewson – Police Officer

A Difficult Mountain Rescue

I became involved in another mountain incident when two very experienced Austrian climbers were at the peak of Mount Kenya and one fell, breaking his leg in two separate places just above the ankle.

Fortunately a ledge just below the Gate of the Mists arrested his fall. Being a doctor of medicine he knew he had a serious injury.

His companion climbed down and made him comfortable, settling him into a sleeping bag and tying him to the mountain before setting off to seek assistance, climbing down from the peaks alone and across the glacier to the Top Hut. From there he faced a sixty-mile hike to the nearest radio at Naro Moru Police Station.

Once the seriousness of the incident had been assessed, the Mountain National Parks team went into action and alerted the Mountain Club of Kenya Rescue teams.

At The Police Training School we went on standby to provide Police Cadets for porterage, when required. We waited anxiously while various strategies were thought through and tried.

One strategy suggested was to drop a rope over the Gate of the Mists, lower the injured climber down the mountain to a height where he could be properly manoeuvred. A helicopter made the drop but lost the rope when it could not be caught and slid down the mountain.

We received an urgent message to get a replacement rope to the rescue camp as quickly as possible. At four in the afternoon a party of ten Police Cadet Officers on a promotion course to Gazetted rank, set off from my office with strict instructions to walk and climb all night and, without fail, get the rope to where it was needed.

Chief Inspector Faisal Sherman, an experienced Cadet and a GSU Company Commander led the party. They delivered the rope within eight hours.

On their return, I debriefed Faisal and he told me what had happened.

'We drove to the tree line at ten thousand feet, disembarked and sorted our loads. The very heavy rope needed to be looped in such a way for ease of carrying for a small party. At around six-thirty as night closed in, we started our walk through the last vestiges of forest, climbing to the moorland and the vertical bog.

'We climbed steadily and as darkness deepened it became more difficult to navigate our way. However we kept going, with only one stop for food and drink. At around one in the morning, thick mist began to close in, reducing what little visibility we had. Added to the darkness of night it made finding our way very difficult.

'But we carried on, moving slowly through the mist and still, we hoped, heading in the right direction.

'As we inched forward I began to hear a constant message in my head.

'It said, "Stop."

'I took no notice, as I knew we had to get that rope to the forward camp by first light.

'The message in my head became continuous and urgent, but I ignored it. The injured climber had been on the mountain almost a week since his fall and our journey was urgent.

'Suddenly the command became strident.

'Adamant.

'STOP.

'With the mist so thick I could not see my hands and feet so I reluctantly gave the order to halt. I arranged sentries for two hours with strict instructions that as soon as we had visibility we would get on the move again.

‘At around four o’clock the mist began to lift and we saw traces of emerging dawn.

‘I still felt concerned about that feeling of restraint I felt just before calling a halt.

‘With great care I checked the path ahead and to my horror saw we had stopped only ten feet from the edge of a sheer fall of some fifty or sixty feet.

‘If we had continued through the darkness and mist we would have walked over the edge to certain serious injury, and possible death for some of us.’

Listening to Faisal, a devout Muslim who would never lie, gave me no reason to doubt what he told me.

Rescuing The Austrian Doctor

Elizabeth Fielding – Police Wife

A New Life

I didn't arrive in Kenya until July 1962, my only previous experience of Africa being two and a half years travelling around South Africa and Southern Rhodesia, hitch hiking from job to job in various cities. My friend who I'd met on those travels had gone back to UK before me and subsequently got a job at The Outspan Hotel in Nyeri. A week after I'd returned home I received a phone call asking, 'Would you like a job at The Outspan handling Treetops bookings?'

Yes I would, and in July 1962 I flew out to Nairobi to be met by Yvonne in the hotel car. Murram roads were not a new experience but I'd not lived at 6,500 feet above sea level before.

I loved the Outspan and quickly acclimatised. Yvonne had a friend, Lew Burton based with the Kenya Police in Kiganjo and they cooked up a plan at George Fielding's request to arrange a blind date with me. George was in Signals Branch, Provincial Signals Officer, and lived at The White Rhino. I'd seen him at the Outspan swimming pool but had not had much contact with him.

We began I think with drinks and a meal at The White Rhino and then it was decided to carry on to Kiganjo for more drinks. I didn't know that Yvonne and Lew were going to stay over at Kiganjo, which left me returning to Nyeri with George. He called his car The Green Goddess. It was a Ford Consul with a bench seat and I ended up changing gear for him as his left arm was otherwise engaged.

To cut a long story short we were married in Nyeri in May 1963 and thus I began my involvement with the Kenya Police.

There was no Police house available at that time, so firstly George was able to move in to my staff cottage at the

Outspan which had room for his daughter Jean, when she came home from boarding school in Nairobi. Eventually we rented a house on Ring Road, belonging to a Mrs Fairley.

Here I remember a night 1964 when George was woken by a phone call. The Army had mutinied down in the Rift Valley and there was a worry that they might also mutiny in Nanyuki, so George was called upon to go down to Nyeri Police Station and issue arms to the Kenya Police. I drove him down in my dressing gown, returning home quickly as our baby daughter was sleeping in the house.

On return our house servant, Robertson Mathenge, was standing outside looking exceedingly worried because he feared that it was the Mau Mau all over again. Luckily the situation was soon under control.

It was a very happy time in Nyeri. I loved my job, being able to go up to Treetops as Hostess when I felt like it, and occasionally The Tree would be taken over by a crowd of us celebrating someone's birthday.

With the arrival of Independence I lost my Work Permit, but in the meantime I'd been introduced to golf and bowls and become very involved in the life of Nyeri Club.

I remember Daddy Probyn always amusing with tales of his homemade aeroplane with a Volkswagen engine. He used to land on a road and taxi up to the garage to fill up. Quite often he'd arrive with sticking plaster on his nose and tell us that his house servant had not got up enough speed when towing the aircraft for lift off. Apparently there was a pine tree in the way.

Saturday night was always at The White Rhino, playing skittles – a shilling in the kitty and winner takes all then stands everyone a round of drinks. Eventually, well after midnight, we would drive home and George used to suggest that it would be better if I took the wheel.

On one occasion I was turning left on to the main road to exit from the pub and coming towards me very slowly on my side of the road was a car with headlights full on. I stopped expecting it to pull over to its left and pass. Instead it pulled up alongside me and an African driver was extremely rude. So George got out to remonstrate and was promptly punched in the nose.

With blood pouring down his face he jumped into the African's car and insisted that they take him to the Police Station. Greatly alarmed I set off in pursuit and was much relieved when the car did actually turn into the Police Station. Here the driver and myself had to undergo tests, walking a white line etc. I was ok but the driver was very drunk and he ended up in court and lost his licence.

TV had come to Nairobi so George decided we would have a set in Nyeri. He brought some of his constables around and gave them a lesson in erecting a very tall mast on our side lawn. On top of that was a TV aerial. My job was to look at the TV set while the aerial was manipulated.

Eventually a snowy picture emerged much to the amazement of everyone, but then there was a time announcement and it was out by an hour. We were receiving Rhodesian TV and the signal was being bounced off one of the glaciers on Mt. Kenya. The TV was soon given up and George's so called "permanent erection" was dismantled.

Independence came and we were all in the bar of the White Rhino at midnight listening to the radio broadcast of the ceremony in Nairobi with mixed feelings. The barman, Mbuthia, broke the tension as offering to buy all of us a round of drinks as the Kenya flag raised slowly up the pole. We all accepted but then had to fudge the expense so that he didn't have to pay for it in full.

Life didn't seem to be much changed. The Club accepted all races and those that came integrated well. One consequence was that the ladies were allowed into the Men's Bar. In the New Year I very nearly blotted my copybook by looking for George for the last dance, and discovering him in the bar with Assistant Superintendent Ben Gethi, then working at Police Training School, Kiganjo.

So I marched up to them and completely without thinking said to Ben "So you're the n……. in the woodpile. I want my husband".

There was a stunned silence from the three of us, and I began to apologise, but Ben just laughed and took it, as a friend would have done. He was an exceedingly nice man. I believe he was mixed Masai Kikuyu, but had been partly brought up by an English family.

This was in the early nineteen-sixties and I liked him very much at the time.

In later years Ben became close to Presidents Kenyatta and Arap Moi and in 1978 became a controversial Kenya Police Commissioner.

He developed close, possibly suspect, contacts with many prominent politicians and involved in actions that caused him to be imprisoned for a year.

Nothing was proved against him and on release Ben returned to his job as Commissioner, but was sacked in 1982. He died of natural causes in 1994.

Nyeri Club survived a few minor crises. There was a time when locusts threatened to completely destroy the golfing fairways. They had already done so at a club in Nairobi, but we were saved by a flock of European storks that coincided with the locust attack and ate the lot. I seem to remember that it took them about three days.

Occasionally a golfer or two would be chased up a tree by the odd buffalo but nobody ever came to real harm.

Alan Dixon – Police Officer

Life in the Kenya Police

I joined the Kenya Police on a two-year contract on 19 July 1953.

My first posting was to Kerugoya, a big station with its own special branch officer who had a propensity for reducing the local goat population with his Land Rover.

Day and night anti-Mau Mau patrols and actions were the prime activity. The preventative ditch around Mount Kenya did not deter gangs and feeders getting into the forest, nor did it stop elephants leaving and causing mayhem at the local Shambas.

I must have been guilty of some misdeed for I was posted to Runyenjes, a police post adjacent to the 5 KAR compound. Whilst on one night patrol I suddenly saw lights flashing and immediately thought we were being fired upon. Quick evasive action saved me from... glow-worms.

At my next posting, Kutus, a Reserve Constable Muranjare got hopelessly drunk and was making a nuisance. This happened just as I was about to leave the station, so I relieved him of his rifle and ammunition and handcuffed him to a telegraph pole.

I went off to carry out my task and returned some five hours later to find him still handcuffed to the telegraph pole, bothered by mosquitoes but sober.

He later went on leave in the Meru district and was arrested by tribal police. Showing his Kipande to prove identity, he protested that he was the son of the Chief. At first the Chief denied knowing Muranjare, but further study of the Kipande persuaded him that Muranjare could be one of his sons – though he asked how he was supposed to know as he had a total of 109 children.

Kutus was on the main road to Embu and one morning I had a frantic call from the gate sentry: the Senior

Superintendent of Police had arrived. Usually the arrival of the SSP was a serious matter, but on this occasion he shouted 'where's the bog?' and made a dash for the lavatory. He came out more leisurely and soon went on his way.

I had news of a reported terrorist gang and went to check it out. I selected what appeared to be a short cut to where the gang had been seen, but suddenly disappeared overhead into water. Solwatan arap Soi grabbed me by the lapels and hauled me out as though I was a baby.

Solwatan was a very strong man and once left two Devon Regiment soldiers wide-eyed when he hauled their vehicle out of a ditch, splitting his raincoat in the process. He also won prizes for throwing the javelin at police sports events.

By mid-1955, the terrorist gangs were coming out of the forests and giving themselves up, so it was time for me to go back to the UK.

Returning to Kenya some months later, I felt as though I had won the lottery with a posting to Mombasa.

I spent the next three years by the Indian Ocean, first in 999 and Traffic, and then at Nyali Police Station. Whilst in 999 I was in the old town one night when the biggest rat I had ever seen started to cross the road. Winding up my window I told my driver to run it over, but instead he stopped and let it cross, saying it was one of God's creatures and had every right to be there. This inspector felt embarrassingly admonished.

When posted to Traffic, I was allocated a Triumph 500 Speed Twin, but had no difficulty in persuading a colleague to exchange my Triumph for his 350 Matchless, which I knew to be a much better road-holder.

I played football for the coast police team and one on occasion during a match in Nairobi I was responsible for a member of the opposing team hobbling off with a damaged ankle.

I played football in much the same way that I played rugby. Imagine my horror when, on being posted to Kitale my Assistant Superintendent of Police was that opposing player. If he remembered he never mentioned it, but it was not long before I was posted to Eldoret.

Eldoret is some 7000 feet above sea level and in my opinion has one of the most agreeable climates imaginable. It had its own airstrip and I was once invited to look for stolen cattle from the cockpit of an Army Beaver spotter plane.

I started off quite unconcerned but as we headed towards the Rift I panicked, fearing we would drop, with stomach-wrenching results. Of course we did not, but just for a little while stupidity reigned, and alas no cattle.

I had no quarrel with Uhuru but believe I would still have been in Kenya had it not occurred, and probably at Eldoret.

After breaking two toes during a football match, when I took it upon myself to take issue with an opponent who had fouled our star inside-left, I was put on the injured list.

Ronnie Benton at Provincial H.Q. recruited me to help with his planning of a visit from the Queen Mother. Whilst all went according to plan, this was not the case when Princess Margaret later visited. Our itinerary and that of the Princess did not always coincide and we had to make some frantic last minute movements of crowd control officers to get everyone in the right place.

On another royal visit, Roy Grant-Smith was deployed to escort the Duke of Edinburgh from the airstrip into town. Roy later told us that he was doing 95mph and still being encouraged by the Duke to go faster.

One day whilst at Nyali Police Station, I received a call from an elderly lady living in a bungalow by the sea. She reported having a snake in her front room and said she would like it removed. This was a new experience for me so I sought advice from my sergeant.

He told me that this is the Inspector's job to take a shotgun and shoot the offending animal. With some trepidation I arrived at the bungalow complete with shotgun to find a python stretched out under a bureau. The lady pointed to three bumps in the snake and told me they had been her three cats. Pointing the shotgun at the snake from a distance of about twelve inches, I blew its head off and returned to the station with what remained of the fifteen-foot long python and the three cats still inside. What a terrible final resting place

Now thinking myself an expert, when, shortly afterwards, a call came in from a new marina just up the coast to say they had a snake in the bar. Out came the shotgun and off to the marina I went. There I saw the python stretched out in front of the bar with the barman drained of colour as far away as he could get.

Again, off came the snake's head, but this time my shot splattered snake blood and gore all up the wall and over the ceiling of this newly decorated bar in this brand Marina. I decided an early departure was probably wise.

This animal story reminds me – once when I was in Embu Division, I had been playing football in Embu and set off back to Kutus just as dusk descended. The driver and myself were in the front of the open Land Rover with two armed Constables in the back.

We came over a rise in the road and our lights picked up the shining eyes of some large animals in front of us.

One Constable said, 'Goats.'

The other said, 'Not goats. Lion.'

I still believe today that it is possible to change from fourth to reverse gear in a Land Rover or we came to a sudden halt covered in a cloud of dust.

It must have been a whole pride of lions ambling across the road.

Setting off again off again we were four anxious travellers until past the point where the lions crossed.

When in Nyali an elderly African villager once came to report that some of his hens had fallen down a well and asked if we could help. I knew it would be another job for the Inspector.

We arranged a beam and rope that allowed me to descend into what might have been a well but was dry now.

Sure enough, I found a few hens and I passed them up. We had some local villagers bystanders who had come to see the fun and were calling for me to be left down the hole. But the old chap was so delighted to get his hens back that he berated the jokers and had me hauled up and thanked me in great gratitude.

I had a somewhat similar experience when I was at Kerugoya in Embu District, but this time a hospital porter had disappeared.

In Emergency days it was not unusual for someone to go missing, so initially we took not much notice of the report.

However, when we heard that the porter's barrow had been seen near the long drop toilet for some days we went to have a look. The upper structure had collapsed and I could see him lying dead at the bottom.

Poor old inspector's job yet again.

I went down and landed beside him and stood several feet deep in human ordure. I got a rope around him and called for him to be hauled up.

The rope came back down for me. At the top I climbed out of the hole and looked at myself.

What a state.

I had muck from the bottom of the long drop all the way up my legs from boots to thighs. And the man's dead body, after about a week down that awful hole, had become full of maggots that abandoned him and dropped onto me during his journey to the surface.

Having been pulled from the hole by my Constables, I walked, filthy and smelling and fast as possible, back to Kerugoya Police Station. I handed my clothes and maggots over to our dhobi man and had a wonderful cleansing shower. Possibly the best I ever had.

I decided that if ever have to go down a hole like that again, I'll make sure I am pulled out first.

I do not smoke but I on this occasion I made an exception and smoked a whole cigarette to try and get rid of the stench and can tell you that cigarette smoke is not the biggest hazard to your health.

Twenty minutes at the bottom of a long drop, beats cigarettes by a mile as a danger to your wellbeing.

Whilst stationed at Nyali I was notified one morning that the shop at Nyali Beach Hotel had been burgled and a considerable amount of property stolen.

A day or two later a plain-clothes Officer came and said he had received some good information regarding the offence. He had been told where the man lived.

Using the information we set up a watch that night on the assumption that the thief would move in or out with the stolen goods to store or sell. We were correct and apprehended the offender with his haul wrapped in a sheet and slung over his back.

When challenged he slashed at my officer with a knife, cutting his trousers without marking his skin.

Not at all pleased by this we arrested him in a forthright manner and took him to the police station. He was bounced up the steps into the report office and the along the corridor stopping only when he collided with the wall of the cell we pushed him into.

In court next morning the prisoner admitted the offence of burglary and when asked if he had anything to say before sentence was passed he replied, 'Yes. The police beat me.'

I could not deny he had been roughly handled and felt greatly relieved when the Resident Magistrate looked sternly over his pince-nez and said, 'Well you probably deserved it. You will go to prison for three years.'

I learned an important lesson that day and thereafter insisted on my staff always preferring a charge of assault where violence had been used against them when making an arrest, rather than immediate heat of the moment retaliation.

Arthur 'Sparks' Lawton – Police Officer

A Muddy Safari And A Helpful Masai

In 1952 at the height of the rainy season and during the early days of the Mau Mau Insurrection, my driver Ngubi and I set off from the Provincial Signals workshops Nakuru for Elburgon to set up a mobile radio command post for a forthcoming operation against the Mau Mau.

We had only two-wheeled drive vehicle and arrived late at Njoro for an update from Inspector John Toft on the best forest route to Elburgon.

John was well known in the Rift Valley and recognisable from the gold earring he earned by sailing round the Cape.

We were soon on our way following a muddy track in Elburgon forest, but making slow progress as we bogged down several times over the first few miles. Unfortunately our vehicle carried only a standard vehicle jack, not the reliable Tanganyika Jack, so we had great difficulty in making way.

We did our best by jacking up and placing brush wood under one wheel at a time and going only a few more yards before getting stuck again. This occurred so many times over the hours that followed.

It became dark and in the pouring rain the work of jacking up was no fun. However we kept on the move until in the heart of the forest the jack decided it could not operate in the mud any more and after screeching and slipping down every time we tried to jack up the vehicle, it finally gave up the ghost.

The forest was dark wet and we had been told, full of Mau Mau.

We had no alternative but to walk the remaining five or so miles.

Around two in the morning we came out of the forest on to a wide-open plateau, into even harder rain. Imagine our surprise when over the ridge in the plateau came a group of Masai driving cattle.

It was impossible for them to miss us and one spoke sufficient Swahili to make Ngubi understand that we were only a mile away their Masai Manyatta and we should be his guest for the night. This sounded a very good idea and before long before we reached a group of mud huts.

We were taken into one that appeared to be occupied by an unpleasant looking old crone. She did however move her goats from one part of the hut and put down a couple of hides for my bed.

Our Host returned with a typical Masai Gourd full of the most revolting concoction I have ever tasted. Ngubi made an excuse to visit Africa so avoided the mixture, which I later found out was the typical Masai mixture of cow's blood and what have you.

The old crone threw some more dried dung on the fire. It produced no heat, but plenty of smoke.

I went to bed, but goats continually interrupted my sleep by pushing in and wanting their corner of the hut back and I think the fleas and ticks enjoyed me as their substitute goat food as they brought their families over to enjoy.

Eventually the sun rose and, believe it or not, my host came in with a sort of tin pot with hot water mixed with tea leaves and milk. He had no sugar, but the hot and warming tea gave comfort and I could almost imagine the tea leaves were porridge.

He indicated it was time to move and to our surprise offered to show us the way from his Manyatta to Elburgon.

The rain had stopped and we enjoyed quite a pleasant walk arriving at the Police Headquarters with our Masai, carrying his Spear, Simi and calabash.

The District Commissioner happened to be visiting as part of the joint anti-terrorist operation and almost threw a fit when he saw our Masai and wanted arrest him for being a well-known cattle rustler he had been trying to catch for months. And he should not have brought his spear into Elburgon.

It took all I could do to keep the Administration Police from taking him away.

Eventually the District Commissioner that agreed my host had been very cooperative, and he had no proof that the cattle had been taken from a European farm, so very *very* reluctantly warned the Masai of the penalties for cattle rustling and told him he was free to go.

I thanked the Masai for all his help and asked if I could repay his kindness with money or a gift.

To my surprise he said no to money but asked for the cravat I was wearing.

I said he could have it with pleasure and showed him how to tie it.

Off he went, turning every so often pointing at his cravat and doing a leap in the air.

I wonder if that is how the famous Masai leaping dance originated.

Graham Tudor – Police Officer

Policing The NFD

The Northern Frontier Police were a Para- Military Force with military style uniforms in khaki drill. The hats normally worn were either French style Kepis similar to those of the Foreign Legion, or broad-brimmed bush hats, sometimes with one brim turned up, Australian Army fashion.

Military security for the massive and turbulent NFD land area had been Army responsibility since the early days of British governance of Kenya. They faced and fought large marauding gangs of well-armed tribesmen from Ethiopia or Somaliland raiding for livestock or women.

The Kenya Police always had a presence in the Northern Frontier, operating with the British officered King's African Rifles, often as guides and interpreters during The First World War and later when faced with inter-tribal battles and cross border raids.

In 1935 the Army handed permanent responsibility for NFD security to The Kenya Police. This new Civil Authority took on the same training and patrol methods originated by the Army in the nineteenth century during desert and bush wars in South Africa and The Sudan. Some of the drills, such as forming square, went back to and before The Napoleonic Wars.

Patrols were carried out in skirmish drill fashion with the Platoon Column covered and shielded by advance, flank and rear guards. Equipment and provisions were carried by an accompanying pack camels or occasionally mules, depending on the tribal area.

European Police Officers would go on outpost duty for months at a time. For instance the Fort Banya stint to cover a section of the Ethiopian Border was three months at a time.

At home base, regular skirmish drills were practiced and drummed into squads of Askaris with action right or left, front, or rear, to face an enemy attack from any direction and, of course, forming square.

Although the NFD Headquarter Bases had Police Stations in the traditional sense, Police platoons went out on six to ten day camel or mule and foot patrols from the Forts.

Life in those lonely desert or mountainous lava rock areas was a completely different world to down-country policing in the growing towns, cities and farming areas.

Forts and Outposts were, or could be, more of a problem than their usual worth elsewhere in the colony. Distances were so vast that the provision of water, rations and medical assistance would need so much transportation.

Marsabit, for instance, had two Northern Forts, Banya, near Lake Rudolf and only six miles from the Ethiopian Border and Sabarei about fifty miles to the west along the Frontier.

In addition, we had Camel Patrol Station known as the Rakhoub Unit in a central position near Lake Rudolph.

The Inspector in charge at Banya would regularly visit Sabarei with a foot patrol, always playing a game by sneaking up to the Fort pretending to be an enemy assault.

The Sabarei tower sentry would invariably spot us and call the duty bugler to blow the alarm. This would bring the Sabarei personnel to man the ramparts with fixed bayonets.

Great fun at the end of a long march!

When I served at Marsabit in 1952, the legendary Abdi Farah was still a Sergeant Major serving in the field. His nickname was 'Kula mawe' – 'Eat stones' in Swahili – his famous answer to trivial requests from his men.

Even after his retirement the name stuck and when he built a shop in a remote spot in Isiolo district, he called it Kula Mawe. As happens in Africa, a flourishing village settlement grew up also called Kula Mawe, with its name printed on all the Kenya maps.

Many of our Askaris, such as my driver for two years, Corporal Abikar, were from the Frontier Somali tribes. If my memory serves me correctly he was a Degodia and one of the classic old school Askaris we were so fortunate to have in the Frontier Police in those days.

He became tired of driving and asked to go into plain-clothes duties. I transferred him, but he found that not to his taste either after getting into trouble for losing his revolver, so I put him on general duties where he was quite happy.

Corporal Abikar

Another old favourite in the NFD police was Sergeant Bakari. He was taken prisoner of war by the Italians with ASP Jack Carter on the day war was declared with Italy in 1940.

Sergeant Bakari had a great fighting record during many actions against Somali Shifta in the NFD.

On his retirement in Garissa in 1952, he was eternally grateful when I helped him obtain a shop traders licence, the first non-Arab or Indian in the township.

He once told me over one of his regular coffee visits, 'Never trust these Somalis, they lie to you. Look at me. The main good in me is from my mother and she is a Bajun'

A great guy.

With staff like that my Police safaris were always fun, whether on foot, camel or vehicle. I never found it boring or monotonous with such good company.

And, of course, I had the sight of all the fantastic wild game that abounded over the whole Frontier.

Nor were we short of action with the odd skirmish against rifle-armed gangs of around two hundred tribesmen not uncommon.

Charles Long – Police Officer

The Husband's Story

I joined the Kenya Police in 1953.

During my Home Leave in 1957 from Nakuru my father and I met up with some friends in the Kings Head, our local pub in Tamerton Foliot, near Plymouth for an evening of darts, draughts, cards etc. with many a beer to wash down the country fare of pickled eggs, winkles, crisps and cheese sarnies.

The next day I awoke with a severe stomach pain, which I took to be indigestion, but which our local doctor pronounced to be severe appendicitis and told me to get to hospital immediately where they rushed me into the operating room and removed a badly inflamed appendix.

Recovering, but in severe pain and hardly able to move, I really appreciated the kind and professional attention I received, especially from Margaret, a very pretty student nurse.

Before being discharged at the end of a week I asked Margaret to meet me that evening for a chat and a drink. She agreed and over the next few weeks we found we had so much in common in books, films and sight seeing that we bonded and I took her home to meet my Mother and sisters. She, in turn, took me to meet her parents.

With only a few weeks leave remaining after leaving hospital I made up my mind and in the last two days, while passing a jewellers shop, I asked her to marry me and choose an engagement ring. She said 'Yes', chose a ring and I returned to Kenya at the end of my Leave to a barrage of disbelief and advice from my well-meaning friends.

Margaret and I agreed she should finish her training before getting married, which in view of the short length of time we had known each other seemed sensible. So we kept contact by writing to each other for two years before I could arrange for our Kenya Wedding.

I received permission to marry from my General Service Unit Boss and arranged a date with Margaret for our wedding to be held at the Church of the Holy Family in Nairobi, followed by a reception in the GSU Officers Mess, for which I ordered a three-tier Wedding Cake from a local restaurant called The Teahouse of the August Moon.

As Margaret's parents would not be present, Paddy Thompson, my Boss, agreed to stand in as her father and give away the Bride. He and his wife Eleanor invited Margaret to stay their home until the wedding in ten days time

Margaret Henry who worked in Rift Valley Police HQ agreed to be the Bridesmaid.

Thus with all settled, my wife-to-be arrived at Embakasi Airport on 15th July 1959 for the Wedding on 25th July, giving us ten days to get to know each other again.

Although, of course, we had never spoken for two years, we had written every two or three days and kept our interest in each other alive.

She arrived in Kenya carrying a few clothes and her wedding dress in a small white suitcase and a handbag. When we left almost ten years later in May 1966 we had four children and six tons of luggage.

The Wedding was a great success, with many of my Police friends and acquaintances present, along with local civilians from areas in which I had been stationed. After the wedding we all went to the GSU Mess for a celebration that lasted for far longer than I thought.

Eventually we were able to break away and drive off on our honeymoon. A mile down the road I stopped to untie and throw away the tin cans, old boots and shoes, and rub off the chalked graffiti with which it had been decorated.

We drove off down the Mombasa road through clouds of red murram dust, dodging the potholes, we had to screech to a halt at one stage as a huge elephant decided to cross the road in front of us, causing me to go into a slow steady reverse.

After a delightful honeymoon spent at Lawfords Hotel, Malindi, we returned to my house in Nairobi, to be stopped by an armed GSU Askari guarding the property because it had been broken into during our absence.

It later turned out that some thieves had poisoned Bruce my Alsatian and broken in to gather up all our wedding gifts and other valuables and put them in a blanket.

At this point my house servant, who lived in a Rondavel in the garden, must have heard a noise, because he came out of his house and saw by bright moonlight a man inside my house passing a large bundle out through the window to an accomplice.

My servant grabbed his spear and threw it, just missing the accomplice who screamed. Both men fled leaving their loot on the ground.

The next day, in some fear for the state of my bank balance following our very expensive wedding reception, I called in to the Mess to pay my bill, which when it presented to me was inscribed in red Paid In Full By Mess Members.

What an exceedingly great bunch of guys.

The Bride's Story – Margaret Long

While a student nurse at Greenbank Hospital, Plymouth, one of my patients, suffering severe appendicitis, was Chief Inspector Charles Long of the Kenya Police.

We got on very well together and at the end of his stay in hospital he asked me to go out with him. This I did and just before he returned to Kenya in October 1959 at the end of his leave he asked me to marry him.

This surprised me, as I had only known him for about eight weeks. I had first seen him whilst dashing up and down the ward, and had noticed a spark between us despite the difficult circumstance, although I found him an intriguing character, as I knew he came from Kenya, about which I knew nothing. I knew he was from Africa, and just different in some way.

To make his proposal, he took me one evening after my duty ended to Plymouth Hoe. He picked me up from work and we called in at Ivor Dewdendy's for takeaway pasties and a cup of tea and drove to Plymouth Hoe.

We sat in a shelter out of the wind, ate our pasties, drank our tea and watched the sun go down. We discussed Charles's impending return to Kenya and that we must make the most of the time left together.

In the middle of this conversation, he slid off the bench onto one knee and proposed.

Of course, I felt such surprise I was almost speechless. I probably said, 'YES,' before I thought of anything else.

We agreed that I should remain in England to complete my two years of medical training before joining him in Kenya.

At the age of nineteen or twenty this seemed a big decision, but not difficult to make. For the next two years we wrote to each other every two or three days, keeping the Royal Mail in profit. We were both working hard, me at my exams and Charles at his Police duties, so the two years passed faster than you would think.

In July 1959, having gained my State Registered Nurse qualifications and an additional Orthopaedic Nursing Certificate, with my parent's blessing I flew to Kenya on my first ever plane flight with my wedding dress and clothes in a small suitcase.

Chas met me at the airport and took me to meet Senior Superintendent Paddy Thompson and Mrs Thompson who had kindly invited me to stay with them until the wedding in ten days time. In addition Paddy agreed to act for my father at the wedding, and being Chas's Boss, granted him fourteen days local leave for the honeymoon.

My first impressions of the, until then Great Unknown of Africa; the heat, light and smells were ones of delight and I knew then that I'd been hooked by this wonderful country of Kenya.

Of course, I felt both excited and apprehensive. After all, apart from those ten weeks in Plymouth, we didn't really know each other. After a two-year separation and had to start all over again.

The next few days passed in a flash, what with shopping, meeting new people and looking over my new home-to-be where Chas lived in a lovely two bedroomed bungalow, on the General Service Unit's base at Embakasi, where he was a Company Commander.

Our Wedding was in the Church of the Holy Family, now the Nairobi RC Cathedral, followed by a reception at the GSU Mess. This was the first time I saw Chas, his Best Man, Jerry Moorcroft and Paddy Thompson in their dress uniforms, all wearing swords.

I was suitably impressed, as I did not know swords were a part of a Policeman's uniform. We later used Chas's sword to cut our Wedding Cake, a beautiful three tiered and highly decorated cake with two Police batons marked "His" and "Hers" alongside it ready for our first fight.

This must have been an example of GSU humour.

A large number of people attended our reception, including farming friends from the various areas where Chas had been stationed, Police and others none of whom I knew. So I, naturally, got lost in a haze of introductions.

Eventually it was all over and we were able to go and change and get ready to drive three hundred and seventy miles down the Mombasa road to Malindi.

Having been brought up on the edge of Dartmoor I was used to open spaces, but the wide horizons of Kenya, the herds of elephant, wildebeest, giraffe, deer, and the leopards were all mind-boggling and I loved it all.

Amongst other things, seeing the huge loads of wood, water carriers that were carried by the local women, impressed me.

Malindi is a delightful place for a honeymoon and Lawfords Hotel, where we stayed, was excellent.

Later we felt very lucky to spend our last three Kenya years in Malindi where Chas was based as Divisional Commander of the North Coast Division from 1964 to 1966.

While on honeymoon thieves broke into our house and our dog poisoned but thanks to our house servant nothing was stolen. He saw the break-in happening and chased the burglars off with his spear.

Later, as a precaution Chas taught me to shoot at tin cans on the fence posts using his revolver, which gave me a bit of a shock to my delicate upbringing.

My worst new African experience was the outdoor toilet. I found having to nip to the loo in the early morning while a dozen or so African prisoners armed with machetes cut the grass all around the house very disconcerting.

Chas's house servant did not take kindly to having a new Memsahib. Once when I was cleaning my shoes he very gently removed the brush and polish from my hands saying that I could not use them as, 'These belong to the Bwana.'

Our life in Kenya was wonderful in those days, but not always easy. Chas was away on duty quite often, for a week at a time and it could get lonely in some up country stations with no nearby friends or family.

However the arrival of our children filled my days, one being born in Nakuru, one in England, one in Nairobi and one in Mombasa. When we left Kenya in 1966, I, who had arrived alone in 1959 with a small suitcase, left with a husband, six tons of baggage and four children.

In 2009 we took our whole family to Malta to celebrate our 50th Wedding Anniversary. We numbered four married children and twelve grandchildren.

And in 2014 we all gathered again to celebrate our 55th Wedding Anniversary

Life in Kenya was funny, exciting, and a wonderful adventure. I shall always be thankful that I took that first step into the great unknown, with no regrets then or now.

Gerry Moorcroft, Eleanor Thompson, The Groom, The Bride, Margaret Henry, Paddy Thompson

Mike Smart – Police Officer

Tea In Nairobi

When based at Police Post 41 on General Hawkins' farm in the Thompsons Falls area, I received an order to escort Lord Gray, a guest of the General, down to Government House in Nairobi, to stay with his daughter, wife of Sir Evelyn Baring, the Governor of Kenya.

I went to the General's house to confirm details and the following day, together with two of my Askaris, returned to collect Lord Gray and various plants he been given.

After a few minutes he stepped into his Rolls Royce and we set off, following in our Police Land Rover across red dirt roads of the Laikipia Plateau, with little problem in keeping up until we reached the Nairobi to Nakuru tarmac road, when it became a chase at between eighty and ninety miles an hour to keep up.

It became easier when we reached the outskirts of Nairobi and arriving at Government House I drove round to the greenhouse area where Lord Gray joined us to supervise the unloading of his plants.

When we finished he invited me in for a cup of tea. I dismissed my Askaris to the Lines and followed His Lordship along various corridors to a drawing room. Sir Evelyn and Lady Baring were already entertaining two other guests.

Sir Evelyn introduced me around, showing some surprise at my presence. He showed great interest that I commanded a Police Post in the Thompsons Falls area and questioned me very deeply on the situation.

He showed great interest in the general setup for patrols and following up on incidents and my knowledge of the local European Settlers and how I got on with them.

Luckily I had experience of mixing with people of his status, having crewed in Britain on a yacht belonging to our local Member of Parliament and visiting both his London home and The Houses of Parliament where I met and chatted with various Members and Ministers.

I found Sir Evelyn to be an absolutely charming gentleman. He had a very gentle way of questioning me, so I did not realise until later how thoroughly I had been interrogated.

After about half an hour, Sir Evelyn passed me over to an Aide who looked after me until I left to drive back to my Police Post.

This little jaunt made a good change from my usual day of patrolling forest and bush up on The Laikipia Plateau and I couldn't help thinking that if you go down to Nairobi you never know with whom you are going to have a cup of tea.

Bryan Coleman – Police Officer

A Big Buffalo And Difficult Bull

During my time at Uplands Police station in the mid-fifties, I used to shoot meat for my Askaris, using a very quiet .22 rifle.

In the evening, before dark, I would travel down to the old railroad track on the escarpment and whatever poked a head out of the bush became meat for my Askaris. I always took two Askaris with me to load whatever I shot into the back of my short wheel based Land Rover.

Normally I would get a Bushbuck, but on one occasion when I couldn't find anything to shoot I decided to wait until after dark and use a spotlight.

I found nothing, but on the way back, a couple of eyes reflected at the edge of the bush. I assumed it must be a Bushbuck and let fly with the .22. The eyes disappeared and my two Askaris ran over to see what I'd shot.

They seemed to take a little longer to return, so I called out, 'What are you doing?'

They shouted back, 'Hii ni nyama kubwa, Bwana.'

'What do you mean, "Lots of meat"?'

'Hii ni mbogo, Bwana.'

'A buffalo?'

I went over to look and sure enough on the ground lay a young cow Buffalo. My bullet had entered through an eye and straight into the brain. I had never ever seen Buffalo in this area before.

Now we had the problem of how to load it into the Land Rover. Instead we decided to butcher it on the spot making it easy to carry and return to the Station with enough meat to feed my Askaris for a couple of weeks.

This story of a lucky shot in the dark may surprise you, but I guarantee, no more than it surprised me.

On another occasion when stationed with C.I.D. I had to carry out and investigation in the Uplands area after the Lari Massacre. At the time I lived with my parents' in a house on twenty acres along the Thika Road over the valley just past Taylor's Brewery the Tusker Beer Company.

I had decided along with my Police career to become a cattle rancher, so I bought three young heifers, and put them on the 20 acres and was told I needed a bull to go with them.

During my investigation in Uplands I found a herd of cattle with a good-looking half-year-old Brahma bull, which I purchased, but with the problem of getting it home.

I used a closed-in Police van to go to and fro from Nairobi to Uplands, and with no other transport available to me needed, quite illegally, to try and use the Police vehicle.

Of course, if I'd been caught I would have been in big, big trouble.

But if I wanted to get the bull to my father's farm, I had no choice.

So what the hell?

With the help of a couple of Askaris and some locals I managed to hobble the young bull, and shove it in the back of the van.

After a great deal of pushing, swearing and general excitement, we eventually got the damned thing in and as settled as a young bull could be under the circumstances.

Being a big animal, the poor bull's head ended between the passenger seat and the driver's seat with the weight of its body in the back making the van's front wheels look as though they wanted to leave the ground.

We bounced the van a couple of times to check if the van would be reasonably steady when driving and I decided to take the chance.

Of course, the bull's weight did make the steering very light and I could only go about ten miles an hour.

Get In, Damn You

I went via Muthaiga road, past Muthaiga Police Station and onto the Thika road.

As we went down into the steep valley near Mathari Mental Hospital, gravity pushed the bull's head forward.

I managed to get down safely and hoped the bull would shuffle back along the van floor when we reached the flat road at the bottom.

Going Downhill

Going up the other side I noticed his head slide backwards and looking over my shoulder I saw his arse-end sliding out the rear door.

I stopped the van, but with only myself and two Askaris we found it almost impossible to shove him back in, all the time hoping that no one would see me in a police vehicle, with the rear end of a big bull sticking out.

Going Uphill

To help with the problem I backed up to a nearby gum tree so he could not escape and along with the help of my Askaris pushed the poor old bull back into the van.

After four hours we finally got home, now with the problem of how to get him out. After some thought I came up seemed to be another good idea.

Tying one end of a rope to his back leg and the other end a tree trunk I pulled slowly away.

I felt really sorry for the poor fellow when he slid out of the van and onto the grass.

The bull turned out to be useless. He didn't wink his eye enough and was too young to know what sex was. I couldn't afford a herdsman so I sold him and the cows to a farmer who was a better cowboy than me.

So ended the story of my ranching career, never to be repeated.

I always felt if that young bull could tell his side of the story, I guarantee it would sound better than mine.

Mike White – Police Officer

Upcountry Life

My first posting when I left Police Training School at Kiganjo was to Kitale. I travelled by bus with another Policeman, John Revell from Kiganjo to Nairobi, staying the night in the Mess and next day continued to Kitale, also by bus.

The dirt roads were very slippery, due to heavy rain, and on several occasions we had to get out and push. We didn`t make it in one day and had to spend one night sleeping on the bus as we had slipped into the ditch and waited until morning to be pulled out.

We eventually arrived in Kitale about noon and the Officer In Charge, Ted Wells, assigned me to the Traffic Office where the incumbent Traffic Officer, Kit Wells, informed me that he was two days late departing for leave and was leaving on the taxi, 'Right now'.

He gave me a simple briefing. 'This is the Office. There are the files. There are the forms and that`s the typewriter``.

A typewriter?

I don`t think I had ever seen a typewriter, let alone used one.

His parting words were, 'Oh. Yes. You have a driving test to do at two o'clock'.

And he was gone.

A driving test? Me? I don`t have a driving licence, I only have a UK licence to drive a motorbike, how can I do a Test?

I called him back and asked him what to do?

'What to do? You type yourself a Drivers Licence right now.'

So, with stiff fingers I attacked the old sit-up-and-beg Imperial typewriter and fifteen or twenty attempts and two hours or so later, I had my first full Kenya Driving Licence.

The Testee duly arrived and we settled into his clapped out old Peugeot 203. I directed him to drive to the first turning and make a left and immediately realised that something was wrong.

'Have you been drinking, young man?' I asked.

'Ndio, Bwana, but only a little to give me courage, as I have heard that you are very kali.'

'Me? Kali? Not me. It must be the other guy.'

I should have arrested him, but how could I have pinched the first civilian I encountered on my first Police job, especially as I had, myself, just committed forgery by printing my own Driving Licence?

I told him to come back the next day, which he did, and I passed him.

That Driving Licence served me well for fifty years from Kenya to Bahrain and on to the Isle of Man, for retirement, where I had to take my very first Driving Test because my Bahrain licence was not accepted in Britain.

On another occasion, as Duty Officer one night, I had a call from a local bar to say that a Land Rover was stuck and could I help. When I arrived the vehicle was high on a kerbstone in an area being developed and the paving had not yet been laid.

The driver, Scotty, had reversed too fast and driven over the kerb upon which the vehicle now teetered. As there were several people around we managed to manhandle to vehicle off the curb. Scotty, the manager of a sawmills up in the hills, drove off and, watching him, I came to the conclusion that he had been in the bar a little too long.

I ran back to the Station, found our driver and Police Land Rover and followed Scotty's route, through and out of town and after half a mile found him parked at the roadside, fast asleep.

I decided to take Scotty home as my tour of duty was now over. So I told my Station Driver to take our Land Rover back and I would return in the morning.

Scotty's Land Rover was a bit of a rust bucket and didn`t have enough petrol to get us to the sawmills, so we ran out of gas really deep in the sticks.

It was a lovely moonlight night with very little cloud so I woke Scotty up and told him we had to walk the last couple of miles to the sawmill. He was staggering a little and I had to support him occasionally.

At one point I turned round and took hold of him for the umpteenth time that I saw a leopard padding along behind us, about twenty yards away and off a little to one side, perhaps eyeing us for supper.

'Scotty,' I said. 'We're being tracked by leopard.'

In a slurred voice he said, 'Oh, don`t worry about that. We see them all the time up here. It will only have a go at us if we stop or fall down.'

I carried him the rest of the way.

I spent time in a Police Post up in the Suk at a place called Psigor. A transport firm based in Kitale called Kaka ran a lorry once every couple of weeks through Psigor and up to Lokitaung on Lake Rudolph, bringing food for sale.

At one time I had a fair stock of provisions but fancied some Digestive biscuits and sent a shopping list back to Kitale on the returning lorry, on which, to save space, I wrote DIG.BISCUITS for short.

A few days later the lorry came back with my shopping in what I thought was rather a large paper bag for two packs of biscuits.

In the bag I found two five-pound packs of Spratts dog biscuits with my original written food order clipped to the bag, so my attempt at shorthand order had been deciphered as DOG biscuits.

The rains started early and heavy that time and lorries could not get through with my rations. I ran very short of food, except for biltong and fresh meat, but one cannot live by meat alone.

I began to eye the Spratts dog biscuits and wondered what I could do with them.

I can tell you – I found I could do a great deal.

I soaked some to soften them and added a bit of Bisto to eat them as a thick soup. The yellow ones were quite nice with a little marmalade but the black ones were totally inedible.

I can still remember the grit grinding as I tried to eat them. They seemed to be made of charcoal, but I got through almost a bag and a half before my next lot of rations arrived.

Megan Edwards – Police Wife

Flying With Eddie And Government House

In November 1959 I spent a truly enjoyable weekend at Eldoret for their annual Battle of Britain weekend with Eddie, my pilot husband. With an enthusiastic crowd I witnessed Eddie's competent and skilful airmanship flying a Police Airwing Cessna when he demonstrated air-to-ground support in a mock GSU anti-terrorist operation.

It was well done, with Eddie dropping coloured smoke bombs and ground troops attacking with rifle fire. What with the smoke, the rifles banging, Eddie flashing around in the sky and the "dead" enemy, great fun was had by all.

I found it all very exciting as, although I'd seen Eddie taking off and landing many times, I had never seen him doing serious operational flying. Eddie had joined the RAF for pilot training in 1941 and learnt to fly with the RAF at The British Commonwealth Air Training Scheme in Canada.

We had a hectic time during that weekend, but did not join the festivities at the final ball. We preferred to go to bed in preparation for an early take-off next morning to avoid the heavy thermals for which the Rift Valley is renowned. Rising sun warms the Valley floor and produces quite heavy turbulence and up draughts all along the Valley walls.

Flying in those days was not my particular forté and this was only my second trip in a small aircraft, so it wasn't long into the flight I experienced the double discomfort of pressure on my bladder and at the same time began to feel airsick.

So I told Eddie that he needed to put down at Naivasha airstrip or take the consequences.

'No way am I putting down at Naivasha. It'll take ages to lose height then regain enough to get us over Suswa and

Longonot. And it'll add too much extra time to our flight. There's a flare tube in the back. Use that.'

I had no other option.

The indignity of scrambling over the rear seat of a Cessna 180 to find and perform in a flare tube was no mean feat. And bouncing around in mid-air didn't help.

Eddie was lucky I managed to suppress the vomiting and asked myself, 'Why were Adam and Eve fashioned so differently and why so undignified?

That was nothing to the embarrassment I felt the following week at a Government House cocktail party for the great Freddie Brown's Cricket eleven when Eddie regaled Sir Patrick and Lady Renison with the details of my distress.

Lady Renison enjoyed flying and thought it hilarious. Her husband was sympathetic, as he, like me, preferred the comfort and safety of terra firma.

Due to Eddie's work in the Air Wing, the Governor frequently invited him to Government House as a thank you for duties performed.

In addition, when Geoff Ellis, one of Eddie's friends from his frequent flights to the NFD, became ADC to Sir Patrick, Geoff would invite us around when The Governor was away and the house empty.

We'd get a call and Geoff would say, 'Come round for a game of snooker, Eddie. Bring Meg with you and she can play a few tunes on the piano.'

So we'd sally forth; Eddie pleased to be snookering; Megan delighted to be to tinkling the ivories on a White Grand in the White Drawing Room, would you believe?

If I wished to lift the piano lid I'd have to remove the large collection of signed Royal Family photos displayed and set them aside, then remember which to replace where when I finished playing and closed down again.

I was always glad when Geoff was on house duty. He had a penchant for pickled onions, so when I'd done some pickling I'd always give him a jar. One Sunday morning after a Government House session, I told Geoff I'd drop off a jar on my way to work on Monday.

I set off in my Morris Minor and must have taken a couple of corners rather indelicately because the jar, sitting in the foot-well, fell over and soaked the brown paper and string lid I'd learnt to use from my mother. By the time I reached Government House, my Morris was reeking of onions and vinegar.

I draw up at the side entrance.

Askari approaches.

I hand the jar over.

The aroma is certainly not Elizabeth Arden.

'Hii ni kwa Bwana ADC Ellis,' I say and make a quick exit down the driveway.

David Hewson – Police Officer

Constable/Driver Korinyang

Korinyang was one of those naturals that one comes across from time to time. He was a Turkana from the Ngiwatella Clan, a Section led by Chief Nakinei. The Section had the reputation of being the best armed, the most militant and the most difficult of the eighteen named Sections of the Turkana tribe.

They were well known for their lack of respect for the Government and the District Commissioner and his minions. Korinyang and his fellow Turkana Policemen, while on leave from the Force were just as likely to lead a raiding party against the local enemy as they were to turn a blind eye on the wickedness of their own tribe.

He was a tall, slim, but well-built man, approaching middle age. In uniform immaculate, out of uniform a different picture. On leave he reverted to his tribal way of life. He fitted his hair into a cow-dug snood, painted it with blue ochre, fitted in three ostrich feathers at the top of his hair-do, fitted a metal skewer into the back in case strange insects created an itch.

He placed an ivory ball in the hole under his lower lip. He carefully folded his uniform shorts away and donned a dirty shuka, took up his wooden pillow cum stool, his fighting stick and spear and set off on foot to find his Manyatta in the back of beyond.

His leave over, he would be back in the Police Lines on the appointed day ready for work, once again the immaculate Korinyang.

Like so many of the warlike tribesmen he was putty in the hands of his wives. Under tribal law he was entitled to as many as he could afford in bride price to their fathers.

Police regulations required all wives to be registered in his Record of Service, a booklet that commenced on his enrolment and accompanied him for the rest of his service. This document listed wives, along with promotions, punishments, commendations, periods of leave, postings and medical records.

I remember driving with him for some fifty miles while we discussed what had made the single wheel track in the dust ahead. There were no bicycles in that remote area we surmised, yet we were puzzled, what created the track? The problem was finally solved when we turned a corner to discover a lone Turkana tribesman pushing a wheelbarrow.

Korinyang was a driver with long experience in the Northern Frontier District. He had returned to his home area after some ten years on the Eastern side of Lake Rudolf. I was new to the Frontier way of life and used Korinyang's experience when necessary. Turkana was his mother tongue, and in the main he was honest in his interpretation from Turkana to Swahili.

He had a sense of humour and was adept at pulling the leg of the fainthearted. I remember him telling one particularly nervous down-country driver to watch out for a man-eating hyena that lurked on a particular spot on the road between two Police Posts.

His advice to the Jaluo driver was to take a good rope and at nightfall climb high into a tree and tie himself to a branch well out of reach. Under no circumstances should he sleep in the cab of the vehicle as this particular demon hyena was extremely clever and well able to open doors and would undoubtedly eat any unwary driver. It was better, Korinyang said, to be forewarned. The driver took his advice and spent an uncomfortable night tied to a tree.

Korinyang's knowledge was of a practical nature. When held up on the wrong side of the Tarash River at the Kakuma crossing, mosquitoes and persistent showers of heavy rain pestered us. With the river running deep and fast we had no hope of a crossing for a couple of days. The ford at this point was V-shaped down a steep bank and across a broad sand river bottom then up a steep bank opposite.

Korinyang's advice was simple, dig a trench in the sand at the top of the river bank, lie in it and cover the whole body except the face in sand and then pull a sheet over the face, rebury the hand and sleep.

It is an uncomfortable way to spend a night, but better than being eaten alive by mosquitoes. We spent three days at the crossing before we were able to move on.

When crossing flooded rivers we never took chances. It is too easy to be caught in mud or to drop into a pothole and be swept sideways across and down the river. It was a standard always to assess flooded rivers by walking through before committing ourselves in the vehicle.

On another occasion he was driving a Land Rover and we came to badly swollen stream. We both crossed on foot, I was perhaps more cautious and certainly less experienced in negotiating swollen rivers. I asked Korinyang what he thought. His reply was 'Effendi it is possible. The problem is the fan. The water is deep and the fan will distribute the water across the plugs and we could kwama.'

'What about taking the fan belt off?' I asked.

He laughed and said, 'There is an easier way,' and unfastened his belt to slip off his uniform shorts.

Standing in his underpants he opened the bonnet and hung his shorts over the radiator grill and fastened the bonnet cover over the shorts to hold them in place.

I walked ahead through the water indicating sunken logs and deep potholes while he drove slowly behind me, the Land Rover lurching on boulders and into potholes. He remained steadfastly in bottom gear, taking no chances with a suddenly stalled engine or waves of river water inundating the engine.

We crossed with ease, and set off again. His shorts soon dried on the bonnet as we drove along.

I should have known that Korinyang's skill with engines

and vehicles was legendary. On one safari his lorry suffered a cracked differential while crossing the Chalbi desert between Moyale and Marsabit.

The oil drained away and the vehicle stopped in the hot lava desert. On board, as part of his load he carried bunches of bananas. He laboriously forced bananas through the plughole in the differential, driving short distances to mash them up and then forcing in more. He and his vehicle eventually limped in Marsabit battered but unbowed.

According to his Service Register he had four wives properly registered and permitted to reside in Police Lines at any time. His senior wife – aware of the regulations but knowing her husband – was determined always to keep an eye on him.

She would spend time out with the family herding their cattle, camels, sheep and goats, instructing the junior wives and the children then would mysteriously turn up back at The Lines without warning to ensure he remained on the straight and narrow.

The Police Station Sergeant Major was in awe of her and she was always allocated her own house when she arrived. Every time I enquired why Korinyang had two wives in the Lines at the same time I was told that one had just arrived or was just leaving.

When I first met Korinyang he was a Constable Driver in the Police and was stationed in his home District of Turkana. His first love was the five-ton diesel lorry allocated to his care, which became his pride and joy.

He looked after it as a mother hen would look after her favourite chick. He was meticulous in checking everything – engine, oil and water levels, hoses, tyres and tubes, heavy jacks and spare tyres. The distances he drove in remote and lonely areas were long with little chance of seeing anyone or any vehicle. He made sure his breakdowns were rare.

I can picture him now; immaculate in his starched shorts and khaki tunic, his kepi set level on his head, the cap badge shining, his rifle ready to hand, his steady eyes searching the road ahead for hazards, his blue overalls behind his seat to be donned should need arise.

Hanging on the bracket for the rear-view mirrors would be two charguls containing drinking water – sweeter than the brackish water available in the local wells – cooling in the breeze of the vehicle's passage.

Korinyang stays with me always.

An earthy man with quick repartee and infinite practical knowledge – a man to have at one's side in times of trouble and in times of peace.

John Hughes – Police Officer

The Queen In Kenya

On Tuesday fifth of February nineteen fifty two, Princess Elizabeth and Prince Philip spent the night in Tree Tops, the game viewing tree house overlooking a water hole on the edge of the Nyeri Forest in the Nyeri District of Kenya.

Next morning the Royal party left to return to the Royal Lodge at Sagana, a gift from the people of Kenya, where they were spending a short holiday on their way to Australia.

At that time they were completely unaware of the momentous news from London and it was only later that morning the 6th February, that Prince Philip took the Princess out on to the lawn and broke the news to her of the King's death and that she had become Queen.

In January I had returned from long leave and posted to the Police Training School at Nyeri Station as an Instructor and living with my wife at the White Rhino Hotel in Nyeri, whilst awaiting a house.

It was then decided that I should take over the running of the Nyeri Police Station for the Royal visit. Security was then a concern as although the Mau Mau Emergency was not declared until October, the Mau Mau were very active in the district.

In fact on one night, shortly before the arrival of the Royal Party, the Mau Mau had wired fast the doors of 30 huts in Nyeri District belonging to various Kikuyu Headmen, Tribal Police and Kikuyu who opposed them, setting fire to the huts and burning alive their occupants.

That morning, the sixth of February, somebody in Nyeri had picked up the news of the King's death on a BBC World Service news broadcast and the place was alive with rumour and speculation pending an official announcement.

We were standing by waiting for developments, when I received orders to set up a Police roadblock at the junction of the Nyeri and Nanyuki roads. When the Royal car passed on its way from Sagana to the Nanyuki airfield I proudly saluted the new Queen, being one of the first to do so.

As a corollary to this story, friends of mine who lived at Timau, just North of Nanyuki were getting married on this Wednesday and a large gathering of Settlers from all the surrounding districts had arrived to celebrate the occasion.

During the wedding the bride's parents received news of the King's death, but decided to withhold the news until the newly married couple had left for their honeymoon, in order to avoid putting a damper on proceedings.

It must be remembered that in those days there were very sparse communications in Kenya and even the local radio station only broadcast at certain hours.

Once the news came out the wedding reception ended and all the Settlers left for their farms. This, as things turned out, was a most fortuitous circumstance. It later became known that the Mau Mau had planned that night of the wedding to set fire to the farms throughout the Timau and Nanyuki districts and the cattle herders were to hamstring animals in their herds.

At that stage many Settlers had little knowledge of Mau Mau activities and how far their Kikuyu employees had been involved in the oath taking. As it was, their unforeseen return to the farms stopped most farm workers from carrying out their acts of sabotage, although the cattle herders hamstrung some cattle. Hamstringing means the cutting of the tendons in an animal's hocks and leaving the mutilated animal to stand on the stumps of its legs.

Mike Smart – Police Officer

A Sad Day At Lanet Police Station

New Years Day 1955 was the normal beautiful Rift Valley weather at my Police Station, which stood on land about three miles south of Nakuru in the Rift Valley, just north of where the Nairobi to Kisumu road crosses the railway line over a bridge.

I was Officer Commanding the Station and as it was quiet in the area it should have been a relaxing day for us all.

Taking advantage of the relative peace by enjoying a coffee in my quarters (a corrugated iron hut about 12ft X 20ft, hot in the day and cold at night) I heard a light aircraft flying over.

The Kenya Police Air Wing was close by, off the road opposite the Police Station, which leads to Thompsons Falls. Being an ex RAF pilot and always interested in aircraft, I went outside to see what it was up to and saw one of our KP aircraft buzzing the Balfour Beatty Construction Company Camp, probably in celebration of the New Year, diagonally opposite my Police Station.

I watched it bank and come over the entrance to the Camp towards a new telegraph pole set up on the road near the gate in the last few days and, to my horror, hit and snapped pole. The plane crashed and burst immediately into flames.

Shouting for help from my off-duty Askaris I ran over the railway bridge, but was unable to get near, as the whole area around the aircraft was alight with spilled burning fuel.

I raced back to the Police Station and informed Nakuru what had happened, before returning to the accident site.

The fire had died down somewhat by this time and I could see two people inside and knew I had just lost my two friends Pakenham-Walsh, known as Pak, and his wife Barbara, now both dead.

As you can imagine I had a hectic first day of the New Year – a date fixed in my mind that brings back sad memories for me on the anniversary of that tragic crash every year.

Adrian Jones – Police Officer

House of Mystery – Strange But Absolutely True

I was a 999-car commander on the nightshift in Nairobi town centre.

Just after two I received a radio message to contact the control room by landline for a special job. This always meant we faced a special problem.

I spoke to Charles Bunce and he instructed me to go out to Muthaiga to a certain road and find a specific name board and to go up to the house to check things out.

I found the house, detached and in its own grounds and all in darkness.

I switched off the car lights and said to my Crew, 'Come on then.'

For the first time ever, they refused, saying. 'This is house is a bad place. The situation here is not good and we will come in with you. It is a bad house and we will stay out here while you make your check.'

My corporal drew his revolver and stood guard by the car and radio, saying, 'If you need me I'll be here.'

I did not question his attitude, as I know that Africans have extra sense about strange or dangerous situations.

I went to the front door and found it unlocked, so I went inside and shone my torch and found a panel fitted with all the downstairs light switches.

Turning on every light, I saw a circular staircase at the end of a wide corridor that opened up into a furnished lounge area with doors going off into other rooms.

I went upstairs and checked the four bedrooms then came down again and went around the ground floor. Opening the doors around the furnished lounge, I passed through a kitchen and breakfast room, a dining room and study. I could see it was a very well appointed dwelling, probably for a rich family.

The furniture was covered in dustsheets. I lifted them all and peered underneath to make sure no intruders may be hiding.

On every floor lay a covering of undisturbed murram dust showing only the tracks of my own footsteps.

As far as I could see, the whole house seemed covered in dust as though the place had been vacated and undisturbed for quite a while.

Passing along the corridor to leave the house I saw a line along the wooden panelling and found a flush door, which I opened to see steps leading down into a dark unlit cellar.

I found it quite unnerving to be underground in this strange place with only my torch for company and light.

In the far corner a small fire of dying charcoal embers glowing in a circular fireplace. I put my hand close and sure enough they were warm.

But, again, I saw only my own footprints on the cellar floor, despite a layer of thick dust covering the floor slates.

I shone my torch around. A small white feather, in pristine condition lay on the floor exactly in the centre of the room, in such a position I felt it had been deliberately placed.

And on the wall I my torch showed up a medium sized Christian Cross that had been turned upside down.

The hairs on the back of my neck began to tingle.

Glad to get out I hurried from the cellar and ran up the stairs, slamming the flush door behind me.

On a small table in the hall sat a black Bakelite telephone, also covered in dust and obviously untouched or used for a considerable time.

I picked it up and to my amazement found it directly connected to the 999 Control Room.

In shock I realised that this must be the telephone from which the original emergency call and still locked to the Control Room switchboard.

The House Of Mysteries

The Control Room Constable answered immediately. I asked to speak to Charles Bunce and, still in shock, told him what had happened and what I had seen and how the original emergency call had come from this telephone, although not apparently touched for a long time.

Charles said, 'This line is still being recorded.'

I said, ' Ok, but according to the dust, no one has used this phone recently, so I can't understand how the call could have been made on this line. Apart from that, all in the house seems in order, with no obvious break-in, although the front door was unlocked and I have no key to lock it again. I am leaving the premises now.'

It was now a quarter past four in the morning and Charles asked me to return to the Control Room and write a report.

Before leaving the house I returned to the kitchen for a drink of water from the tap.

In my report I stressed all the strange things I had seen.

I went off duty just before dawn and thinking the incident over, could now understand why my car crew had not followed me into the house.

About two in the afternoon, I was awakened and told to dress and taken by a Police car back to the scene, to be faced by a real circus, including an irate Ambassador, three of his staff and two Assistant Superintendents all waiting to give me the onceover.

Also attending were men from the telephone company, the electricity company, the water company and a telephone engineer.

It turned out that the house was owned by the Embassy of a major European country.

The Ambassador started the questioning, waving his hand and shouting.

'How did you put the lights in?"

'I used the light switches.'

'You couldn't have done. The house had no electricity.'

'Well it did when I was here. You can ask my car crew.'

'We already have done and they confirm you switched the lights on, but we don't believe them, so be careful how you answer, because the electricity was turned off four months ago, as were the telephone and the water. This means you could not have turned on the lights, used the telephone or had a drink of water. You are lying.'

I said, 'I can only report to you what happened and my telephone call was recorded. Check for my fingerprints on the telephone and check the cellar.'

We went down into the cellar to find a clean and cold fireplace empty of ashes and the feather had disappeared and the Cross, now back where how should have been, the right way up.

For some reason this absolutely convinced the Ambassador I was lying and in a state of extreme excitement he accused me of causing the death of a high-ranking official back in his own country, the man who had lived in this house.

It seems he had dropped dead at a party three or four thousand miles away at the precise time I opened the door and walked in. The Ambassador, still excited and irrational, now blamed me for the man's death and wanted me charged with murder, for some unspecified thing I had done whilst checking the property.

At this ridiculous suggestion the two Assistant Superintendents stepped in.

After a considerable amount of discussion with everyone putting in a pennyworth I was returned to my flat and able to catch up on a bit more sleep.

I never heard another word about this very odd and disturbing incident and have often wondered what actually happened during my search of that house.

Ken Wilby – Police Reserve Officer

An Unexpected Birth

By April 1961 things had settled a bit but The Land Freedom Army, successor to Mau Mau, remained active and nasty and the KPR was heavily involved in day to day policing the Nairobi Area, allowing experienced Regular Officers to investigate the more complicated and more difficult cases.

I was posted to Parklands Police Station then under the command of the totally unforgettable Superintendent of Police John Kearney.

My main duties were to work on 999 Motor Patrol. I was usually issued a very elderly Morris Oxford Estate codenamed Northern Six for this purpose, which no doubt reflected the degree of confidence my superiors had in my ability.

When not on duty with the KPR I worked as a purser with East African Airways flying along the routes to London, Bombay, Aden, Johannesburg, Salisbury, Ndola, the so-called DC3 "Coastaliner" service that took two days to fly all along the African coast to Durban.

I certainly enjoyed that trip, although the coastal thermals made it uncomfortable for our passengers who were not so enthusiastic. Also, I often had pleasant day-trips to Dar es Salaam, Mombasa, Entebbe, Aden and Mogadishu.

On this particular evening on duty in Nairobi, I was in command of Northern Six when l received a call to report a dead woman lying on somebody's lawn.

On arrival I found an African woman heavily bleeding, but still breathing.

She had given birth to a live child but had not passed the placenta and appeared to be dying before my eyes.

I remembered a little while previously seeing Doctor Jules de Mello demonstrate a similar condition on a Cadaver in the Ngong Road mortuary where the mode of death was similar and had shown how the death could have relatively simply been prevented.

Accordingly – and blessing Doctor De Mello – I applied tension to the placenta. It happily came away and allowed the powerful uterus muscles to close and stop the bleeding.

Because the lady's position was poor to say least, I decided not to wait for an ambulance, but loaded her into the rear of Northern Six and went as fast as the old car would allow to the Pumwani African Maternity Hospital where I handed over my, by now, unconscious patient.

Thence back to Parklands to report and go thankfully off duty

Then across the road to the Mayfair Hotel where Mr Fernandes, the head barman, brought me the first of a couple of large Tusker Exports.

And so home my wife, who complained bitterly about the bloody state of my uniform and handed it straight to the house servant for a good wash.

Next day I had a memorable interview with Paddy Kearney about the state of Northern Six with its rear seats covered in blood.

That same day I called the mortuary to check and she was not there, so I went to Pumwani Hospital, where I was told that both baby and mother were alive and doing well.

The next month I received a Letter Commendation from Assistant Commissioner Ken Akker, which pleased me greatly.

Telegrams: "ASCOMPOL", Nairobi
Telephone: 22251
When replying please quote
Ref. No. .../6/47.....
and date

NAIROBI AREA HEADQUARTERS
THE KENYA POLICE
P.O. Box 30051, NAIROBI
27th May, 1961.

Dear Wilby,

The capable and cool manner in which you recently rendered assistance to an African woman in childbirth has been brought to my attention and I wish to congratulate you on this most efficient action.

It is more than probable that your action helped to save the lives of both the mother and baby and there is no doubt that your capable handling of the affair was in the highest tradition of the Police service.

Well done.

Yours Sincerely

(M.K.AKKER)
ASST.COMMISSIONER OF POLICE,
i/c NAIROBI AREA.

Inspector (R) K. Wilby,
Northern Division,
NAIROBI AREA.

Anonymous – Police Officer

The Ileret Incident – Northern Frontier District

In March 1952, Assistant Superintendent Ernie Wright, stationed at Fort Banya, near the Ethiopian border, received news that a small party of about twenty-five Ethiopian Gelubba tribesmen had crossed into Kenya.

These ruthless raiders had occupied two villages to rape, murder and kidnap women and children and to steal cattle, while the men were out with their herds.

At about 3am Ernie set out for the area with two lorries, one carrying himself and eighteen Askaris, the other with Inspector Graham Clark and twenty Askaris, all well armed with rifles and two Bren guns.

On arrival at around 4am, Ernie halted and parked his vehicles fives miles from the villages and divided his force to approach both villages by foot.

Ernie formed his men into skirmish order and approached his target village. The Gelubba, well armed with Italian weapons from the Second World War, opened fire and showed themselves far more numerous than first thought and moved to surround his party. Outnumbered and outgunned, Ernie, retired and set up a defensive position on the slope of a nearby ridge.

Meantime Graham Clark, at that time, aged twenty-two, had found his target village deserted, but, hearing the shooting, hurried his force towards the sound of battle and the dust raised by stampeding cattle. At the same time he saw a new larger party of Gelubba also racing towards the fight.

By this time there appeared to be up to three hundred Gelubba fighting Ernie's small force, now reduced, with one Askari dead and several wounded, one badly.

On The Ridge

The Gelubba had cut three Askaris off so Ernie left his defensive position and went down the ridge alone to rescue them.

He managed to get two Askaris back to the safety of his position. The other escaped to meet and join Graham Clark's approaching force.

The Rescue

Ernie went out alone a second time to bandage and bring back a wounded Askari under heavy and sustained fire from the Gelubba. During this time a bullet passed right through the crown of his hat, skimming, but not touching, his skull.

Thoroughly outnumbered and under extreme pressure, Ernie withdrew his men up a gulley and met Graham Clark coming to reinforce him. The Police party continued a fighting withdrawal and managed to extricate their small force, including the dead Askari and their wounded, without losing any weapons to the Gelubba.

Both Ernie and Graham Clark cared for their wounded in the heat of battle, taking personal risk to pull in and give first aid whilst under heavy fire. Although they had been forced to retire, they returned to the scene a few days later and discovered that the Gelubba had fled back into Ethiopia, having sustained a large number of casualties, about twenty dead and many wounded.

First radio signals to Marsabit Divisional Headquarters from Fort Banya reported that Ernie Wright and Graham Clark had been killed. But they managed to eventually extricate themselves from the battle, although running short of ammunition in a fierce six-hour engagement that continued until around one o'clock.

A significant factor in this action was that although in constant engagement under heavy fire for almost six hours in blazing sun and in desperate thirst, every Askari showed courage and discipline throughout, a great testament to their training and faith in Ernie and Graham.

Ernie retained his hat showing a neat bullet hole through the crown and later gave it to his son.

Both officers received decorations for their bravery, with Ernie Wright awarded The George Medal and Graham Clark the Colonial Police Medal for Gallantry. The Sergeant and two Constables also received the Colonial Police Medal for Gallantry for their part in the fight at the same Investiture from the Governor of Kenya, Sir Evelyn Baring.

During the Investiture Ernie met and later married Lady Sarah, a friend of The Governor's daughter.

Ernie Wright retired to England and died aged 89 in 2012.

Graham Clark returned to Glasgow, his hometown and is current President of The Kenya Police Association.

The Investiture - Four Brave Men

Insp Graham Clark Sgt Leo Shule Const Ethinyon Barua ASP Ernie Wright

Const. Ali Abdi, also awarded the Colonial Police Medal for Gallantry, was on home leave in Somalia at the time of the Investiture

Sara Wright – Police Wife

Marriage, Children and A Kenya Household

Thomas was born in January, and a family who had gone on leave lent us their ayah. A small boy arrived at the back door and said he was our Shamba Toto. I really didn't need a gardener, but there was no arguing with Maina, who stayed with us for the next seven years. I have always loved gardening and in Kenya, with two rainy seasons a year, there was almost nothing you couldn't grow, and I loved the speed with which things worked.

We really did live like kings, two servants and a gardener, us two, a baby and a grand piano. When Thomas was three months old we went on home leave. At that time we were doing a tour of four years and six months leave. The thought of living for six months in England with either of our sets of parents wasn't very thrilling, so we decided to go home as slowly as possible.

We found a German cargo boat. There was naturally no doctor on board and room for about ten paying passengers, although there was only one other couple, and a wretched giraffe in a very tall cage on the deck, which destined for a zoo in Germany. I suppose it had a keeper but we never saw him.

Our journey got off to a rather sticky start. It turned out that our steward (the only steward) had been an Anti-aircraft gunner in Hamburg. 'Do you know Hamburg?'

'Yes,' Ernie replied. 'I did a lot of town planning there in 1944.'

'Mein Gott. Maybe I shot at you!'

'Well, you missed.'

We went into all sorts of ports, picking up and dropping cargo. We travelled very slowly and the following gentle breeze travelled at the same speed, so the smoke from the funnel went straight up. Passing camels overtook us in the canal. The poor giraffe dreamt of Amboseli and cool nights. So did we.

Travelling back to Kenya after our leave became complicated when President Nasser nationalised the Suez Canal, which became off-limits. So we left our heavy luggage to follow as best it could and flew to Nairobi, where we spent the next four years. Ernie worked in H.Q. In the end we bought a house quite near the Mess, as we had to find somewhere big enough to put the piano.

By now our household had been increased by Adan's wife, a fat-tailed sheep, a new ayah who became a great friend, her small daughter, a dog, and of course Maina. Nairobi wasn't as much fun as Fort Hall. Ernie was very busy, there were some horrible incidents, but we made lots of friends. David was born when Thomas was eighteen months old and to celebrate his birth we all ate the fat-tailed sheep, which dealt with one problem.

I don't suppose my life was all that different from anyone else's life: looking after two babies, dealing with domestic problems, entertaining a certain amount, going on safari not very often, but wonderful when we could. Mau Mau was gradually winding down and eventually we took leave, this time only three months.

We came back to Mombasa, Ernie's favourite place after the NFP, which was not a really suitable place for two small children.

Mombasa was wonderful in every way. We left the piano with Mrs Catling, the Police Commissioner's wife. Adan and his wife left us and went back to the NFP. I think the presence of so many Arabs was uncomfortable to many up-country Africans. Memory in Africa is very long.

Our two little boys began school, so we didn't have our dear ayah Mwana Mvua, but she produced a female cousin, Salama who had a small son always known as Smiley Way.

Our first Mombasa house was horrible – I used to sit on my bed and watch ticks climbing up the walls into the roof. Goodness knows what else went on in the roof. The house was hot and stuffy.

Our next house was much better. It had an upstairs, so the bedrooms were cooler and it had a nice garden. We spent happy hours on the beach, particularly at Nyali with the children. The boys and I swam almost daily in the pool at the Chini Club. Lying in the water looking up at the huge walls of Fort Jesus built by the Portuguese in the 15th, listening to the swifts screaming overhead, knowing you were going to eat the most delicious fish for supper, was just about as good as it gets.

We had two very happy years there. Both the boys swam like fishes; Ernie played hockey, squash and cricket and worked very hard. I was allowed to score for the cricket matches he played, which was made easy for me because almost the entire team was called Patel.

The Emergency came to an end, and so did our time in Kenya. In 1963 Kenya became independent and as Ernie was an expat officer, he was able to take redundancy. It was for us both a sad and difficult decision and if we'd not had the boys we might well have stayed. But we needed to think of their future and knew that couldn't be permanently in Kenya.

So we packed up the piano for the last time and returned to England. We'd had a wonderful life, full of colour and excitement, doing things and seeing places and people we never would have done in England and we were truly grateful. The piano is in my sitting room as I write.

Avtar Mutharu – Police Officer

Scotland Yard And Interpol Headquarters

When I was on a Colonial Police Course at MPTS Hendon in 1960, I was sent to the Yard with instructions to meet a senior officer visiting from Kenya.

The reason for this visit was not clearly explained, but I was assured there was nothing to worry about. When I arrived at the right office I came face to face with ACP Tom McBrailey whom I had once previously met at CID HQ, Nairobi as junior Constable when I had taken care of the revolver of a deserter Contract Inspector.

I had a flash back of that episode, and wondered what would happen now? However, after a warm and welcoming handshake I sat down at a table with ACP McBrailey and an officer of the Scotland Yard forensics department.

My ACP, being on home leave, had decided to look at the possibility of introducing an "ID Kit" into the Kenya Police. This gadget, made up of many transparent slides, depicted different shapes and sizes of varied face anatomical features.

The idea of the exercise, from ACP McBrailey's viewpoint was for me to describe the facial features of an African in Swahili, so that the Yard technician could build up an image of a wanted person. The 'wanted subject' chosen was Peter Okola Ochieng.

From my description in Swahili to McBrailey, the Yard's forensic technician made some progress. But he became stuck, as he could find no slides of African anatomical features, especially noses, in the Kit.

ACP McBrailey concluded that there was need to develop a specific ID Kit for Africans. I don't this happened in Kenya as independence approached faster than anticipated.

At the end of my Hendon course I took leave to travel around in the UK and added a brief trip to Paris. After a visit to the Eiffel tower, the Lido nightclub and walks around the city I became bored.

Completely out of the blue and quite spontaneously, I decided to visit the Interpol Headquarters. So I took a taxi and arrived at the gate.

I introduced myself at the reception desk and, to my surprise I was well received and escorted to a senior officer who passed me onto an officer who spoke good English and gave me a three-hour tour through several departments and generally shown around.

I was finally taken to the Director. After a short meeting with him he gave me an autographed copy of booklet about Interpol. I later thought that it was a cheek on my part, as, had I requested this visit through proper channels, as I had no official status to warrant such an approach, it would have probably been declined.

On my return to Kenya I never mentioned it, lest it backfired.

I felt my experience in the Kenya Police was very unique. The skills acquired and experience gained transferred easily to my later civilian career on leaving the Force in 1967, after nearly fifteen years a Policeman.

I joined the Pharmaceutical Industry in sales and worked in Eastern Africa, based in Nairobi and covering Kenya, Uganda, Tanzania and Ethiopia. I thoroughly enjoyed my work and the responsibility.

The 1972 expulsion of Uganda Asians when Dada Idi Amin announced prompted my departure from Kenya.

With my family I came to the UK at the end of 1972 and joined Welcome Foundation of UK and also worked for Bayer of Germany. I thoroughly enjoyed the Pharmaceutical profession and retired in 2000.

Bryan Coleman – Police Officer

My days at Uplands Police Station

I transferred from Kiambu to Uplands Police Station after being disciplined for continually sneaking off to Nairobi to see a girlfriend. I enjoyed my time at Uplands because, surrounded by forest, to feed my Askaris I used to do quite a lot of hunting for game in my spare time.

One day whilst down in the Rift Valley and driving along the Narok road with my African Inspector John, the exhaust pipe on our Land Rover came loose.

We were doing about 30 miles an hour and the sound of the engine went from a quiet purr to a loud noise that sounded like a machine gun. Inspector John panicked and jumped out of the Land Rover. My heart sunk as I thought I had lost him. I stopped and looked behind, and luckily saw John limping down the road full of dust and dirt. I asked him why he had jumped out and he answered that he thought we were being ambushed.

I used to do a lot of patrolling on the Escarpment down in the Rift Valley. On one occasion in the late afternoon, we were sitting above the little forest station situated half way up the Escarpment road when a VW Beetle drove.

Up and out jumped a man and woman, who proceeded to lay a blanket on the ground and take their clothes off.

After they had settled down on the blanket I decided enough was enough and fired a few rounds beside them. It did not take them long to hop back into the Beetle. They left their clothes where they had hung them up on the tree, and off they went.

I have often wondered what happened to them. I did try to find their names by checking their clothes, but without success. Incidentally, there were signs along the Escarpment road that read 'Tourists Beware of Armed

Terrorists'. At a later date, somebody took the time to change them to read 'Terrorists Beware of Armed Tourists'.

Another incident that happened on another patrol in the same area was when we came across a broken down car. The owner Mr Patel told me that the car had stopped and would not start again. I tried to start it but with no luck. I told Mr Patel to stay in the car with his family, as this was a dangerous area.

I started off on my way to get help, but after 100 yards I was alerted to the fact that Mr Patel was following behind me.

I asked him, 'What about your family?'

'No problem Sahib, I have locked them in the car so that they're safe.'

Mike Smart - Police Officer

You Never Know What Christmas Will Bring

At the end of 1954 I found myself in charge of Police Post 41 in the Laikipia Area at the north end of the Aberdares. It was an interesting Area with quite a few raids on the local European farms during which the Mau Mau came down from the forest and hamstrung whole herds of cattle. They then disappeared back into the forest with a few carcasses. Leaving me with the grim task of putting down the injured cattle left struggling on their haunches.

I also had to contend with quite a lot of through Mau Mau traffic going towards the Aberdare Forest from the area to our west and seen by African farm guards. They would fire a few shots to chase the armed terrorists away and alert me.

On an alert I would go out with my patrol of around ten Constables and sweep the area. Sometimes we contacted a gang or captured a wounded terrorist or a straggler.

Over the five months I commanded Post 41 I came to know the local Farmers quite well. One of them, Mrs Christopher, organised a group of loyal Kikuyu known as The Torchbearers who acted as security guards, mainly in Thompsons Falls Township. These men were supposedly loyal, but we all knew they had taken the Mau Mau oath, whether freely or not.

Mrs Christopher approached me at the end of November requesting that I take some of her Torchbearers on patrol in the bush. I was not keen but thought what the hell and agreed.

I arranged for a patrol into an area of bush owned by one of the farmers that I knew to be part of the terrorist through route. We went in at dusk on the 24th of December; me armed with an old Sten gun, my Sergeant with a .303 rifle and seven Thompsons Falls Kikuyu Torchbearers armed with Simis and Pangas. In addition my Sergeant carried a large backpack with a very heavy radio.

We crossed a field and went into light bush. As the bush became thicker the noise made by The Torchbearers increased, as they had no experience of moving quietly under these conditions, so I signalled a break to set up camp for the night.

I woke them about five in the morning and assembled them reasonably quietly and set off, leading my patrol through the bush. After about a hundred yards we entered a small clearing. Suddenly two men armed with Pangas appeared on the far side about ten yards away from me.

I shouted, 'Simama!' but biggest one turned and ran.

I fired a burst at the smaller man as he tried to follow his companion. I hit him and he dropped. I ran past him and fired another burst but the tall man had gone.

Returning to my patrol, I checked the short man and found him dead. I think the Torchbearers were astounded and gabbling to each other at my speed of reaction and probably thought the whole area must be thick with Mau Mau.

I got on the wireless and after some alcoholic Merry Christmases managed to get through and report the occurrence.

We stayed at the scene until a rather annoyed Police Inspector from Thompsons Falls – who did not appreciate a callout early on Christmas Day – arrived with several Askaris to collect the body.

I took the Torchbearers back to the Falls and returned to my Police Post for a few Christmas drinks in the comfort of my quarters and a day spent not in the bush, but in a far better way than I expected.

David Hewson – Police Officer

Punch Bearcroft

The Kenya Emergency was declared by the Governor on 20th October 1952, a day that was to become Kenyatta Day in 1962.

The first Anti Terrorist Operation reach to Police Station level, codenamed "Jock Scott" after a notable trout fly, provided a top secret coded list of people to be arrested and placed in detention that night.

I was stationed at Rumuruti at that time, a station area on the border of Central Province the main Kikuyu homeland. I went out and brought in all my wanted persons on my list, except one who was absent from home and never returned.

An airstrip at Rumuruti was used by the Beef Barons of the area for travel between their ranches and Nairobi or Mombasa on the coast.

Soon after The Declaration of Emergency I was asked to provide housing for a Police Pilot; a Reserve Officer who owned his own Piper Cub, a single engine, four seater high winged light aircraft.

I agreed and within a few days my houseguest arrived.

I met him at the airstrip. After discussing security he taxied his plane down to the Police Station compound where it could be properly guarded when not in use.

At the time I was aged twenty-four and the man I met was a few years older. He wore shorts, a khaki shirt and jumper, a Police cap and Police socks with desert boots. An irregular guise – as irregular as the wearer – I soon learned.

He pulled a grip from the back of the plane and having locked the aircraft and placed the tassled markers at certain spots, picked up the grip in his left hand, put his right hand in his pocket and walked over with a grin and introduced himself as Punch Bearcroft.

He shook hands with his left hand in an awkward manner, but I took no real notice. It was some time later I realised that he had no right hand, which had been severed at the wrist.

Over the years we were to become firm friends. In 1957 I was Best Man at his wedding to Nola, also a pilot. I never asked him how he lost his hand and he never volunteered. There was one uncomfortable moment some months later when I volunteered to help tie his shoelaces. He just laughed and said, 'No, I can manage, thanks.'

Over the period of the next twenty plus years I flew hundreds of hours with him, both as a passenger on long flights, or on operations such as food drops, message drops, often landing where there were no airstrips, on the beach in a desolate area of the South Coast between Malindi and Lamu, at Oropoi under the Turkana Uganda escarpment.

The first time I flew with him I realised just how skilled and indomitable he was.

Having a plane at Rumuruti was useful for two reasons. It looked for stolen stock and for Mau Mau gangs moving into and from the Aberdare Forest and across the plains of the ranching area.

I was intrigued to watch how he flew a light aircraft with only his left hand.

Once settled in the right hand passenger seat I watched with interest just exactly what he did when he settled into the left hand pilot's seat.

Attached to the right hand end of the "steering- wheel" was a length of webbing strap fixed with a brass buckle, taken, I surmised, from an old army haversack.

He completed all his pre-flight checks making the necessary adjustments with his left hand. When ready he pushed the stump of his right arm into the webbing strap.

A quick quizzical look and a grin to enquire whether I was ready, a check of my safety belt, door and window as he leaned across and we were off.

This was my first flight in a light aircraft and it was exhilarating. He was even then a superb pilot and knew exactly what he was doing.

Pre-Emergency he did freelance work as an aerial photographer and under that old Piper Cub he had fixed a proper aerial camera.

One morning, a few days after his arrival at Rumuruti he decided to fly over Mount Kenya and take a series of pictures of the Mountain and its peaks, glaciers and tarns.

This was no simple task and although we were only about forty miles from the peaks as the crow flies the peaks are seventeen-thousand-feet above sea level. The single engine Piper needed considerable time to make that altitude.

We were up at four in the morning and it was very cold. After coffee I saw him off the ground at the airstrip and went back to bed. Sometime after nine I heard a plane approaching and drove up to the airstrip to see how the pilot and the little plane had faired.

After a good landing he taxied in and I went ahead to the Police Station. He switched off and having completed setting his flags he removed the camera and went off with it tucked under his arm to unload the film.

Sometime later I walked over to the house for a mid-morning cup of coffee and to enquire regarding the success of the flight. Punch was sitting reading. I asked him how it went.

He looked at me, grinned and said, 'I forgot to put the bloody film in.'

As the Emergency progressed more and more use was made of light aircraft and the Police Airwing grew and so did the type of aircraft.

One Flight of aircraft flew from Nairobi with a second Police Air Base in Central Province at Mweiga on the Eastern side of the Aberdare mountain range, from where Punch led the air offensive against the Mau Mau. A third

Police Flight was based at Nakuru on the western side of the Aberdares.

Two episodes come immediately to mind that took place at Mweiga.

The first was the bomb. In those early days the Nyeri wing had three aircraft, Punch's Piper Cub and two similar aircraft.

Punch, in his wisdom, decided that it would be possible to manufacture and drop a bomb on Mau Mau gangs sighted moving through the forest. With a bit of ingenuity he could manufacture a bomb "in house" and fit it to a homemade rack attached between the wheels of a Piper Cub.

He fabricated a number of mock up bombs and tried them on various types of rack, eventually finding one that worked. The next step – the bomb and fusing mechanism – were designed and after tests found satisfactory. But only one bomb made a successful drop.

The second episode grew out of Punch's attraction to thunder flashes. He always carried a supply of these military firecrackers – allegedly for scaring elephants and other game from isolated airstrips, also for dropping on terrorist gangs sighted in the forest below.

A couple of miles from the Police Airstrip at Mweiga was situated a largish military camp for The Kenya Regiment and the Lancashire Fusiliers.

After a particularly extended party at the Outspan Hotel in Nyeri, Punch and his companion decided it would be a good idea to test the security alertness of the military.

Parking their vehicle some distance away they crept back to the camp and tossed a couple of ignited thunder flashes through the barbed wire fence. There was no immediate reaction so they tossed in a couple more.

The second pair of thunder flashes drew an immediate reaction. Whistles were blown and shouts were followed by bursts of indiscriminate small arms fire. For a short time it was a though World War Three had broken out.

On my transfer from Rumuruti I was to lose contact with Punch for a number of years and our paths did not again cross until I was posted to Police Headquarters and Punch was posted to Nairobi to command the Airwing in the absence of the substantive officer on leave.

As bachelor officers we lived in the Officers Mess on a hillside overlooking the City. From there we made our off duty forays into the Night Clubs, Restaurants and Curry Houses of Nairobi.

It was at this time that I got to know Punch well. I spent considerable time flying with him as an escort for visiting VIPs from other Colonial Forces, from the Carabinieri stationed in Italian Somalia, as well as various British politicians.

Punch was famous throughout Kenya for being a great pilot and a great character. Even people who had never met him had heard of his exploits and knew all about him.

A great character, a great pilot and a great man.

Arthur C. Williamson – Police Officer

The Right Side Of Justice

In mid-June 1953 I responded to a Kenya Police advertisement in the *Daily Telegraph* and only a short time later went for interview at the Crown Agents in Millbank, London.

The Kenya Police needed to expand fast after some horrific murders of European farmers and families by armed men of the Kikuyu Mau Mau terrorist organisation and the consequent Declaration of a State Of Emergency. The Mau Mau also turned their ferocious methods those people of their own Kikuyu tribe, who refused to join or support the insurrection.

A few days later I accepted the offer of a position as an Assistant Inspector in the Kenya Police.

Why did I join up? Probably because of boredom, frustration and the lack of an obvious future as a civil service cartographer in Whitehall and partly a sense of seeking adventure. In those days most people of my age had just missed the war and there was a sense of having been invited to a Party and then it seeing it called off.

I flew to Nairobi with three other police recruits where we were temporarily booked into a Nairobi hotel an overnight stay and, next day, our first introduction to life as Kenya Policemen.

First to Colony Headquarters to take the Oath and be kitted out – revolvers and, strangely, shoulder holsters only – and to an Indian tailor to be measured for uniforms. Then we drove to the Police Training School at Gilgil in the back of a small pick-up truck, all of which gave an impression of disorganisation and *ad hoc* arrangements. Not an auspicious beginning.

We arrived at Gilgil to find our School sub-standard accommodation still in the process of conversion from stables. This is where we were to live with no recreation facilities at all other than some *ad hoc* Football.

Without personal transport we endured a *Beau Geste* like existence and I can't remember any senior officer visiting other than for Passing Out Parades.

The issue uniform was virtually a khaki boiler suit, a Police peaked cap coupled with a intensive six-week training course run entirely by Reserve Police Officers apart from one Inspector who lectured us in Police Law, based entirely on the Indian Penal Code and McNaughton rules, also from India.

This may seem surprising in Kenya, but was a hangover from the early days when The India Office in London had responsibility for governing British East Africa. This use of law based on India remained after formation of The Colonial Office and the early 1920s change from British East Africa, a Protected Territory, to The Colony of Kenya.

None of this was what we had expected, but the experience remained an adventure and there was the one weekend volunteering to stay with a European family on the Kinangop as a farm guard, our first experience of community life outside the Police Force.

Gilgil itself was a rude introduction to Kenya and eventually there was a not very grand Passing Out Parade and subsequent postings to the wider Police Force. I went with Pete Freeman to Kiambu, where I remember on our first night we slept on a Billiard Table in the Kiambu Club.

It was another surprise that no accommodation had been planned or made available and we were both beginning to feel like uninvited guests to Kenya.

The following morning we were transported to our respective postings, mine to Githunguri and Pete's to Gatundu and as we had no idea and weren't told where these places were it might as well have been to the moon, however we were both soon to be enlightened.

I was taken to Githunguri by Jim Stewart, the Kiambu Inspector who when we arrived went through in short order, the rudiments of managing a Police Station. Githunguri was also the sub-Division Headquarters and there I met the District Officer, Richard St. J. Matthews a Kenyan who also was stationed at Githunguri.

Jim Stewart returned to Kiambu the following day to Kiambu. As an Assistant Inspector I was to be Station Commander at Githunguri – after only six weeks training at Gilgil, a daunting task.

The Githunguri and Gatundu areas, apart from being the home area of Jomo Kenyatta, were hotbeds of Mau Mau actions and beliefs.

My first impression was of a place at the back of beyond with the Police Station built entirely of whitewashed mud Rondavels; three used as living quarters for European officers and a fourth as an Officers' Mess. But these mud huts did have the luxury of glass windows and concrete floors.

Station mules brought water from a local stream. Lighting was entirely by Tilley Pressure Lamps, fuelled by paraffin, including the perimeter static searchlights.

Our telephone connection did not work and remained so as copper wire makes excellent bangles for the African women. So we communicated three times a day on short-wave radio powered by a small two-stroke engine. A very temperamental Villiers I think.

On reflection I can see that the whole muddled business was a run on a minimum budget with few people seem to know what they were doing. Fortunately, the Kenya Police had a small experienced cadre of regular Inspectors originally either from Palestine or ex-UK Police who literally bore the brunt of those very early days.

I later discovered that prior to the State Of Emergency the Kenya Police had no responsibility for the Tribal Reserve areas, that duty being undertaken by the Civil

Administration using Tribal Policemen and Government appointed local Headmen.

This meant that senior Police Officers had little knowledge of either the conditions in the Reserves nor the problems to be encountered and solved by newly arrived Assistant Inspectors on two year contracts, with no experience of Africa and its tribal system and languages.

However, for most of us, being thrust immediately into the sharp-end was clearly real pioneering. The success with which these young "two year wonders" was probably due to the Crown Agents careful selection process and that most newly arrived Policemen had previous military experience during National Service.

In addition to the asset of having Richard Matthews as District Officer was the fortunate arrival of Chief Inspector Ron Crossland as sub-divisional commander at Githunguri. Recently posted from the NFD this ex-Metropolitan Police Officer was a hard taskmaster and excellent Mentor who taught me much about Colonial Policing and turned me into a confident Kenya Police Inspector.

His insistence on extensive night patrols to demonstrate a police presence in the Reserve was only one of the many lessons to be absorbed.

Githunguri Police Station

We all had a very steep learning curve. Looking back I'm surprised that most two-year wonders in the Kikuyu Reserves made such a good fist of it.

I recall a late October morning in 1953 reports came in of a serious Mau Mau incident at a village in the north of our Station area abutting the Aberdare Forest. I went off in the Station Lorry with a Mkamba Corporal and eight Askaris to investigate.

After an hour of bumpy ride later we arrived at the village. Never having been to this place before, I knew nothing of the area. To be frank I had little real idea of what I was supposed to do, nor how big the opposition group would be.

The village Headman and quite a few of his Kikuyu Home Guard led us along a small path toward the Forest line pointing and jabbering away in Swahili. My limited knowledge of the language meant I understood very little of what they meant, except that they all seemed very frightened and I soon to found out why.

The path we followed was about fifty yards on the downside of a Ridge to our left and led directly into the impenetrable looking rain forest about a hundred yards distant. At this point the sound of a large number of people ululating and coming up the other side of the Ridge reached us.

The Headman and his followers immediately took flight: clearly not a good omen.

Rightly assuming the opposition, knowing we were there, must be advancing up the other side of the Ridge gave me little time for thought. Fortunately having been in the military and read a great deal about war, I knew that gaining the high ground first was important and made a run for the crest of the ridge.

In the excitement of the moment and with limited knowledge of Swahili I called out to my Askari the word

'Kwenda' for 'Go,' instead of, say, something for 'Come on,' meaning to order 'Follow me.'

Apart from my Corporal, who realised what I meant, stayed with me while the rest took off. I vaguely realised what had happened, but by that time events unfolded at an unprecedented speed, with the opposition pouring over the ridge in dramatically increasing numbers.

Looking back, it seems I could have been in a Sid James "Carry On" film script.

The Leader of the opposition gang, later said to have numbered more than one hundred and fifty, was wearing a Police uniform of blue overcoat with Slouch Hat and carrying a standard issue SMLE rifle, probably some of the spoils Naivasha Police Station raid.

We were about thirty yards apart at the time. He raised and aimed his rifle at me. He fired his first shot at me, removing any doubts that I should have immediately fled with my Askaris.

I no longer needed any convincing and remember the thought shooting through my mind that this must be the most stupid way to die.

Fortunately he missed and I had a 9mm Patchett sub-machine gun and my Corporal a Sten and we both opened fire. Frankly foregoing any idea of a calling out a legal challenge seemed to make no sense under the circumstances.

So we two charged the one hundred and fifty, spraying 9mm bullets. The gang hesitated, then turned and ran. If we had hit any of them it wasn't obvious as none fell. But then we weren't hit either; in spite of exchanging shots at such close range.

On the other hand it is well known that accurate shooting at targets up or down a slope is known to be notoriously difficult.

During the fight I heard the sound of a Bren gun firing, whether at us or not we hadn't time to speculate. The Bren may have been one of those stolen during the Naivasha raid.

By this time the rest of my patrol, seeing how the action was going, were desperately running to our aid with the gang retreating at speed into the forest, with us hot on their heels.

In those early days we were completely unaware of how astute the Mau Mau could be and their very effective tactic of dispersal to later reassemble at an agreed place stood them in good stead over and over again.

Needless to say, chasing them was hopeless, as they had no intention of making a stand. After about two-hours of fruitless search we gave up and headed out of the forest to the village.

Although of the on the surface this seems a disappointing encounter and little seemed to have been achieved, the reality is that the action was successful on two counts.

It proved to the local loyal Kikuyu that the Police were very willing to challenge the terrorists, something very necessary in those early days, and secondly it gave the Askaris confidence in me and formed a trusting bond, which remained throughout my service.

There is a weird corollary to this story. The Leader of the gang we fought was one Kariuki s/o x, later caught and charged with the attempted murder of a police officer – me.

Months later I received a Summons to appear at the Supreme Court as a Crown Witness in his Trial and this is where, again, we seemed to enter into "Carry On" mode.

I arrived at the Court and against all the rules passed him in a corridor and was surprised at his joyous greeting, almost as though we were old friends.

He was really pleased to see me as the only person he recognised in or around the Court from his part of the country.

Needless to say I sort of responded in kind. What else could I do? After all, weren't we nearly old friends, having met and survived in difficult and dangerous circumstances?

The Court found him guilty, but happily and strangely, to my great relief, with only a sentence of hard labour rather than a more dreadful fate.

This pleased me because in prison he would almost certainly be taught a trade such as carpentry, stone masonry or even as a car mechanic and on release would have a prosperous life after all.

The Kenya Prison Service usually taught all long serving prisoners a trade, not only for use in Prison but when discharged they would earn a very good living and presumably become useful members of their communities. In my experience all the best tradesmen had served long Prison sentences and were excellent at their trades.

So some good may have come out of our first rather chaotic encounter.

Arthur Williamson

Going on long leave in the days when one took the Union Castle Line from Mombasa to London, via Suez was great fun; three weeks cruising, all expenses paid except for drinks, and then the return journey still to come. The Red Sea was an ordeal with a small baby who was suffering in the heat. We had a cabin on C Deck at the time. After that it was worth paying extra for A Deck and air conditioning.

Aden was a good place to shop and we didn't pay duty on arrival in UK, as we were not resident there. We enjoyed bargaining with the shopkeeper and always ended up with a drink, usually Coca Cola, to seal the bargain.

In Port Said the bum boats people would come aboard. We bought a large copper table from them once and George managed to get it through the Mombasa customs without paying duty by insisting that we smoked a lot and needed it for an ashtray – all done in Swahili of course and great good humour.

Returning to Kenya Ron Thompson – I think of CID or Special Branch – was with us and the passenger allocated to share his cabin was a very young Roman Catholic priest. By the time we got to Gibraltar Ron had sufficiently indoctrinated him so that he went ashore with the rest of us in search of alcoholic bargains.

We bought the odd bottle of whisky, but the priest came back later than us, staggering under the weight of a box load. Ron had told him that as he was going up-country to isolated missions he would need the alcohol for offer to passing travellers.

On that voyage John Newman was due to join us – I think it was at Marseilles, and Ron managed to put it about that he was the Bishop of Lokitaung, travelling incognito. A lot of people believed him, including the ship's purser.

Eventually of course the VC10 took over from the sea voyage, but even that had some funny sides. Once when we were all delayed at Nairobi looking at our plane on the runway and wondering what was the problem, the pilot who we knew, of course appeared. Waving a small screwdriver said he was going out to fix it. Shortly afterwards we boarded and when the plane was revving its engines prior to take-off a little voice was heard from a child saying "Mummy. Is this when we pray?" We nearly all relieved ourselves in laughter.

George was posted to different provinces quite frequently. We had some brief spells in Nairobi, firstly living at Kileleshwa in a bungalow with mud walls and a tin roof, exceedingly noisy when it rained.

In Lavington George and I went to look at a house before we moved in and I was impressed by the parquet flooring until we stepped on it and were immediately beset by fleas. Robertson solved the problem – mansion house polish and paraffin did the trick.

On our final stay in Nairobi, now with 2 small children and a large dog we were given a maisonette six floors up in a large block. Ron Thompson rescued us by letting us have his "shack" one of the few remaining old style colonial buildings up on stilts. Through the slits in the floorboards we could see the wild life underneath.

David Hewson – Police Officer

Force Sergeant-Major M'rindari

When I went to the Police Training School in 1951 as a recruit, M'Rindari was the Force Sergeant-Major; the most senior non- commissioned rank in the Force. His responsibility at the Training School was for training in drill and discipline, particularly among the African rank and file. Like the fabled British Army Regimental Sergeant-Majors he was a kind and knowledgeable disciplinarian.

He was feared by the African non-commissioned officers and held in awe by the recruits. His command of Swahili was wide and when he spoke it was like a burst of machine-gun fire, woe betide anyone who hesitated when he roared. But he also guarded the privileges of the African Police officers, and fought just as hard to ensure that authority did not erode these privileges.

Six feet tall, built like a watchtower with not a vestige of fat, M'Rindari was massive and in 1951 the only African non- commissioned Police Officer permitted to wear khaki uniform. He was also one of the few African Police permitted to wear boots.

In uniform he made an impressive sight. Starched khaki shorts, without a crease anywhere, except the knife-edge at front and rear made recruits fervently believe that he never sat down.

Starched tunic with a high collar fastened at the neck, also without a single crease except at the right elbow from constant saluting, a black belt and cross strap polished bright as glass, navy blue puttees with shining black boots. On his head he wore a red tarbush or fez, not as tall as a general duties Police tarbush and made wider and of better material.

Under his arm he carried his wand of office; a thick heavy Malacca cane topped with a silver knob engraved with the Force crest.

Later in my service I was posted back to Kiganjo Training School and for a time commanded Junior Training Wing, a Section that included responsibility for recruitment, enlistment and training of Police Constables and promotional courses for Corporals and Sergeants. Force Sergeant-Major M'Rindari was still at the Training School and I found an opportunity to read his record of service.

He had joined in the early nineteen-thirties as a member of the Boys Brigade and on reaching the age of eighteen had started his pensionable service and, over the years, worked up the ranks to his exalted position as Force Sergeant-Major.

His service had been wide and he had picked up a number of commendations, including the Colonial Police Medal for Meritorious Service. He had also collected a number of punishments, and I noted that early in his service he had been sentenced to "six strokes" for some misdemeanour.

In those days their senior officers could still hand out corporal punishment to serving African Policemen, but such punishments were abolished in the year nineteen forty six.

During my second time of service at Kiganjo I came to know M'Rindari well. He was still the Force Sergeant-Major, but his uniform had changed and he was permitted to wear the khaki uniform, white shirt and black tie of a member of the Inspectorate, as well as a highly polished black Sam Browne belt.

One incident, in which M'Rindari was a principal, sticks vividly in my memory. The Training School had a constant turnover of recruits, and each intake looked forward to their Passing-Out Parade.

Besides being a spectacle of smartly trained and turned-out young men there were also a variety of shows presented to the guests and the families of recruits.

These parents and siblings travelled long distances to witness that proud moment when their young men became fully-fledged Policemen with an important position in life and a future away from the grind of village life and stock herding or farming.

After the last squad had marched off to the music of the Kenya Police Band, various displays got under way. The more serious such as precision marching drill and arms drill displays, riot drill and physical training took place first. Lighthearted events such as tribal choirs, tribal dancing and the like followed these.

And how many Policeman can get into a Land Rover? It was not unusual to see up to thirty Constables come tumbling out as the Land Rover drove slowly across the Parade Ground.

In one of the most popular displays – the Silent Drill – showed a squad of thirty men going through a series of drill movements, both in stationary and on the march, apparently without a single verbal order being given.

The whole Silent Display took fifteen minutes from March On to March Off and required great concentration.

In training for the event recruits memorised a sequence of drill movements and one man in the centre rank whispered the time count between each. With the Display Squad in the Parade Ground centre, the audience could not to hear the subtly expressed orders.

All Silent Drill training, closely supervised by Force Sergeant-Major M'Rindari, began with the drill movements executed on the tap of a side drum. The Constables counted off each interval – one two-three – until the next tap and so on right through the whole schedule until it became second nature.

Silent Drill training took place in a secluded place behind the barracks. On one occasion as Orderly Officer for the day and making my periodic patrol of the barrack area I heard drum taps, so decided to check the progress of this new Silent Drill squad.

I rounded the corner and saw the Squad Sergeant and his whole troop facing towards me.

M'Rindari stood with his back to me, holding the side drum above the head of a recruit constable, snapping detailed instructions at the poor man, with each order punctuated by a sonorous bump on the unlucky man's head.

With the drum poised high for a final blow, the Squad Sergeant managed to catch the 'Old Man's' eye.

M'Rindari whipped round with the drum at his side, poised for a salute. But by the time he completed his turn I had gone back round the corner.

I saw nothing.

The incident was never mentioned.

Men like M'Rindari are gems of leaders and any recruit with whom he dealt knew they had him always on their side.

By the time he retired some years later he had achieved the rank of Chief Drill Instructor at the Police College. He returned to his home district of Meru to be appointed as a Chief of his clan area.

Bill Smith – Police Officer

Cattle Theft

Like almost all other recruits at the Police Training School in 1951 I wanted to be posted to the Kenya Northern Frontier. We dreamt of forts looking like those used by the French Foreign Legion and camels and palm-shaded oases.

In the event, I went to Soy in the Eldoret Division of the Upper Rift Valley, a Station and a Police Station built just before World War One to protect the first European Settlers.

After World War Two an influx of new Settlers moved into farms twenty or more miles from Soy. When I arrived they were being plagued by cattle theft with incursions from the Nandi, Elgeyo and Marakwet, tribes who lived in nearby districts separated from the European area by a range of hills.

For people of those three tribes, cattle were literally sacred as well as being their means of living and a cultural identifier. Other tribal youth, such as the Masai qualified as warriors by feats of daring such as killing a lion with a spear. Young men from the Nandi, Marakwet and Elgeyo tribes qualified by acquiring cattle, usually by theft.

When I arrived at Soy Police Station the Officer In Charge was Sebi Fadamullah. He was that rare thing in the Kenya Police, a Nubian. I soon learned that Sebi was a man of parts. He was a full Inspector, unusual then for an African. He was charming, clever and a brilliant shot and had competed in international competitions.

Sebi policed the Soy area well but the new European farms were too far away to deal with stock thefts. I therefore decided to go on safari and set up camp near the Post Office at Moiben, the small township twenty miles from Soy.

The established way to deal with stock theft employed a dual approach. One group of detectives would try to track the stolen cattle while another group questioned the Rancher's herdsman to learn what they could about the thieves and the possible destination of the stolen animals.

Tracking thieves almost never worked. Firstly, by the time the theft was reported to us the tracks were long gone. Secondly, the thieves swept the ground behind them, obliterating any signs of their passing.

I realised that the key to success, as in so much police work, lay in gathering information. Obviously the stolen animals did not simply vanish and because cattle played such a large part in the lives of the three tribes they would not just be slaughtered. Ergo somewhere in the tribal homelands the animals were alive but hidden. I set about recruiting informers who I paid from my "Goat Bag", a widely used term for money.

The main source of the fund in my care I owed to my predecessors at Soy.

When they located stolen animals being kept by suspects the Police were entitled to impound all the stock belonging to the miscreant until the case was solved. Nature took its course and we claimed all newborn calves.

When I took over the herd were kept – free, gratis and for nothing – on land belonging to a retired, Colonel Swinton-Hume, a gentleman well-disposed to us.

Suspect cattle thieves were brought to Moiben Police Post for interrogation. The word interrogation covers many procedures. Nowadays the TV generation may think of an austere room where detectives and suspects are seated at a table with a tape recorder. Behind them stands a uniformed police constable for security.

At Moiben interrogation was quite different and invariably took place in the open air. African detectives wearing shorts and a blanket covering their shoulders would sit on the grass with the suspect inside their circle.

From time to time those involved would turn their heads and spit a stream of tobacco juice behind them with unerring accuracy.

At first there would be general talk about cattle and their welfare. Then talk would pass on to the keeping of cattle and so to naming particular animals and where the suspect had acquired his. Lastly the questions would be about the animals we believed to have been stolen.

The relationship between suspect and detective varied and could be quite extraordinary. I was present when a suspect suddenly got to his feet and said, 'Yes I stole the cows from Bwana Mustard and drove them over the hills to my land. The cows I stole and spirited away myself". He glared at the ring of detectives and added, "Which one of you could do that?"

A master of interrogation was a Nandi Assistant Inspector called Arap Tanoi. He was what the Nandi called a Laibon, or witch doctor and credited with supernatural powers by others of his tribe. He was stocky for a Nandi with a commanding presence. Sharing a bottle of Tusker beer around my campfire I learned a great deal about my job from him.

After three years I had no unsolved cattle thefts on my books. By then the Mau Mau had murdered some Europeans and Africans loyal to the Crown. I volunteered to serve in an Emergency Area and left the comparative tranquillity of Soy for the mayhem of Fort Hall and spent my time tracking a very different kind of quarry.

Warren Martin – Police Officer

Female Mutilation And The Caring Side Of Policing

In 1956 I was a Police Officer in Embu at Kerugoya Police Station.

At that time it was common practice for young girls of the tribe to undergo a Clitorectomy.

Due to the work of the Resident Doctor at Kerugoya, a Kikuyu and a remarkable man called Doctor Kiinya and the Colonial Nursing Sisters, the Kiama Court, composed of the most Senior Tribal Elders, outlawed the practice in our Police Sub-Division.

The Kiama Court had authority to pass only Local Ordinances that had full Power of Law, but only with relevance to the Local Area, not having been passed through the Kenya Legislative Assembly

Doctor Kiinya, and Sister O'Connor, the Senior Nursing Sister, had no hesitation in calling on me when they needed help.

Between us, we managed to persuade the Elders that they must agree to take action after the Nursing Sisters took them to witness childbirth by a young African woman who had been circumcised as a young girl.

They were appalled at what they saw. Although the Tribal Police were excellent at bringing information regarding Consequential unlawful Ceremonies it fell to the Kenya Police to enforce the Ordinance. On one evening I arrested one hundred and thirty-two women performing the operation on young girls and the Assistant Commissioner of Police was very pleased when he checked my Petty Crime Register on his next Station Inspection.

It took us about six months to bring the practice of female Circumcision to an end in our Sub-Division and later other Sub-Divisions followed with Local Ordinances.

All this took place with our Area still under the Mau Mau Emergency Regulations, with terrorist gangs still active in our forests and villages.

We achieved this in the bad old days of the British Empire. I wonder what it is like there now?

In Britain we have had only one female mutilation prosecution since the offence has been on the UK Statute Books since 3rd March 2004.

13th March 2015 a Jury took just thirty minutes to acquit the Doctor concerned in the first and only case so far brought to court.

Alastair Tompkins – Police Inspector

Extracts From The Book "A Beat Around The Bush" By Alastair Tompkins, Woodfield Publishing, 2003

I joined The Kenya Police in 1953 and went straight to Gilgil Training School to learn about policing with the rest of my intake. We'd flown out together and, at Gilgil, went through an interesting training course to make sure we became proper cops.

In one of our duties, we had to stand night guard and protect the camp from attack. You wandered around alone, armed and ready, but nothing ever happened. As nights by and it became colder, this, at first exciting task, became extremely boring.

Then one night my friend Dave, patrolling the perimeter, heard something moving just outside the fence. He stood still, straining to catch more than the slight rustling sound in the bush or grass.

Could he have been mistaken?

No.

He heard it again.

With shaking hands he drew his revolver.

He heard the sound again, moving slowly from right to left through the darkness.

Oh my God. It's for real. This is the Mau Mau

Trying to sound stern and brave, Dave made the barely remembered Swahili challenge, 'Simama – nani wewe?'

Of course it is unlikely he'd get a reply along the lines of, 'It's me, a Mau Mau.'

Without response and the rustling edging closer Dave opened fire, shooting off six shots, with the fusillade greeted by a loud. 'Moo.'

'Oh my God, I've shot a cow,' he shouted.

Shining his torch he could see the animal ambling towards him, blinking in the bright light, seeming completely unruffled at being shot at.

Dave hissed several psttt noises to encourage it forward in order to make a detailed inspection. Shining his torch and peering through the fence he could see not a mark upon the cow.

This spoke volumes for the accuracy of his shooting.

On hearing shots, the camp had immediately woken and immediately stood to. Reinforcements rush to Dave's perimeter section to find a very red-faced Police Cadet and a contented cow, happily munching grass.

A few months after initial training I went on a special jungle warfare course conducted by Captain Barton of the British Army during which we were shown what to do if ambushed in a vehicle.

For this exercise we had an old Canadian Army truck with an observation hole above the passenger seat for Captain Barton to watch and control. On in this exercise, Barton would bang his hand on the cab roof and shout 'Ambush Ahead,' or 'Right,' or 'Left.' At this, the driver slammed on the brakes and we had to jump out the opposite way, leaving the vehicle as cover against the ambush.

The African driver had a crucial role, but didn't speak English and Captain Barton didn't speak Swahili.

The first time we tried, Barton banged the roof and yelled, 'Ambush Left.' As we tried to jump out on the right, the driver roared into reverse.

Clinging to the truck sides we tried again with an 'Ambush Right.'

This time the driver slammed on the brakes catapulting us to the floor of the truck. Before we could recover the lorry lurched and roared ahead.

By this time we were almost collapsed in laughter and it took many disjointed words between a furious Captain

Barton and the driver to secure a semblance of mutual understanding.

After lunch we tried a different form of ambush. We split in two with one section in the truck, while the other set up an ambush from long roadside grass. I joined the ambush party, armed with ten-inch long thunder flashes as grenades and rifles with blank ammunition.

In grass so long we couldn't see well, we decided to lob a few of our large imitation grenades, so not give away our position by standing up to shoot. Our opponents would then leave the truck and we would pick them off from our long grass ambush.

We thought this a brilliant plan.

We heard the grinding gearbox of the clapped-out truck approaching and tossed our grenades and heard three loud bangs then silence.

So we waited.

Then Captain Barton voices came loud and clear, shouting, 'Fire. Fire.'

Since we'd not yet fired a shot, we took this as an order and, still unable to see a thing, blazed away. Tucked down in the grass, the noise nearly deafened us.

Then Captain Barton's voice came through again, still loud and clear, shouting, 'No. No. It's forest fire. You've set the bloody grass alight.'

A year or so later at an operational meet to discuss a recent minor cock-up, one young Inspector attending, named Brown, whispered, 'We'll have to sack him.'

The Superintendent conducting the meeting overheard and sarcastically comment, 'Thank you Supol Brown for those words of wisdom.'

From that day on Brown took the nickname, Supol, the radio code for a Superintendent. All his mates used the nickname and the Mess barman started making out chits for Supol's drinks and food, to be settled at the end of the month with the Mess Secretary, who had obviously not heard of the nickname.

The real Superintendent, married and rarely in the Mess, queried why he had been sent a bill for several hundred shillings, and was not amused to discover the reason.

Brown, at that time based at an operational Police Post received an angry call on the radio, saying, 'One. Come at once to see me and to settle your bar bill. Two. Cease immediately using the name "Supol".

Brown apologised, but explained that the Land Rover had broken down, so there would be some delay.

'Listen very carefully Brown. I don't care if you ride here on a donkey. You will be here tomorrow without fail.'

Brown could not resist the opportunity. He borrowed a docile donkey and a three-ton lorry and next morning, dressed in his number one uniform, dropped off around the corner from Divisional HQ.

He rode the donkey through the gates to a present arms salute from the sentry on duty.

Dismounting outside the Superintendent's office, he asked the secretary to tell her boss he had come to report as instructed. She had no need to tell him. His voice roared 'Inspector Brown. Come in here. What the hell do you think you're playing at?'

John went in and saluted.

'I'm not playing at anything, Sir. I'm merely obeying your order, which, Sir, considering the current security situation is unwarranted.'

The Superintendent nearly exploded.

'Get out of here Brown. In a couple of weeks I'm going on leave. When I return I do not want to see you in this Division. Is that clear?'

'Yes, Sir, but I only obeyed your order.'

'Out, Inspector Brown, out, out; get out of my office.'

As expected, Brown soon received a new posting.

John Hughes – Police Officer

Colonel Hanna's Cook

Towards the end of October, 1953 I took over command of Mweiga Police Sub-Division with the task of co-ordinating the Security Forces' efforts at preventing stock theft from the Settled Area farms by Mau Mau gangs.

Living in the Mweiga district at this time was Colonel Hanna, a retired British Army officer, a pre-war Regular soldier commissioned during the war years. He was Irish and, having risen through the ranks from Private, very much on his dignity and now living in a Kenya district populated largely by retired Generals and Indian Army Brigadiers.

Hanna owned a small residential property on the side of the Amboni Gorge and his wife, renowned as an excellent cook, passed her skills to her African kitchen helper. He learned well and he became equally accomplished.

Sometime in February the Mweiga Police learnt that a Mau Mau gang was getting food from Hanna's property. Many older Kenya houses upcountry had kitchens detached from the main house due to the fire risk.

Hanna's kitchen at the rear of the house and on the edge of the gorge could be easily approached under cover. On the evening of Monday 15th February 1954 three Police officers from Mweiga Station, scrambled quietly up the forge below Hanna's house and set up an ambush.

Before they had time to get properly into position they saw three Mau Mau making for the kitchen from further up the gorge.

The Bren gunner opened fire, but unfortunately in the scramble up the steep scrub-covered gorge, the barrel locking catch had been knocked open without him realising. As a result the gun barrel flew off with the first shot and the terrorists fled.

A check of the kitchen revealed food in cooking pots ready for the gang, so the cook was arrested and charged with aiding the Mau Mau.

On 23rd February I handed over the sub-division and left for a five week Kikuyu language course at Kabete before returning to Mweiga to pack for transfer to Kisumu on the shores of Lake Victoria. This posting took me about as far away from a Kikuyu speaking area as possible.

I looked in at Mweiga Police Station to see how things were and accepted an invitation to their Mess for tea. Imagine my surprise when they produced a very superior cake.

Wondering how these chaps had managed such an improvement in their culinary standards I asked how this had come about?

They said 'It's a waste of talent for Hanna's highly trained cook to sit around in cells while waiting to appear in court, so we impressed him to cook for us in the Mess.'

Of course, before long, in the natural course of events, the cook needed ingredients and it seemed obviously easier to send him to do the shopping, rather than some Police Inspector lacking domestic knowledge.

So they allowed the cook to shop alone at Mweiga Duka for what he wanted and, for a time, all progressed in a satisfactory manner for all concerned.

Some time later that month – fortunately after I left for Kisumu – the inevitable happened and one morning Colonel Hanna came face to face with his erstwhile cook in the Duka and the Pawpaw hit the fan.

In high dudgeon Hanna roared into Nyeri to confront the ACP in charge of the province, "Glorious George" Hadingham.

I never did hear exactly what happened next, but I am sure that the Mweiga Police Inspectors never lived so well again.

Adrian Jones – Police Officer

Catch Us If You Can

Sometime in 1960 I was duty Officer, Central Province and working in Nyeri Operations room.

A British Army SAS unit on night exercises told us they were going up Mount Kenya after dark and they were going to be pursued by a GSU team, whose job it was to find and surround them somewhere up on Mount Kenya.

'No way will they catch us where we are going,' was the SAS final boast on leaving.

GSU, as per plan, waited a few hours and then over the radio came Punch Bearcroft, saying, 'Listen out for me on the radio.'

He had taken off from the Nyeri airstrip shortly after eight. Ten minutes later he called with a map reference, saying, 'They've set up camp and lit the fires to cook their dinner.'

The GSU team set off and a few hours later came back to the Ops Room, highly delighted that they had captured all the SAS and sent them packing back to Nairobi with their tails between their legs.

Mike Wade – Police Officer

Witchcraft at the Police Station

Witchcraft is not something one comes across every day, especially in the reasonably large Rumuruti Police Station.

One morning my Senior Sergeant reported that a Constable who had been on guard duty overnight was very poorly and unable to rise from his bed.

Making my way to his quarters, a hut shared with another unmarried Constable, I felt shock at seeing him shivering, muttering incoherently and in a very bad state.

My first thought was Malaria, but as he had been fit and well only a few hours before, it seemed unusually rapid. Nevertheless, I administered a couple of Mepachrine pills, piled on more blankets and sent for our vehicle to take him down to the doctor at Thompson Falls.

While waiting for the vehicle I questioned the Guard Commander and discovered that around midnight the previous evening the Constable, now ill, had stopped an off-duty Police Constable sneaking back in, presumably after visiting a nearby accommodation area which housed a number of women and children.

An altercation had ensued which, according to witnesses, ended with the defaulting Constable placing a curse upon the sentry.

Much to my surprise, the poor chap died in his Police Station hut, before we could get him to the doctor. However, a subsequent report by the local Medical Officer assured me that he had died of cerebral malaria.

This information was received with some scepticism by both my Second in Command, a Kikuyu inspector, and my Staff Sergeant, a Nandi, who suspected some kind of witchcraft. They added, that the offending PC came from a Kalejin Can well versed in the black arts.

This untimely death brought morale amongst the junior ranks to a low ebb.

To find time for further investigation I assigned the offending PC to a patrol that would take him from the station for at least five days. I learned little about the incident during that time, but learned a lot about witchcraft and decided my best course of action would be to get the man transferred.

However, things came to a head much more quickly than expected. Two nights later, I awoke to loud banging on my door with the news that a Corporal was trying to drown himself in the nearby river.

Hurrying to the scene I found the Corporal stretched out on the bank and held down by three men. His condition seemed identical to that of the deceased Constable.

Wasting no time I bundled the Corporal into the Land Rover and managed to get him down to Thompson Falls where he was sedated and taken into care by the Medical Officer, who again diagnosed malaria, despite a witness claiming that the man had been cursed.

After a brief conversation with the Division Commander I arranged a temporary transfer for the offending Policeman to Division H.Q.

Before I set off I sent a runner to summon a Laibon of the Samburu tribe I had become acquainted with in my General Service Unit days.

My driver and I delivered the man and his kit safely to Headquarters and made our way back towards Rumuruti. A mile or so out of town the driver insisted we stop and search the vehicle in case anything harmful had been left.

We lifted the cab seat cushions and discovered four newspaper wraps of what seemed to be powdery tree bark.

It appeared harmless, but when we arrived back at Rumuruti Police Station during the evening parade, I took the opportunity to address my men and make it clear that I thought the probability of somebody dying from a curse was absolute nonsense.

To reinforce my assertion – being certain my driver would not keep a good story to himself – I produced one of the newspaper wraps and poured the contents over my head, declaring that if I dropped down dead, they could certainly believe in the curse.

I experienced absolutely no effect apart from dirty hair, although my wife later said, ' If you go down with Malaria again, you're lost.'

I'd suffered recurring Malaria several times in Rhodesia and she worried it may return.

The following day the Samburu Laibon arrived.

What followed was sheer pantomime and akin to something from the film, "Sanders of the River".

But given the deaths and what had gone on before I felt it worth a try.

A circle of Askaris was formed, hands were joined and we were treated to a throwing of bones and waving of a fly swat in a performance that ended with the Laibon dramatically pointing to a patch of flowers surrounding a sand bagged emplacement.

Following the direction of his finger I searched in the flowerbed. Low and behold I found and pulled out half a dozen wraps similar to those hidden in the Land Rover.

I immediately dropped them onto a cooking brazier burning nearby.

That brought the show and the incident to an end.

Whatever the rights or wrongs of the whole business, it certainly brought success and high morale to the extent that for the following Saturday morning inspection went well, with everything neat and tidy, even to the extent of Second in Command's eight year old son lining all the Station's children up for inspection also.

Two African Police Officers from the Headquarters Witchcraft Unit – a surprise to me – turned up. They spent the day listening to people and nodding sagely before departing, never to be heard of again.

As for the Corporal, I am pleased to say he recovered and seemed no worse for his experience.

Witchcraft?

I really do not know, but the mind can play funny tricks now and again.

The flywhisk still hangs on my office wall as a reminder.

After a lifetime spent in either the Police or Investigative business, it is wonderful how in spite of many hairy moments one usually remembers the one-liners with affection.

Whilst in charge of the Marine Section at Kilindini I had the duty of boarding all incoming ships to check various items, such as firearms and harbour regulations, a task I usually carried out with the Chief Officer over coffee or breakfast.

On one occasion on board an American cruise liner the Officer invited me to finish my paperwork over breakfast in one of the deck restaurants.

Having previously eaten aboard a French vessel, I merely ordered orange juice and a couple of boiled eggs.

Minutes later, a smiling black stewardess returned with the juice and a dish containing mashed up eggs.

Without thinking, I asked, 'What happened to the shells?'

'Gee,' she said. 'You Limeys are funny eating the shells too.'

And during my time in a General Service Unit I knew an elderly Mkamba Sergeant Major we called the Retread, because he had retired from the Kenya Police and re-joined for the Mau Mau Emergency.

We were chatting one evening round the fire and he told me about his father who, during the First World War, had been with the Police in German East Africa.

I asked him about differences between the two Forces and which was the best.

He said, 'Well Bwana, of course I was only an Mtoto, but saw that the German method of discipline was better than the British.'

'Why?' I asked.

'Because,' he said, 'with the Germans you knew exactly where you stood. They gave harsh but immediate discipline. With the British, you are never certain whether you will be punished or given a new pair of socks.'

I don't know why he chose socks as his example, but I always remember the way he spoke with amusement.

Mrs Susan Mansfield – Police Wife

My Two Brushes With History

You may recall that sometime early in 1951, an International Situation came to crisis point; Ruth Williams's marriage to Seretse Khama, Ruler of Bechuanaland and their subsequent exile ordered by the British Government.

This crisis had been pretty much caused the U.K. Government of the time and certainly made worse by what seems today to be a rather unacceptable attitude to interracial marriage.

In order to increase the number of Police able to maintain independent actions on the matter, a number of Kenya Police volunteers were seconded to Bechuanaland, my husband Derek and Maurice Silcock among them. I think the timespan there was about six months in total, this incident being early summer as far as I remember.

I do not recall being told any great detail of this tour of duty, but I know Derek did contribute to the smooth running of the journey into UK exile by carrying baby Jacqueline in her carrycot up the flight of steps and into the aeroplane.

To be sure, a small deed on the scale of History in total, but a brief moment of involvement, none the less, and a kind and courteous gesture on a sad and difficult occasion.

Another small brush with History occurred on sixth of February the following year.

The Derek's Police Station was one of those on the radio relay network and towards midmorning the Radio Operator burst into Derek's office, declaring he had important news: The King had died in his sleep at Sandringham.

Princess Elizabeth was at that time undertaking an official tour of Kenya on behalf of her father, because of his failing health. I believe that she had spent that night watching Game from the hotel at Tree Tops.

Timing is the essence of this story. It is obvious that Derek heard the news quite a while before the Queen was told by Prince Phillip at Sagana Lodge, during the same afternoon.

Derek's Radio Operator had, of course, swiftly passed the message onward before leaving his post to tell Derek.

So long ago now and so much water has flowed under so many bridges.

David Hewson – Police Officer

Beginning of Mau Mau and One Hundred Pieces Of Silver

When Kenya's Emergency was declared, on 21st October 1952, I was the Inspector-in- Charge of Rumuruti Police Station in the Laikipia District of the Rift Valley Province. On that day, each Police Station Commander in the affected areas received, in code, a list of people living in the Police Station area who were to be detained at seven o'clock that evening.

Operation "Jock Scot", the precursor of the Mau-Mau Emergency, was activated. My immediate boss was Superintendent Pat McCann, a dour Scotsman, but a patient and painstaking investigator who taught me the basics of good statement writing. He missed nothing, was a patient and careful investigator and skilled in framing telling questions. I was able to tell him that all my chickens, except one, were in the bag.

Very soon after the Declaration of Emergency, the first of a number of vicious murders of European settlers and their families took place about four miles from Pat McCann's Headquarters in Thomson's Falls.

This first case became known as the Meiklejohn murders. The victims were a Dr. Meiklejohn and her elderly husband, a retired Commander from the Royal Navy. She was a doctor of medicine and had, as was so often to be the case, been called out during the night by her house staff on the pretext of treating a sick member of her farm staff. She was brutally murdered and left with her dying husband close by. Their attackers ransacked the house and made off with their booty, which included cash and the firearms that were available.

Other killings followed this initial murder. A case that particularly angered the settlers in Laikipia District was the murder by the Mau-Mau terrorists of the Ruck family. The attackers had used a ploy similar to that used on the Meiklejohns, and when Mr Ruck had gone out to help the allegedly "sick" farm labourer he was attacked and killed.

The raiders returned to the house to kill Mrs Ruck and their two young children, who were murdered in their beds, one being chopped in half at waist level. Again the terrorists returned to ransack the house and steal all available firearms.

At the same time as the murder of these Europeans the terrorists also murdered a number of Africans in the District. Those who had refused to take the Mau-Mau oath; a particularly obscene oath that was anti- European as well as anti those Africans who refused to side with the Oath administrators and their alleged fight for land.

At the time I was investigating a series of brutally horrific murders, one of which was of an African schoolteacher who as a devout Christian had flatly refused to be intimidated into taking the bestial oath. He was horribly murdered and his body defiled and dismembered then disposed of in a waterhole and left to rot.

After about three weeks parts of his corpse had been recovered from the water hole and used in an oathing ceremony. This so disgusted some of his friends that they broke their oath of silence and agreed to give evidence. This in itself was a singular breakthrough for the Police as silence on the pain of death was the rule.

The doors and windows of those who broke their oath had their houses wired tight shut at night and the thatch set ablaze so all inside perished in a particularly sadistic way.

As can be imagined these and other cases caused an outcry from the farmers and other Europeans in the District. This was particularly so where the murdered Africans were trusted servants and had died rather than betray their employer.

As a result a Task Force of local army personnel moved in and sweeps were made in an attempt to find those responsible for the murders and to find witnesses prepared to give evidence in Court against those responsible.

Anyone who has lived in Africa will know that there is always a witness to any incident, no matter how isolated the circumstances, or how dark the night. The Task Force set up an Interrogation Centre. Although I was not involved, the Centre was on the edge of my Police Station area, and any problem that might develop as a result of it being there would land on my plate in the long run. In the business of policing information is a valuable resource and I made a point of instructing my staff to keep me informed of everything that happened in the Centre.

Rumours began to reach me of indiscriminate ill treatment of the inmates and my African Police were decidedly unhappy with what was allegedly taking place. Stories regarding baby python and women prisoners made me decide to go and look for myself. Together with another Inspector I went on an official visit to the Camp and what we saw horrified us.

I had no responsibility for the Unit concerned and faced the problem of what should we do about what we had seen. After discussion we decided to report the matter to the local Magistrate, a settler and a local cattle rancher as well as a former Colonel in the Kings African Rifles and man in whom we both had the utmost faith.

I explained to him what we had seen and the appalling state of some of the prisoners. Many were unable to walk; the marks of their beatings were obvious and they did not appear to have been fed.

Most were old men and old women bemused and terrified by their ordeal. Whether the python had been used as alleged we did not know, as we were unable to speak to the women alone. The Magistrate told us that he would report the matter direct to the Commissioner of Police in Nairobi. We returned to Rumuruti Police Station and waited. We did not have to wait long.

Two days later I sat in my office taking a statement from a witness in one of the Mau-Mau murder cases when two senior plain clothes Police Officers walked in.

I knew one; he was the Senior Superintendent in charge of the Police Divisions in the Lower Rift Valley, he introduced his companion as the Director of Intelligence Special Branch, an Assistant Commissioner of Police. The two Officers acted with complete formality.

After the introduction I was asked to produce my Cell Register. They both left the office. It was my assumption that they had gone to check the prisoners in the cells against the Cell Register to see if there was any illegality. They did not invite me to accompany them.

They returned almost immediately. The Director asked me why there was a prisoner in the Cells who had been in custody longer than twenty-four hours. I explained that the man was charged with murder and the Magistrate knew I had him and was making a special trip that afternoon to remand the prisoner into Police custody for two days and then to the Remand Prison.

The Director of Intelligence tossed the Cell Register onto my desk and with the parting remark, 'Hewson, why don't you clean your own Stygian Stable before you complain of others," he and his companion left.

The following day I received an order to take the Divisional Police three-ton lorry my own Police Station vehicle and a Hospital Dresser to the Interrogation Centre. There I was instructed to load up those prisoners sick or badly injured and escort them to Maralal, a remote District Headquarters some seventy miles north of Rumuruti.

I was told that the District Commissioner, Maralal, would meet me and give instructions on how the prisoners were to be dealt with. We loaded some twenty sick and injured people together with their meagre belongings onto the vehicles, and set off on our journey.

After the removal of theses people the Centre closed.

Ten miles out from Maralal the District Commissioner met us together with some Tribal Police to act as guards. He guided us to a remote area close to the Maralal Airstrip. Stacked on the ground were a few tents, some coils of barbed wire and steel pickets. We were told to pitch the tents and set up a perimeter fence around the camp.

When all was ready, the prisoners, who had been resting on mattresses in the shade, were moved into the tents. We collected wood for a fire and soon had pot of boiling to make tea for the prisoners.

One old man thanked me and asked what was to happen to them. I told him that I understood they would remain in the Camp, under the control of a District Officer and guarded by Tribal Police. The Hospital Dresser would look after them until their health and their feet had recovered from the bastinado treatment they had received.

I told him that as far as I knew, they would then be released and sent to their tribal Reserve.

When I had completed all arrangements I left the prisoners in the care of the District Commissioner whom I knew as a fair and honest man and returned to my Police Station at Rumuruti.

I heard no more for some weeks then one morning I received another visit from the two senior officers. They arrived, as before unannounced and entered my office. Without ceremony the Director of Intelligence advised me as follows. 'We have completed our investigations, and there are ten persons who will be charged with assault occasioning actual bodily harm. The case will be held here in the Court at Rumuruti and Crown Counsel will prosecute. A Senior Resident Magistrate will come from Nakuru to hear the evidence. You will act as Court Orderly.' Having delivered their edict and advised me of the date of the Hearing, they left.

On the due date both Senior Resident Magistrate and the Crown Counsel arrived together. I took them to the Court

Room where all had been set out for them. The ten European accused arrived, all smartly dressed in suits and ties.

When the Director of Intelligence to arrived I saluted and without further ado he said, 'Hewson, all ten will plead guilty. They will be fined one hundred shillings each and you will hand over their fines'. He then handed me one thousand shillings in notes and left.

The ten prisoners sat in the dock next to me. As I had been told, they were jointly charged with one assault occasioning actual bodily harm. When asked each man pleaded guilty and at the conclusion was fined one hundred shillings.

No complainant attended.

The case took only a matter of minutes. The Magistrate asked no questions regarding the nature of the assault. Neither did the State Counsel offer any information.

I paid the fines as ordered, and there the matter ended.

Some years later I was serving as a Staff Officer in Police Headquarters in Nairobi. To satisfy my curiosity I went to the Records Office and asked to see the Police Rewards and Fines Fund Register.

There on the appropriate date was an entry for one thousand shillings drawn for the Director of Intelligence.

Kind And Diehard Police Surgeons

On a Christmas day in the early fifties I was on traffic standby duty. After an accident it became necessary for me to have a lorry driver examined for being under the influence of alcohol and arranged for him to be examined by a police surgeon.

I took the driver to the office of the surgeon and waited for his arrival. After inordinate wait the Doctor finally arrived.

I immediately realised this would be fun as the surgeon himself had obviously been drinking. He almost staggered around his office looking for instruments, meanwhile he lighting a cigarette and taking a few long puffs.

He needed to take the suspect's temperature and inserted a thermometer into his mouth and took few more puffs on his cigarette. He then very courteously offered light with a lighter to the lorry driver, obviously thinking that he had given him a cigarette.

The driver laughed.

I cringed.

The examination was over. The Doctor recorded the driver was not sufficiently under the influence of alcohol, therefore no blood sample was needed. The surgeon exchanged greetings with me and the driver, and left presumably to resume his own Christmas drinking session.

On another occasion I needed to have an African driver examined. An examination was arranged, and a message came through from the 999 controller to take the suspect to the Nairobi European Hospital, where a Doctor would examine the suspect. I thought this odd, as the Doctor would have normally seen the suspect at his Nairobi Area office.

Nevertheless, I proceeded. On arrival at the Casualty Department the Doctor came to examine my suspect. The Doctor was annoyed and embarrassed and the poor African driver puzzled and frightened. Not surprising as he was clearly over the limit.

The Doctor asked me to take my suspect to King George Hospital, the dedicated African hospital, saying he would only see the suspect there, not at the European hospital.

I dutifully complied and waited and waited at King George hospital. After almost two hours the Doctor arrived, by which time the suspect had changed from a 'Lord' to a 'Judge' – at least visibly – and was certified sober.

The Doctor gave me a sarcastic look. I responded with an equally sarcastic smile and thanked him, disappointed at the system of race-separation, even in law enforcement. Sadly there are many other such instances, where race took priority over justice.

Traffic was a department where one came across all manner of public, not predominantly the criminal type as in other police formations. So it was good learning ground for interpersonal skills in dealing with variety of behaviour and attitudes.

One evening, whilst on standby duty, I was writing an accident report in an office not far from the public counter, which was always manned by a constable. I heard some commotion, then thumping of the counter.

I went to look what was going on. There stood a bulky white man – a typical sunburnt white Boer type farmer from Eldoret area – demanding to see a European Inspector to report an accident.

I explained that I was the duty officer and that I would attend to him.

He insisted that I should call a European Inspector; otherwise he would report me to the Commissioner. At this juncture the Officer second in charge of Traffic Department walked wearing civilian clothes. He was in the habit of coming to the office in the evening to catch up with paper work.

He identified himself to the complainant.

The Boer promptly responded, 'Well, get on with the job and take down my accident report.'

The Boss: 'No This officer will take your report as soon as he is free.'

The Boer: 'But he is not a European.'

The Boss said, 'He is Duty Officer,' and walked away to his office.

I told The Boer to wait in the waiting room; not a very glamorous place for anyone and certainly not for the Boer who insisted that the African whose statement I was recording should wait and he should go first.

I refused.

At first he was furious, but then common sense prevailed and he calmed down. When I finally took his statement, he read it through and signed, saying it was a well written.

He was probably too embarrassed by then to do anything else. It probably was far above his own educational standard, as he seemed only semi-literate to me. Such incidents of arrogance and racial bias were not uncommon, especially when there was influx of settlers from the White Highlands into Nairobi around the time of the annual Royal Agriculture Show.

Another 'opposite end of the spectrum' occasion occurred under somewhat similar circumstances when, one evening, I heard a very soft spoken and polite voice from a gentleman wanting to report an accident.

I was not engaged, so I went over to the report office counter. Who should I see there, but none other than Sir Michael Sylvester O'Rourke, a polite cool customer.

I saluted him and duly addressed him.

He asked, 'Do you know me?'

'Yes Sir,' said I, 'you were the Commissioner of Police when I joined the Force in 1953.

After the due reporting formality, he had a brief social chat with me and this fatherly figure parted company with a warm handshake and drove off to his home in Langata in his Peugeot 203.

In one unusual incident, my crew and I were on patrol around three in the morning one night in the Nairobi red light district.

Normally this was a quiet time and occasionally difficult to remain watchful.

While driving along a straight stretch we noticed an unusual quite bright figure in the middle of the road.

The crew and I became suddenly alert.

I switched on the Police sign on the roof of the car and slowly advanced to see a white man marching vigorously in the middle of the road towards us, absolutely naked but for a pair of black full boots.

As the car got face to face with him, I stopped. He also stopped and saluted.

I went over and interrogated him. It was revealed that he was a British army soldier – a Johnnie – from a camp on Thika Road, in an out- of- bounds area. He explained that he had been to a brothel. There was a dispute over settlement of the fee for the services rendered, which had resulted in him being stripped naked of his apparel by a group of women who had also stolen his pay packet

After due checks and search we recovered poor Johnnie's property, and restored his dignity.

We handed him over to the Military Police and his tormentors were conveyed to Eastleigh police station. My car crew dubbed him "Mzungu Masai".

It was sight to remember but hard to believe.

Another night at about four in the morning when returning to Traffic Office from the scene of a serious accident I was driving through Kariakor, Nairobi, when I came across a Land Rover being driven very erratically.

It was literally swaying from one side of the road to the other, travelling fortunately, in the same direction as me.

With flashing blue beacon and siren ringing I somehow managed to bring it to halt.

I approached the driver who remained seated. He had two passengers, one in the front and one in the back. All had long scruffy dreadlocked hair and stunk high of alcohol. If confronted in a forest they could have been surely taken for active Mau Mau. I must admit at one point that, being alone, I felt scared.

Both the driver and the passenger were literally begging to be allowed to go. They disclosed their identity when asked. Both were Special Branch Assistant Inspectors and claimed to be on an operational mission.

I was in a quandary. Should I radio for help or let them go?

They dropped the names of their senior superiors. Some I had heard of but never met, including a very senior officer. I faced a difficult and ambivalent decision that could have led to neglect on my part. I took a chance.

In those days it could well have been operational matter relating to Police pseudo-gangs, which were prevalent at the time. So I chose to let them go if they promised to be good boys, hoping they did not end up in a crash.

They also promised to keep quiet about the incident. I did not want to jeopardise my own future by showing valour over discretion in this case as I would have been noted in the upper echelons for interrupting a Special Branch operation.

It was a gamble that, fortunately, did not go wrong.

If I'd been in a fully crewed a 999 car it could have been a different matter and I may have taken them in.

But one of the two above-mentioned Assistant Inspectors was later rewarded for his participation in operations leading to the capture, conviction and hanging of Dedan Kimathi, a most wanted Mau Mau terrorist.

As a multiracial Force, the largest section of The Kenya Police was indigenous African of many different tribes.

In order to be all tribes inclusive, a carefully balanced tribal composition headcount was maintained.

Europeans made up the second largest contingent with the smallest contingent being Asian, including coastal Arabs.

Amongst the three racial groups were many fine, fair and dedicated officers. It was my pleasure to have worked alongside or under some of them as a team. One of the earliest African officers I met was Inspector James Juma in 1948 when I lived at Karatina, when I was still at school.

Juma used to take his cycle for repair to the same shop as I. In January 1953 I met him again at the PTS as a recruit where he was an instructor.

The other legendary policeman at the PTS was Michael Arrum, under whom I served at the Force Headquarters in early 1960s.

My experience in the Kenya Police was very unique. The skills acquired and the experienced gained was easily transferable to my civilian career that followed on leaving the Force after nearly fifteen years. I joined the pharmaceutical industry in sales, and worked in Eastern Africa, based in Nairobi, and covering Kenya, Uganda, Tanzania, working for Wellcome Foundation of UK and Bayer of Germany. I thoroughly enjoyed the profession and retired in the year 2000.

Bryan Coleman – Police Officer

The Funny Side Of My Kenya Police Career

I joined the Kenya Police directly from leaving the Prince of Wales School in 1949 and despatched to Kiganjo Training School in January 1950.

My roommate was Brian Matthews, ex Metropolitan Police and our room was about three down from the Mess and nowhere near the bathrooms. The windows in the rooms were only about two and a half feet off the ground, so when we came in late we never bothered to go all the way down to the toilets, but instead relieved ourselves out of the window.

One night whilst asleep I woke to the sound of running water. Looking up I saw Brian standing facing a full mirror against a wall opposite the window.

I yelled, 'What the hell are you doing?'

'I 'm peeing out the window.'

'The hell you are, you're peeing on the mirror.'

After graduating from Kiganjo I stayed PTS as they thought that, still only aged seventeen, I was a little too young to go out into the big world.

I was given the job of Farm Patrol covering the Nyeri and Nanyuki areas to check on their security at the very beginning of the Mau Mau insurrection. With a short wheel Land Rover and four constables, off I went.

At the first house we came to I walked up onto the veranda and knocked on the door. As I did, I heard one hell of a row coming around the corner. There, to my surprise, were five big German Shepherds that didn't look too happy.

I hopped over the railing and onto a pepper tree so I could climb onto the roof, hoping the residents would appear. Well wouldn't you know it, they had gone to Nyeri for the day and then on to the Outspan Hotel and a movie.

With nobody else around my brave constables weren't about to get out of the Land Rover, so there I sat until 11pm. When the owners returned, they stopped at the Land Rover and asked my Askaris, 'Wapi Bwana?'

The Askaris pointed in my direction and the dogs were called away. I must say it was harder climbing down that tree than getting up it. We had a good laugh and a drink and the owners told me the dogs would not have attacked me in any case, but it was still a lesson I never forgot – make sure the owners are at home, before you start stamping round their property and getting into trouble.

From Kiganjo I transferred down to Mombasa and lived at Mvita Mess, on the top floor with all of the other Police Inspectors. To get to our rooms we had to pass the bar, which not only had the booze, but also an African Grey parrot. You can just imagine what kind of language it learnt.

Every month we had a Ladies Night to which the Assistant Superintendent of Police and the Senior Superintendent of Police, plus guests, would bring their wives. Usually when this happened, one of us living in the Mess would volunteer to put the parrot in his room.

On one night when we had forgotten to arrange this, I thought the next best thing would be to put it in one of the toilets, located down the corridor. Next thing we knew, the Senior Superintendent of Police's wife returned from the toilets demanding to know who was in the toilet next door using such disgusting language. I calmed her down and took her and her husband back to show them the culprit. She never did tell us exactly what the parrot had said.

I used to own a Harley Davidson motorcycle and often rode to the Nyali Beach Hotel on a Saturday night, with Alan Martin for a few beers and a dance).

One night, when we were ready to go home, we passed a big party in one of the rooms. An American guy invited us in for a drink called a 'Horse's Neck'. It tasted pretty good and what with the beers and a few Horses' Necks, we were well on the way to heaven. So much so that we both found it hard to kick start the bike. We gave it a push start and off we went.

On the way home I had to run off the road to avoid hitting a steamroller parked on a corner and found myself hurtling through a coconut grove. Somehow I managed to avoid running into any of the trees. I drove straight through two hedges running down both sides of a driveway, back into the coconut grove and back onto the road without a scratch. I dropped Alan home and went back to Mvita House.

Alan's mother rang the next morning wanting to know why he was fast asleep with his arms around the toilet bowl and head on the seat. Someone else called wanting to know why my Harley was decorated with hedge.

I never did have another Horse's Neck.

While stationed in Mombasa I was given the job of Spiv Squad, along with Charge Office duties. This meant I had to round up vagrants and also incorporated bar control, covering the Kilindini Road and Fort Jesus Road, plus several other areas.

With ten Askaris and a three ton lorry assigned to me my instructions were to try to get at least thirty petty crimes a month. Vagrants in those days were defined as any person after 10pm on the streets without a shilling in his pocket.

I also used to arrest the local prostitutes soliciting on the streets. On one occasion I, sitting in the lorry outside the Star Bar on Fort Jesus Road at around midnight, I noticed two good looking young European blondes approaching the Bar and decided to investigate.

When they saw me they turned down the alley next to the Star Bar and started to run like hell.

I sent my Askaris after them and followed, picking up stuffed brassieres, blonde wigs and handbags. When my Askaris caught and arrested the pair, the two men were wearing only underpants. In those days it was illegal to impersonate a woman.

We took them back to Makadara Police Station where I charged them and put them in the cells for the night. The following morning I made them dress up exactly as I had seen them the night before, including the makeup, and put them before the Magistrate, Mr Balderson. When he saw them he immediately remanded them back into custody until the following day and instructed me to make sure that they appeared in front of him dressed as before.

The next morning Mr Balderson invited his whole family and all his friends to court so they could hear the charges. He sentenced both men to six months in jail.

It turned out that they were stewards working on the Dunnottar Castle cruise ship that was docked in Kilindini Harbour.

After six months they were picked up on the Dunnottar Castle's next visit to Mombasa.

Elizabeth Fielding – Police Wife

A Wonderful Life In Kenya

We spent time in Nakuru, living in a palatial bungalow with a large garden. It looked a perfect home. Arriving from Kisumu with all our goods we managed to make up the beds for the first night there and fell into them, exhausted.

Some time during the night I woke and being unfamiliar with the layout of the room turned on the light. The beautiful wood-panelled walls were thick with big brown cockroaches. War was declared and in spite of everyone telling us that we would just have to live with cockroaches as they did, we eventually succeeded with the aid of Niltox in getting rid of them. And a doctor had previously occupied that house.

The best part about Nakuru was that George needed to go into the National Park around the lake to maintain a radio station and sometimes we went in with him to see the flamingos, colobus monkeys and the other wild life.

On one occasion we saw a young couple with rucksacks marching down the road towards the park entrance, and we stopped to find out what they were doing. They were Norwegian and under the impression that they could walk into the park. So we gave them a lift and a tour around and on exit asked them where they were spending the night. They said they would stay at the Hindu Temple, so we offered them a bath, supper, bed and breakfast with us and the following day they departed.

They were hitch hiking from Cairo to the Cape. Several months later we received a small tin Viking type boat from them with a note saying, "We made it".

Local holidays were always taken at the coast. George and I had honeymooned at Shelley Beach but Trade Winds on Diani Beach was a favourite with us. Norman and June Pring who ran it became friends and one evening we all went off to a nightclub in Mombasa returning on the last Kilindini ferry to cross that night.

It was hot and sticky with a brilliant moon and we decided to have a skinny dip to cool off. We stopped at the beautiful white sands of Diani Beach and undressed in the palm trees.

A few minutes later, swimming around, we were alerted to the sound of voices further along the coast, and we had not taken any clothes down the beach with us. However a voice shouted, and we recognised it as Norman's, calling, 'Are you doing what we are doing?' and of course we were.

One time we went deep-sea fishing and I managed to catch a fellussi, the sale of which at the Mombasa Fish Market covered the cost of our boat hire, rods and the crate of Tusker that came to sea with us.

We also stayed at the Police Leave Centre at Malindi. The journey down was memorable. Driving down from Nairobi our plan was to spend a night en route, but we got no further than Hunters Lodge, because on a diversion from the main road we had an encounter with a large rock that hit our sump and there we were in the bush with a puddle of oil in the sand.

A big Range Rover arrived and George insisted that I went with the children to Hunters Lodge. He was not going to leave our car wreck unattended. So I was dropped off at Hunters Lodge and got accommodation. Eventually George arrived by lorry and the car was taken to a garage to be fixed, leaving us of course with no transport.

Next morning George was up at crack of dawn and hitched a lift back to Nairobi where he hired a little Datsun 120Y and we set off again but had to stop another night en route, this time at Voi Safari Lodge.

To save time we decided to go across Tsavo East to Malindi. We were a bit put off at the entrance by Joy Adamson who had just finished releasing a cheetah. She said that the roads were very wet. Anyway we decided to go on but were stopped by a wash-away.

No bridge. It wasn't too deep and the riverbed was dry so we all got out of the car and George recced a route, and made it up the other side. I'd been thinking we had food and water in the car but it wouldn't have been a good idea to stay in the car if it was stuck in ditch, so I was much relieved especially as it was now getting dark.

We finally got through after sunset on to a proper road, and I remember this long strip of tarmac descending into a dip with a great big elephant standing there. We waited and his family crossed the road to vanish into the bush and he appeared to wave his trunk at us as if to signal us on.

At Malindi our chief watering hole was the Driftwood Club. We also enjoyed a visit to the mysterious ruined Arab village at Gedi, full of butterflies but not a bird to be seen.

We finally had to leave Kenya, from Nairobi in April 1977 as the British Government was withdrawing the part of Overseas Aid that paid George two thirds of his salary.

Our daughter was thirteen by this time and our son ten and we were not too happy at the Kenya Governments decision to no longer use the UK exam systems. But we left with huge regret.

Mike Wade – Police Officer

Not All Criminals Are Bad People

Following my marriage, my wife and I were fortunate in being posted to Rumuruti where I had Police responsibility for the large Northern part of Laikipia District.

With the Emergency coming to an end, crime I had to deal with consisted mostly of stock theft from the European-owned Ranches in my Area of Policing.

I soon discovered that young tribesmen from the Samburu, Turkana or Somali homelands that formed our top border were to blame for many of the thefts. Cattle rustling had taken the place of single-handed killing of a lion, now frowned upon as they were in fairly short supply.

This left only stealing cattle as a way of preparing their rite-of-passage into manhood in their move from boyhood to the elevated status of Moran.

When apprehended they were taken before our local Magistrates' Court and given a prison sentence to be served in a local Detention Centre situated not far from my Police Station domestic lines.

We had little to do with the Detention Centre apart from constantly borrowing whitewash from them, but I well remember two incidents that made us smile.

My wife and I were just finishing dinner when our house servant came and whispered in my ear that we had a naked man sitting on the step.

I went out and, recognising him as a recently convicted cattle thief, and asked, 'Why are you out of prison?'

'The prison is cold and damp Bwana and I do not like the warders. Can I please stay in your Police cells?'

The Detention Centre staff seemed unaware he had gone so I took him across the Station, gave him a couple of blankets and put him behind bars.

Around midnight a Constable woke me to say that a prisoner had just escaped from the Detention Centre and the Corporal Warder needed assistance and that in the meantime my Sergeant Major had readied a Police Search Party.

I went across to the Detention Centre and questioned the Warder. He told me that the prisoner had been seen climbing the wire fence just a few minutes before and the Centre had sounded their siren alarm.

I must confess I decided not to be helpful. I ordered the my Search Party to stand down and told the Warders, they should continue their own search despite the very dark night and if they did not find him by morning we would assist.

After our Police Station morning parade, I sent the Corporal Warden's prisoner back wrapped in a blanket, with a couple of Constables as escort.

A very chastened Corporal Warder retook his prisoner into custody, from my escort, who turned his discomfort into a comical story on their return, acting the incident out as Africans do so well, bringing great hilarity to my Station.

Late one evening on another occasion I received a report that five prisoners were missing. I made my way to the Detention Centre and the Corporal in charge told me that five prisoners who had been sent out under escort that morning to repair a broken culvert on the main road between Thomson Falls and Rumuruti had not returned.

Just as we finished our conversation five weary prisoners, still carrying picks and shovels, came trooping into the yard. It transpired that they had been taken the ten miles or so to the repair site that morning in a local trader's lorry who then went on to Thomsons Falls.

On arriving at the site the escorting Warder said he wanted to do some shopping in the town. Leaving the gang to do the work he carried on with the trader. However, come the end of the working day he had not returned and the gang decided that they had better find their own way back, so tramped the whole ten miles back to hand themselves in.

Rufus Waters – Police Officer

Action To Academia

I was with the initial batch of two-year contract people in 1953 and spent my first days at the Spreadeagle Hotel outside Nairobi before going to Gilgil for training.

My first posting was to Meru and Jim Constant sent me to Kanyakine Police Post, an Area where we had plenty of excitement at that time, with the Mau Mau Emergency in full swing. The guy in charge of Kanyakine, whose name, thank God, I cannot recall, was a strange person – an ardent Communist who led a very active sex life.

Luckily he moved on soon after my arrival, leaving me in charge. My friend Derrick Fitzpatrick joined me as my Number Two. We had grown up together in Ireland and my father gave Derrick a reference for the Kenya Police while his father did the same for me.

Life was a routine of patrols and police post building but once on the way home from a party in the Meru Hotel we were ambushed on the Mile Strip and the driver of our Land Rover shot and wounded.

We all got out OK, but didn't return fire as the Land Rover veered off the road and we were probably too drunk and too shocked to do anything anyway. We tried to get ourselves organized and noticed flames in the valley below.

An African village was on fire and obviously under Mau Mau attack.

Without a word to anyone Fitz took off alone with a Sten gun and I watched in horror from above as he charged through the village, brightly lit from all sides, between the burning huts and driving a herd of people ahead of him. I stayed up on the ridge with our six Askaris and the wounded driver.

I put Fitz up for the Police Medal for Gallantry but I never even got a response.

After a few months I was posted to Nyeri Police Station where I stayed in various roles until leaving the Police in 1957.

Like so many others I was married in the Cathedral of the Highlands in Nairobi. My wife was an Anglo-Irish woman I had known in Dublin. Our first daughter was born in the Memorial Hospital in Nyeri and it was while I was in Nyeri that I bought Cossick, a hundred and ten acre farm on the Moyo Ridge, just below Pura Milk off the road to Thompsons Falls. The farm was incredibly beautiful and incredibly cheap because the Mau Mau had murdered the previous owners. I saw my future life on the farm growing pyrethrum and coffee.

I came from a Police family mostly Royal Irish Constabulary in Ireland prior to Independence, when several of them moved to the Palestine Police. My brother-in-law, Alured Denne Bolton, was blown up in the King David hotel.

We had many family connections in Kenya – Ewart Grogan's brother was married to my aunt – but I decided to get away from the past and make my own life.

I first chose Australia and was registered to enter the University of Western Australia in 1960 but on a visit to Nairobi I met an alcoholic American writer called Robert Ruark, the author of Something Of Value, who expressed horror at my choice and said I should go instead to the University of North Carolina from which he had graduated. So I sold the farm, did as I was told, took the SAT exam and went to America.

I liked the University life and even though my money soon ran out and I had to hold three jobs as well as going to school, I stuck it out. After Bachelors and Masters Degrees in Economics I went to Rice University in Houston, Texas, to get a PhD.

From then on it was the academic life, with stints as a Professor at Texas A&M, Oklahoma State, Wake Forest and the University of Dallas as well as jobs such as Chief Economist for USAID, and lots of global travel on other people's money. I also started a computer company in Fresno, California, which later failed.

I tried but failed to make my first wife happy and we divorced amicably in 1976, by which time our children were gown and independent. After racketing around for a couple of years I found a delightful Dean – a Concert Pianist – at Texas Wesleyan University in Fort Worth. We married in 1980, adopted four children, all sisters, from Korea in 1984, and have had a remarkably happy life since.

We moved to California in 1986 and after a brief time in the Hoover Institution at Stanford I was offered a Professorship at California State University in Fresno, from where I retired in 2007. We live on a small acreage in Clovis – a sister city to Fresno – with our three dogs, three cats, and horse belonging to the young couple who rent the other home we built on the property for our youngest daughter. Three of our daughters live near by.

It has been a lucky and a happy life and although I was only in the Kenya Police for five years, those five years were a strong foundation for all that happened later.

I am grateful.

Adrian Jones – Police Officer

A Witch Doctor, A Misplaced Aircraft And Some Dastardly Reds

For my first posting upon leaving the Police Training School I went to Nyeri Police Station, a building still awaiting funding to complete the inside of the existing shell of the Operations room required to cover the whole of the Central Province.

On my second day I went for my first visit to Nyeri Magistrate's to observe and learn general Court procedures where Des Hunt, traffic Inspector who also held the duty as the Prosecutor for Nyeri Court.

I entered the Court, built as a typical single storey Colonial style official building with windows open on two sides and, as instructed, took a seat next to the dock.

The Senior Resident Magistrate took his place and called for the first Defendant, a scruffy smelly object, who came in and immediately started shouting.

The body of the Court, full of Africans cleared immediately when the man marched in. All the Kikuyu recognised him as dangerous and to be avoided and they all rushed from the room via the door and opens windows.

Now empty of Africans, except for the Prisoner, only the Prosecutor, the Magistrate and me were alone in the Court with the Defendant was still ranting away.

The Magistrate addressed me with the instruction to hit the Defendant, shut him up and get him out of his court.

'Do you mean me?' I asked.

'Yes,' said the Magistrate and left the Court.

This I did and dragged the Defendant out to the cell at the rear of the building. After making sure he'd been properly locked in I returned to Court.

'What's going on?' I asked Des.

'The Defendant's a witch doctor. He came in and put a bad spell on the Court'.

Of course, nothing at the Training School had prepared me for this.

'What happens now?' I asked Des.

'You stay here and look after the Court. I am going on my motorbike to get witch doctor more powerful than the one we have here.'

So there I was on Day Two of my Police career, looking after an abandoned Court all on my own.

After a while Des came back with another scruffy looking African. This man had a bag of bones and some powder that he spread around the Court with plenty of mumbling and incantations.

I followed him around to watch him at work.

After about ten minutes he finished and held out his hand to Des for a one hundred shilling fee. When he left the Court everyone came back in and sat down again, satisfied thins were now safe and I took my place at the back next to the dock.

The Magistrate returned and the case started again and went on quite normally as though nothing had happened to disturb the peace.

So ended my first visit to Court in Kenya.

They appear to have assessed a shootout and decided against such action.

Several weeks later, with the Nyeri Operations Room up and running, on one of my first evenings of duty in the new Ops Room I received a panic radio call from Thika Police Station.

The European Inspector, who had been on the same course at Kiganjo as me, asked for help with a light aircraft that had landed at dusk on the main dual carriageway road near Thika.

It was now dark, so I told him to remove the 'plane from the road and guard it overnight with a by stationing a

Constables. I also told him to make sure it took off at first light next morning.

The pilot turned out to be a lady who had flown up from Mombasa with her handbag, containing a metal powder compact, next to the magnetic compass, leading to false direction readings that threw her off course.

Instead of taking her to the small Wilson Airfield, just outside Nairobi, the compass aimed her northwest towards Thika. Seeing the wide road and knowing she needed to get down, she managed a safe landing in the same direction as the traffic and avoided a serious accident.

She parked her aircraft in the wide central reservation and just after dawn the next day, took off and made it to Wilson without further problem, although the Civil Aviation Authority was not very pleased with her.

A few months later, again on late evening duty at Nyeri Ops Room Nairobi called by radio to say that a Pakistani Constellation aircraft was about to enter Kenya airspace with only one of its four engines working.

The flight path took it over Meru, Embu and Thika to Nairobi's Embakasi International Airport. The pilot was lightening his load by throwing out all seats and luggage in the hope the aircraft would make it safely to the Airport.

I put all Divisions on standby and set up a search for the baggage and seats. The plane landed safely and over the next few weeks we found and recovered everything discarded except for one seat, which had been found by a Chief from the Igoji Police Station area.

He hung on to it and requested he keep the seat as a new throne because he preferred it to his old throne and, anyway, he had found it when it fell out of the sky.

I gave him permission and squared it with the Pakistan International Airline people, who were only too pleased to give it as a reward.

About six months later I transferred to Nairobi Area Central 999, when I became involved in a standoff at the Russian Embassy.

One of the Russian's top men in Australia had defected to the West. And had been moved to a safe house somewhere in Nairobi. The Russians had found out and were about to set off to try and find him.

The Control Room dispatched from Nairobi Central to Muthaiga with instructions to prevent the Russians from leaving their Embassy. I parked my 999 patrol car in a position to block the road leading to the Embassy and, with my crew following, got out about seventy-five yards and blocked the one-way road.

I arrived just in time because the Russian heavies were just getting into a car parked by the Embassy gate.

There followed a conversation between Nairobi Area HQ and the Embassy staff, who asked who had been sent and had seen me shooting accurately and winning in a competition at the Kahawa ranges.

The Russians said, 'Is that the Inspector Jones we saw shooting at Kahawa?'

'Yes.'

After a short interval they withdrew their vehicle and shut the gates.

Mike Hudson – Police Officer

Characters And Eccentrics

Sometimes, if you hadn't been in Kenya very long you might find a bit of confusion over the Swahili language. During my first posting to Fort Hall in the dark days of the Emergency, Inspector Jim Valentine, in charge of Kangema Police Station ran into difficulty. His cook and other African staff were somewhat bemused when he called out for two malaia, or prostitutes to be boiled for four minutes. He should have asked for two mayai, the correct plural Swahili word for eggs.

A very successful roundup of suspected terrorists in Nairobi was code-named "Anvil". To follow up on Anvil, the powers that be launched a new top-secret dawn sweep of the forest, code-named "Hammer One" that planned for the forest edge to be cordoned off by security forces before sunrise.

Les Morgan and Bill Baldwin of 14 Platoon GSU duly arrived at first light and took up their position facing the tree line. Almost immediately a Kikuyu Mzee strolled up to them and said "Jambo. Are you here because of Hammer One?"

ASP Paddy Thompson, a human dynamo, was a big source of irritation for the Inspectorate in Fort Hall over what they considered trivial administrative matters.

Gordon Baxter, who achieved fame when he locked Chief Njiri in his kitchen when Kinyona Police Post came under attack by terrorists, was my great friend.

One evening Gordon and I were grumbling over Tusker and the fabulous samosas at Filo's bar. We semi-seriously considered ambushing ASP Thompson but upon reflection decided to send him anonymously a copy of the American self-improvement book, How To Win Friends And Influence People.

Paddy visited every Police Post in Fort Hall to examine the Occurrence Book and check the handwriting to find out who may have sent it, but being more or less ambidextrous I used my lesser hand to write his address. He never found out until many years later in Australia I put him in the picture. He said he found the book very useful!

Gordon Baxter, a good friend but a rather eccentric character, eventually headed one of the first Asian Combat Units. About three o'clock one morning he arrived at my Police station, Kiriani and woke me up with the news that he had just received some new parachute flares and wished to test them out.

I suggested he fired them over a small bit of uninhabited bush called the Wahandura forest, so we wouldn't disturb anybody. Soon the sky lit up like the Blackpool illuminations.

Half an hour later three terrified Mau Mau, who had been hiding there in safety for about two years, came out of the forest and surrendered.

In the early days of the Emergency Inspector Tim Trafford brightened our lives with Radio Karatina, a pirate station broadcast by Inspector Tim Trafford playing records over the VHF system late at night. I don't think the authorities ever found him out.

A Country and Western ditty called "Don't Give Daddy Any More Whiskey" became great favourite with our Askaris. The Africans weren't interested in the plaintive wailing of the female singer, but loved the background crying of her baby as Mommy wailed out the sad, sad lyrics. They just couldn't hear enough of it.

A very colourful character in the early days in Fort Hall was Geoffrey Hedger-Wallace, a former Guards officer and actor. He was the first Contract Inspector to arrive all alone in the Colony and regarded with distaste by the regular Police because they thought he was paid too much.

He was posted to Mioro, a Police Post on the forest edge in Location 13, Fort Hall and eventually joined by Colin Crowe. A contact of Geoff's from UK days was a famous newspaper columnist, Arthur "Follow Me Around" Helliwell who wanted to go out with a forest patrol.

Eventually, according to Colin, Geoff led the biggest patrol ever to enter the Aberdares set off. He had gathered together a motley crew of Europeans and Africans from assorted Police Stations and Home Guard Posts plus a Black Watch Platoon – all wanting to get in on the act.

With such firepower it must have been the safest patrol ever to go into the Aberdare Forest and would probably have frightened an army, let alone a few Mau Mau terrorists cowering among the trees.

Helliwell eventually produce an article for his British Sunday Newspaper complete with lurid tales invented by Colin Crowe under the headline "I knew fear at every step".

Just another gullible journalist or author who visited for ten minutes and made a career out of imagined dangers and battles.

During their time at Mioro, Geoff and Colin were joined briefly by a very aristocratic Kenya Police Reservist, The Hon. Lionel Reilly Lord, who arrived in an MG. After hanging around for a week, he decided to go to Nairobi for a couple of days and asked his hosts if they needed anything from the big city.

Geoffrey suggested he buy a couple of mugs as the ones they had were a bit chipped. When he eventually returned The Hon. Lionel presented them with a Crown Derby tea service.

Geoff Hedger-Wallace was eventually promoted to Chief Inspector and posted to Kigumo, another Mau Mau hotbed. Geoff's dulcet tones seemed to be always on the VHF and he became christened "The Golden Voice of Radio Kigumo" by his officers from other Police Stations and posts, often frustrated by him occupying the frequency when they needed to communicate with others.

Paddy Thompson was in the habit of calling all Police posts in turn to receive situation reports. One day his calls were continually interrupted by the Golden Voice, Kigumo to control, Kigumo to Control.'

'Wait your turn, Kigumo,' said Paddy repeatedly, as Geoffrey continued hogging the airwaves. Eventually, worn out by the interruptions, the exasperated ASP asked, 'What is your problem Kigumo?'

'Help,' squeaked Geoff. 'I'm under my Land Rover being shot at.'

Fortunately reinforcements came to his aid in the nick of time but it seems to have been near thing.

In his early days Geoffrey was noted for carrying a long gnarled walking stick.

One day on his forest patrol encountered a Mau Mau gang and he discovered, that while he had his stick, he'd forgotten to take a gun.

In late 1958 Arthur Brelsford and I were working in Special Branch Nairobi Area and decided to spend a couple of weeks leave driving through Masai land to Tanga, and travelling along the coast Dar-es-Salaam.

We had been going about four hours in Arthur's little Fiat 600 Topolino when we went over a rock and an engine mounting broke off. We replaced it with the leg of our primus stove and drove for more than a thousand miles without any more trouble.

A few hours into Masai country we became completely lost in the wilderness and couldn't find a turning shown on the map. Eventually we saw an ancient Masai gentleman standing on one leg and holding a spear in traditional fashion.

Not speaking the language we decided to ask him for directions in our not particularly competent Kiswahili.

After a few faltering questions he replied in faultless English, 'About two miles along the road just past a small duka.'

It turned out he had been a Sergeant in the KAR during the war.

The terror of the Inspectorate during the Emergency in Fort Hall was Superintendent Les Pridgeon. He would descend on Police Posts at strange hours to perform inspection, even sleeping in Home Guard Posts overnight so he could make dawn raids on the hapless station commanders.

One day I was sticking pins in maps in the Operations Room following an appendix operation – the Fort Hall doctor originally diagnosed malaria – when I heard conversations between Police Air Wing pilots and Police Posts.

The pilots usually had call signs named after birds, such as "Eagle Red" or "Kestrel Blue". Like Saul on the road to Damascus I had an inspirational moment and decided to christen our bête noire, "Vulture Black".

From then on police posts were warned that Vulture Black would be flying in their area whenever an inspection was expected.

Even Paddy Thompson got into the scheme and warned us whenever he knew Pridgeon was preparing a visit.

Pridgeon never found out Vulture Black referred to him, but one day he visited Mioro when Colin Crowe was on patrol. On Mioro's radio he heard the message, 'A spotter 'plane, Vulture Black, is patrolling over your area today,' and told Colin when he returned from patrol, 'There's been an aircraft trying to call you.'

Sir Roy Welensky, boss of the Central African Federation, visited Nairobi in the late 1950s. Assigned to him as a Special Branch bodyguard was 'Big Jim" Allen. Both men were built – to use an Australian euphemism – like a brick outhouse with a combined weight of more than forty stone or two hundred and fifty six kilos, which equals just over a quarter tonne.

One of the places Sir Roy wanted to visit was the Rowland Ward shop, a place of wonderful treasures, particularly the glassware engraved with African animals.

They were admiring the glasses when Big Jim stepped back and - *CRASH* - down went a display cabinet with disastrous effects on the contents.

Poor Jim looked down ruefully at the mess, working out in his mind how long it would take to pay for the damage.

Almost immediately Sir Roy turned to the manager and apologised for his clumsiness. 'It's quite all right, Sir Roy - accidents do happen.'

It shows what a decent man Sir Roy was.

John Newton – Police Officer

Last Words

Rather than write my own anecdotes I'll use this final page to thank you all for sending in so many great stories, so amazingly well remembered from sixty or seventy years ago.

The idea for this book popped into my head one morning after several telephone calls from wives and widows with queries about something being done by our Kenya Police Association.

Each of these indomitable ladies told me a tale of their time in Kenya; some interesting snippet about themselves or their Policeman husband.

During the third or fourth call it hit me.

This is History.

These stories should not be forgotten.

So I popped off a letter inviting stories, expecting, perhaps, thirty or forty and, to my delight, received well over eighty.

And not a dud among them.

The editing and compiling has been a joy. I devised the method of calling and chatting through the stories with their authors. During these chats I made many friends among our Association, with whom I have never before spoken, which pleases me deeply.

A big benefit of this approach is that by gentle questioning and probing and a bit of added humour, I teased out and expanded half-hidden memories from sixty or seventy years ago that brought even more colour and interest to the way you told your experiences.

Of course, I apologise if I seemed to interrogating you at times.

But we both seemed happy with the end result, and we certainly had many chuckles and giggles along the way.

It has been a pleasure and an honour.

I am grateful to every single one of you.

I am grateful for the stories.

I am grateful for the way you submitted to my digging deep into your past.

But between us, we mined and from the depth of memory brought out many important nuggets of History for our families, our friends and for future generations interested in, or researching the truth of day-to-day Colonial Policing in our beautiful Kenya.

Acknowledgement

Jennifer Reeve

My thanks to Jennifer who gave great help in transcribing and editing the stories submitted on paper. Also for checking and proofing the final draft manuscript with such care and attention. Jennifer worked hard and well with great concentration and I thank her on your behalf.

Buffalo On The Road At Tsavo Drawn By Jill Fielding

Two NFD Women

Avtar Matharu And Friend High On Mount Kenya

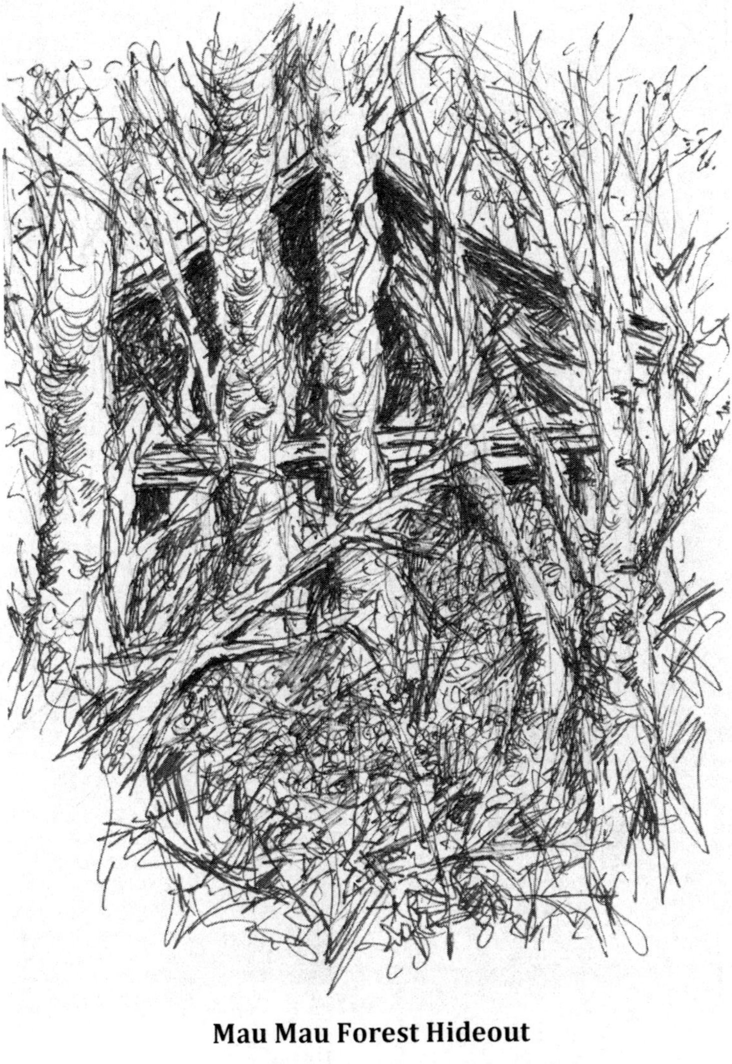

Mau Mau Forest Hideout

Forest Patrol

Askaris On Parade At Githunguri

(Photo by Arthur Williamson)

Cartoons By Peter Herz-Smith – Police Officer

Northern Frontier District Nomad

Northern Frontier Camel Patrol

Mount Kenya